The ball was brilliantly delivered by Giggsy. The keeper had no chance, couldn't hope to keep it out, and I exploded. It doesn't get much better than to score a last minute winner against Liverpool in front of the Stretford End.

D0295556

RIO
MY STORY

RIO
MY STORY

RIO FERDINAND
WITH SHAUN CUSTIS

headline

THE SPORT ENTERTAINMENT & MEDIA GROUP ltd
www.sportentertainmentmedia.com

Copyright © 2006 Rio Ferdinand

The right of Rio Ferdinand to be identified as the Author of
the Work has been asserted by him in accordance with the
Copyright, Designs and Patents Act 1988.

First published in 2006 by
HEADLINE PUBLISHING GROUP

1

Apart from any use permitted under UK copyright law, this publication
may only be reproduced, stored, or transmitted, in any form, or by any
means, with prior permission in writing of the publishers or, in the case of
reprographic production, in accordance with the terms of licences issued by
the Copyright Licensing Agency.

Every effort has been made to fulfil requirements with regard to
reproducing copyright material. The author and publisher will be glad
to rectify any omissions at the earliest opportunity.

Cataloguing in Publication Data is available from the British Library

Hardback (ISBN 10) 0 7553 1532 4
Hardback (ISBN 13) 978 0 7553 1532 1
Trade paperback (ISBN 10) 0 7553 1615 0
Trade paperback (ISBN 13) 978 0 7553 1615 1

Typeset in Sabon by Palimpsest Book Production Limited,
Grangemouth, Stirlingshire

Career statistics compiled by Jack Rollin

Printed and bound in Great Britain by
Clays Ltd, St Ives plc

Headline's policy is to use papers that are natural,
renewable and recyclable products and made from wood grown
in sustainable forests. The logging and manufacturing processes
are expected to conform to the environmental regulations
of the country of origin.

HEADLINE PUBLISHING GROUP
A division of Hachette Livre UK Ltd
338 Euston Road
London NW1 3BH

www.headline.co.uk
www.hodderheadline.com

To Rebecca and Lorenz, Mum and Dad, Anton,
Sian, Chloe, Jeremiah, Remy and Anya.

CONTENTS

ACKNOWLEDGEMENTS

This book would not have been possible without the help of so many people to whom I will be forever grateful.

Thanks to Rebecca and Mum and Dad for always being there for me. And to my brothers and sisters.

Thanks to all the team-mates, coaches and managers I've had throughout my career, from schoolboy football and Sunday League through to Manchester United and England. You've all played your part.

Special thanks to Dave and Kate Goodwin, and Pini Zahavi.

Also to Tony Carr, Paul Heffer, Frank Burrows, Roger Cross, Frank Lampard Snr, Ronnie Boyce, Harry Redknapp, Ian Wright, Iain Dowie, David O'Leary, Roy Aitken, Eddie Gray and Keith Power.

Not forgetting Gavin Rose and cousin Bernard, my two best mates.

And, of course, Sir Alex Ferguson, Carlos Queiroz and Mike Phelan for helping me fulfil the dream every day at Manchester United.

To all the staff at Headline and especially my editor David Wilson, who embraced the idea for this book from the start and never wavered in his enthusiasm.

To my agents SEM, in particular Jeff Weston and Jerome Anderson, who have been hugely supportive of this project.

Special thanks to Chris Nathaniel and all the team at NVA Management for their vision and tireless work behind the scenes.

To Shaun Custis, the chief football writer at the *Sun*, who burned the midnight oil helping to put these words together.

Also to Jane Morris who spent many a long hour transcribing hours of taped interviews.

Last and by no means least, thanks to the staff at Wythenshawe Hospital in Manchester, particularly Mrs Ahluwalia and Meriel Fowler, who helped bring our son Lorenz into the world.

Prologue

It gave ammunition to all those who believed I was one of the game's bad boys. To them I was the flashy rich kid, the champagne-slugging, big-mouthed, trouble-making drug-taker. A footballer without values, a thickie who just got lucky. I don't recognise myself from those descriptions.

Standing in the toilets at the Radisson Hotel, Heathrow, on 18 March 2004, doing what you do, I reflected on how that last cup of tea wasn't the only thing slipping down the drain.

My career was going the same way.

In a couple of hours the FA's appeal panel would decide whether to uphold the eight-month ban imposed on me for missing a drugs test.

If they did I would miss the rest of Manchester United's season, the Euro 2004 Championships with England, and the start of the following season too.

Press interest in the case was huge, and the speculation rife. Were the FA determined to make an example of me? Would other players have been treated the same? I felt like a sitting target.

As I stood there, contemplating the injustice of it all, a large figure loomed into view at the next urinal. 'All right, how you doing?' he asked. I couldn't believe it. It was the FA's prosecuting lawyer, Mark Gay, the man who tried to get me banned for two years.

He wasn't just having a piss, he seemed to be taking the piss too.

'How was I doing?' I thought, 'Fucking terrific.' I wanted to put the geezer through the wall. This bloke was trying to nail me and he was asking if I was all right. No, I wasn't all right. I was far from all right. In fact, I couldn't have been less all right.

Two hours later the ban was confirmed and I was banished from the game. It was the lowest point of my football career.

It gave ammunition to all those who believed I was one of the game's bad boys.

To them I was the flashy rich kid, the champagne-slugging, big-mouthed, trouble-making drug-taker. A footballer without values, a thickie who just got lucky.

I don't recognise myself from those descriptions, but they've all been thrown at me at different times in my life, sometimes all at once.

They come from those who don't know me, who have never met me yet feel they can make a judgement about what I'm like and what I stand for. Yes, I'm rich – how could I pretend to be otherwise? Not as rich as has been claimed, but I've got a few quid. Which international footballer who plies his trade in the Premiership hasn't? I'm not unique.

Yet when you have made money you are apparently no longer a human being. You are there to be ripped to pieces. I don't know what it is – jealousy maybe? I don't understand jealousy. If I see somebody doing well I'm happy for them. If the next geezer to me is earning 50 grand a minute, I'd want to know how he did it and, provided it was legitimate, I'd admire him.

Having money is not a crime and nobody can say I don't know the value of it. I was brought up in a concrete council block on the tough Friary Estate in Peckham, south-east London. It's been described in the press as one of the roughest estates in Europe, although it never felt like that to me.

We might not have had much, but my mum and dad scrimped and saved to give the family the best they could. When I was able to buy my mum a four-bedroom house in nearby Mottingham when I was 19, all our possessions fitted into the front room.

I've been called flash just because I'm from London. You're automatically a cockney wide boy just because you like nice clothes, wear a big watch, have a haircut that's a little different or wear a sparkly earring. That to me is prejudice.

Flash? I wouldn't know where to start.

So I drive a nice car and I've got a nice house – of course

I have. Should I just leave my money in the bank, kip on a mate's floor and get myself a beaten-up Metro? You can't take your money to the bloody funeral parlour. What do people want? Who is the Identikit footballer who is acceptable to the public? The truth is, there isn't one and I've come to realise that.

I have plenty to say for myself at times, like in a dressing-room environment, with close friends, or even to the media if I feel strongly about an issue. But put me in a bar or a restaurant and I'm looking for the corner of the room. I don't want to be the centre of attention.

You won't find me in The Ivy or other celebrity haunts where you know there's going to be cameras. I don't go to those places, I avoid them like the plague. I don't want my picture taken every time I go out. I hate it. And if the photographers start following me around I go looking for the back door.

I'm not the 'look at me' type who holds court and bores everyone to death. Anyone who is successful can go round saying, 'I'm the geezer, I'm the man, look at me. Who wants a drink at the bar? I'll buy the whole place a drink. Give me the most expensive thing you've got.' I don't do that, that's not me.

I've walked into clubs and I've seen geezers I know with buckets of champagne going, 'Oi, over here, mate,' and I'm off to the other end of the place. If we book a table in a restaurant I want the one out of sight.

I like a drink occasionally, it's true, but no more than the next man. And as for being a Champagne Charlie, a glass of wine or a lager will do me.

Talking of Charlie, no, I'm not a drug-taker. Never have been, never will be. Plenty have accused me of it, even before I famously missed that drugs test.

I'll get to the truth of what happened later on, but, no matter how much I protest, there will always be those who think I took something and deliberately avoided the test. Mud sticks. Claiming that I'd forgotten was not a very convincing excuse, even I can see that. As soon as I said it, I could hear the whole country going, 'Pull the other one!'

If I'd been an ordinary fan, getting the train to the office each day and reading the latest sports news in the paper, I'd have thought Rio Ferdinand was on drugs as well. But if I'd wanted to avoid a drugs test I'd surely have come up with an excuse which was a lot better than that one.

It upsets me that I will forever be a drugs cheat in some people's eyes. I don't want my own children or other kids who love the game thinking that, but I'll never be able to convince everyone.

All I can do is live my life as well as I can and, by my actions, persuade the public I was innocent, or at least make them question whether they were right to judge me so quickly.

I want to be known as Rio Ferdinand, quality footballer, not Rio Ferdinand, dodgepot. One of the reasons I want to tell my story is to show people the real me, the person they think they know but probably don't.

It's always been in my nature to take others at face value unless they show me different. But, with me, people have always jumped to conclusions.

I'm not going to pretend I'm an angel because I'm not. I've been in some scrapes, but that puts me in the majority not the minority. I regret some of them and others I couldn't care less about, but I'm not malicious, just a bit daft some-times. A man who's never made mistakes has never made anything.

I know what's right and what's wrong and I have strong values which were instilled into me by my parents. We weren't well off, but my background gave me a wonderful grounding in life.

I didn't become a footballer through luck. Despite the fact that I've been accused of laziness at different points in my career, even by the ex-England manager Sven-Göran Eriksson, I've worked damned hard to get to the level I'm at now. I was always obsessed with the game and determined to fulfil my dream. There are those who want to be doctors, solicitors or fighter-pilots; I always wanted to be a footballer.

Even when there were many who doubted me, I kept focused. I put hours and hours of practice in every day of my life to ensure I succeeded. And I'm not thick either. Just thought I'd get that one straight while I'm here. I loved school, hardly missed a day and got GCSEs in English, maths, drama, PE and science. It doesn't make me Brain of Britain, but it doesn't make me an idiot either.

I love reading and will take anybody on in a debate about world events and modern history. Want an argument about Saddam Hussein, bin Laden, Che Guevara, Nelson Mandela or Martin Luther King? Bring it on. But I can also debate what's happening in *Big Brother* and on *EastEnders*!

I know people don't think of me as being intelligent because of various incidents like the Ayia Napa video (which I'll discuss later as well) and forgetting the drugs test. But the truth is I feel comfortable in any surroundings, talking about most subjects. I can go into any room and speak to anybody, from government ministers to factory workers, and I will always cope.

Obviously there are subjects I don't have a clue about, but you can still have an opinion. I feel strongly about the fact that we went to war in Iraq, for instance. I don't think we should have gone in there unless we were 100 per cent certain it was right. The reasons to get involved should have been black and white, but they weren't and now look at the mess which has been left behind.

I wish the history lessons at school had gone into all that sort of stuff – the Middle East and the tensions in Israel, Iraq and Iran. But all we learned about was mediaeval times. Not a lot of help in understanding the world we live in today.

While I don't claim to be a figure of great importance myself, I was grateful for the opportunity to write my own book so people can pass judgement on me based on information rather than hearsay.

I'm still a relatively young man, but so much has happened in my life that I felt it was important that my generation knew my side of the story. Whatever conclusion you come to in the end, good or bad, at least you've given me a hearing.

That is all I've ever asked for.

He Who Dares Wins

Growing up in Peckham, I always believed anything was possible. We might not have had any money, but dreams don't cost anything. My dream was to be a footballer and nothing and nobody was going to stop me.

I'**m a Peckham boy** and proud of it. It's my manor. It wouldn't be everyone's cup of tea, but that working-class jungle of bricks and concrete in south-east London is the greatest place in the world to me.

The only reason most of the country has even heard of Peckham is because it's the home of the BBC comedy series *Only Fools and Horses*. Del Boy Trotter, the main character, once joked: 'The only people who missed Peckham were the Luftwaffe.'

Well, I miss it. Okay, it's not pretty, and it has always had a bit of a reputation for crime and drugs, but it's my home and I never tire of going back there.

Del Boy had another saying, 'He who dares wins', and that's been my philosophy all my life.

Growing up in Peckham, I always believed anything was possible. We might not have had any money, but dreams don't cost anything. My dream was to be a footballer and nothing and nobody was going to stop me. Yes, you've got to have talent, but without determination you've got no chance and I had it in spades.

I was born in King's College Hospital in Camberwell, next door to Peckham, on 7 November 1978. I was named Rio after the Rio Grande, which means Great River. My mum, Janice Lavender, thought that sounded good. Apparently, I would have been called Giovanna if I'd been a girl! Gio instead of Rio.

Mum was only 17 when she had me, but she was a strong girl. Her Irish mum walked out of the family home in Bermondsey when she was eight. She was one of six kids, but they all mucked in together to help her dad run the house for most of their young lives.

She doesn't even know where her mum is and isn't bothered about finding out either. My granddad is a diamond bloke who now lives on the Isle of Wight with his second wife, my nan, and they are a lovely couple.

My dad Julian Ferdinand's family are from St Lucia. There were ten in his family and one by one they came over to England. He was ten years old when he moved here. We used to go round to Granddad and Nan's house on a Sunday, with all the other grandkids and my dad's brothers. Granddad was quite ill and we would go in and say hello to him and he would give us some sweets. Then Nan would bake us wicked cakes.

Dad was older than Mum by five years and, while little Rio coming along was a shock to both of them, they'd already been living together in Peckham for a while, since Mum was 15, so there was a foundation there, of sorts.

People still call Mum Mrs Ferdinand sometimes, but she never has been. Mum and Dad didn't marry. But she changed her surname from Lavender to St Fort 13 years ago when she married her husband Peter.

When you tell people you come from Peckham you are expected to conform to that image – be a bit of a bad boy or perhaps more of a wide boy like Del or, perish the thought, be like his brother Rodney or their mate Trigger.

Only Fools and Horses and another comedy called *Desmond's*, about a family who owned a barber's shop, were bang on about the sense of community which existed in Peckham. On the sprawling Friary Estate, where I lived at 18 Gisburn House, everyone looked out for everyone else. It might have been tough, but to me it was a warm and friendly place where I always felt safe.

Any adults walking past you would go, 'What's up then, Rio, are you all right?' When I was little my mum only had to ask for someone to look out for me and it was done in an instant. An ear-piercing scream from our third-floor flat was enough. 'Sheldon! Can you look after Rio at the Adventure, please?' and it would be done.

The Adventure was the playground across the road from where we lived, and it housed the playgroup and youth club. It was the centre of our universe, our lives revolved around it. It was the sort of place the kids of today are crying out for. I never realised how lucky we were. Me and my mates, Gavin, Ray, Ahmet, Sevhan, David and Fitzley and a whole bunch of others had a blast there for years.

Mum used to look after little 'uns as a childminder and she'd take them to the kids' club near the Adventure where their mums would pick them up. When I finished school I'd go straight to the Adventure.

There were leaders there who supervised activities after school and during the holidays, and our parents always knew we were in good hands. Also on the estate was a huge grassy area which was our Wembley. We may have been short of money but we certainly weren't deprived.

There would always be kids running around causing havoc, but it was an innocent sort of havoc.

We'd play games like 'knock down ginger', where you'd knock on someone's door and run away. The worst we'd ever do was put a banger through a letter box, which made a hell of a noise . . . as did Mum whenever she found out about it.

It was a very diverse estate in terms of culture. There were white boys, black boys, Turkish boys, Irish boys, African, Caribbean, almost every colour and creed you could think of. If you wanted to find an integrated society we had it on the Friary Estate.

I've heard it said I must be gutted to have been brought up in a place like Peckham. Rubbish. My ideal scenario would be for me to live in Peckham as it was then but with all the amenities that I'm used to now.

I wish my kids could grow up on the same estate at the time that I did, because I honestly believe there was no better place. You learned all about life. You became street-wise but you got a sense of real values as well. You learned social skills to deal with all manner of cultures and to talk openly and respectfully to adults, kids, blacks and whites. You understood about taking the rough with the smooth, but you also learned about discipline and what's right and what's wrong.

Mum is like Supermum. She's devoted her whole life to us kids. Whenever I've needed her she's been there for me. Growing up she made sure I was always doing positive things that stimulated me. She's the best mum anyone could wish for. Mum lives in Mottingham now, which is about a 20-minute drive from Peckham, but she still takes my little brother Jeremiah and sister Sian back to the old estate and the Adventure in the summer holidays. It holds such fond memories.

The estate's not the same now though, the warmth has gone. Everyone keeps themselves to themselves and it's lost its heart. There's hardly any kids play outside there any more. It's weird, almost eerie.

Some kids are so segregated these days and don't understand what it is to be around loads of people from different races as we were. They don't go out to play because their parents are scared of the paedophiles and kidnappers, and the children become cocooned.

Even when it's light kids just go round to friends' houses, often driven there and back by their parents, even if it's just a few hundred yards away. I always played out till it started getting dark and Mum called for me to come in.

The back grass was about 50 yards long, hemmed in by the flats, which acted as a natural boundary, although it resulted in the occasional broken window and some very angry parents.

There were signs up saying 'no ball games' but nobody took any notice. And when the council put trees up to stop us playing some of the older lads just chopped them down. It was our hallowed turf.

People would be out on balconies in the evening watching us and when I had to go in I would then watch from the window because my bedroom overlooked the grass. It was like having my own little corporate box.

We would play massive football games of 13-a-side or even more. No matter what the numbers were you'd play, and if there was one extra you'd have a rush goalie. Yet see a big group of kids today out on the field playing football as it gets dark and you'd think, 'Bloody hell, that's odd.' We had 24- and 25-year-olds playing football with 11-year-olds. If you saw that now you'd maybe think the older ones were kiddie-fiddlers. But for us it was normal, part of growing up.

They put a little purpose-built games area up next to the grass which was brilliant and we would play on that when it was wet. There was a basketball net on it originally, but anybody playing anything but football got eased off. Eventually, the basketball net went the same way as the trees – it got cut down.

As long as I was on the estate Mum was happy, but she didn't like me going off it. A lot of my mates would go to Neat Street, which was about a 20-minute walk away, to play kids from other estates, but I wasn't allowed to go because I was too young. I pleaded and pleaded with Mum, but she wanted to know where I was all the time.

And there was no playing out after dark. Mum used to come out on the balcony of our flat and scream, 'Reee-oh, Reeee-oh' and I knew that was it for the day. If I wasn't in within two minutes of that scream there was trouble. Neither of my parents was averse to giving me a good clip round the ear.

Like many estates, ours could get naughty at times. I once saw a woman who was an absolute drunk get picked up by her boyfriend and chucked head-first on to the concrete floor. There were drugs around, but we knew where the dealers were and we knew not to get involved. Any problems were usually at night which was why Mum always wanted me indoors.

One evening a girl got stabbed to death on the stairs of the block next to mine. She was a really pretty girl and I don't think they ever found out who did it. I was only 11 at the time and it shook everybody up. But you just thought it was because she was involved with bad stuff and as long as you stayed out of it you were fine.

As a kid, I felt immune to any trouble because there were so many people on the estate who were good people and there was real discipline in our family, which kept me on the straight and narrow as much as possible.

Mum's best mate was called Sharon and her daughter Chantelle was my best friend when I was growing up. Sharon used to look after me when I was little and do my hair when I was a baby. I loved it round her house and threw a tantrum whenever we had to go home because I never wanted to leave.

I went to Lympston day nursery till I was five and then Camelot Primary School, which was just behind a housing block opposite our flat. Kids from the Friary either went there or St Francis, which was on the other side of the estate. Camelot was a small school, a one-minute walk from our flat, and had one of the first black headteachers in the area.

I never wanted to skive off. I loved going to school, but not because I was a boffin, more because I enjoyed messing about with my mates. I liked learning too, but fooling about was what I preferred. There are those who will tell you I haven't changed!

I wasn't the most attentive in lessons. I got suspended from Camelot once for mucking about after I'd finished all my work. Mum went ballistic – not with me, but the school and she told them they needed to find more to keep me occupied. I was always finished long before everyone else.

One of the best things about Camelot was the food. School dinners might not have much of a reputation, but ours were brilliant. I would go back for seconds and thirds. Long after I'd left, the dinner ladies would remind Mum of how much I used to love their cooking.

There was a dinner lady called Sasay from Jamaica and another one called Pat who were like my best mates because they had the grub. You used to get sheets of lamb and beef with the best roast potatoes and the fish fingers were awesome. And for afters the arctic roll was blinding. I would be first in the queue and last out of the hall.

I would eat like a horse at home as well. Mum was a great cook and she would swap dishes with other families on special occasions. She'd make, say, a Caribbean meal for someone and they might give us a Turkish one back. It made for a lot of variety.

I got the nickname 'Apples' because I always had at least two apples a day, one on the way to school and one on the way home. I often had an orange as well. And that was on top of everything else.

I still eat loads. My plate is always piled high. Whenever I go to a fancy dinner I laugh at the tiny portions they dish up. Sasay and Pat would have gone mad. To them it would be a starvation diet. Nouvelle cuisine? You can keep it. School dinners will do for me.

I could always get to the front of the dinner queue because I was the fastest kid in school. I was forever tearing about. I had a little Raleigh Burner bike which I was a demon on. One day it got nicked. I'd left it downstairs because the lift was broken and carrying it took ages because it was so heavy.

As I quickly went upstairs into the flat someone's shouted, 'Rio, Rio, your bike!' I looked down over the balcony and some geezer of about 18 or 19 was riding off on it. My dad and uncle ran downstairs, chased after him, caught him and gave him a little slap. Well I was told it was a little slap. I never saw him again.

When I wasn't on my bike I was running everywhere. At my best, when I went to Bluecoats secondary in Blackheath, I could do the 100m in around 12 seconds and the 200m in about 24 seconds, if memory serves me right.

We used to run up and down Friary Road, from the church at one end to the school at the other. I did it in my socks because that made me even faster. I'd pretend I was Linford Christie or Carl Lewis and challenge the other kids. Mum would go bananas when I got home and say, 'What you got holes in your socks for?' and I'd say, 'I was racing, I was racing, I'm faster without shoes.'

I would push my luck with Mum. If I wanted something, she'd usually give in. I once made her take me all the way to Camberwell to get a special haircut.

The cut I wanted was a Nike tick shaved into the back of my head. I must have known they were going to be my future sponsors! All my mates were going to this one barber called J & Johnsons. Mum couldn't believe it when the bloke said it would be a tenner to get my hair done like I wanted. She told me that as well as being the first time I'd been to the place, it would also be the last. The tick looked great but it only lasted for about a week until my hair started to grow back.

Another time, I went on and on about wanting a clicksuit, which was a combination of a baggy shirt and trousers. She saved up for weeks to buy it, but when I got it I only wore it once because by then it was out of fashion. I still feel bad about that.

It's funny thinking back about all the stuff I used to get up to when I was a kid. I really haven't changed that much. Fooling around, running about, eating loads, cool haircuts (I think so anyway), football day and night. That's me all right.

* * *

Gymnastics was a big passion of mine as a kid. I represented Camelot and got selected for our borough, Southwark, to compete in the London Games. I performed on the floor, the vault, the parallel bars and the high bars and won the competition.

The floor was my favourite. It's a dynamic discipline, with all the tumbles and twists involved, and exhilarating when you get it right, though not so much fun if you land splat on your arse. I've not tried to do a summersault for a few years, but back then I could easily do the type of celebration Robbie Keane does when he scores for Spurs. I could do three or four back flips in a row, no problem. LuaLua's routine is a good one at Portsmouth. I wouldn't even try that one now – I'm too long in the body.

I was spotted at a gymnastics contest by someone from the Central School of Ballet in Farringdon who offered me a scholarship. It was Billy Elliot stuff and I jumped at the chance, even though I was only ten. I knew I might get some piss-taking from other kids, but that didn't bother me, although I used to tell them I did dance rather than ballet to cover myself. But I didn't feel like a cissy or anything. I've always been open-minded and prepared to try anything.

I thought joining ballet school would be exciting because I would be travelling out of Peckham and seeing different places. Because Mum never let me go off the estate it was a big adventure.

There were loads of birds at ballet school, which was also one of its attractions. But there would also be male adults getting changed in front of us, prancing about stark naked. Me and my mate were sure they were all gay.

It might have been a strange place all right, but ballet school was also very disciplined. You couldn't talk in class and you couldn't have a laugh either; you were there to work.

I would go up to Farringdon four times a week. I'd get the bus straight after school with a couple of other lads and not get back until 10 o'clock at night. Eventually, Mum got us sponsored by a local cab firm to take us there and back because we were coming home too late.

I went to ballet school for four years, doing jazz dance, contemporary and normal ballet, but, what with football training on a Saturday and a game on Sundays, it all became too much. In the end, Dad said I had to slow down and do one or the other. Luckily, I picked football.

Ballet has stood me in good stead in my football career. It has given me an edge in terms of flexibility, movement, co-ordination and balance. I'd say to any boy worried about taking it up, give it a go. Don't worry about the mickey-takers – individuality is what life's all about.

Dad moved out when I was nine and my brother Anton was two. He and Mum never really had fights. If they did they rarely happened in front of me or Anton, but I later found out they hadn't been getting on.

When Dad told me he was leaving, he was in the bath and I was brushing my teeth. He just said, 'Look, I'm going away for a while, but I'll still come back and see you.' At the time I just shrugged my shoulders and thought, 'Fine, if he says he'll be back to see me, he will be.' I've never properly understood why they split up. It's their own business.

Dad's day job was as a tailor, hand-cutting clothes all over north and east London with his two brothers. They always wore good gear, and my dad used to spend most of his money on his threads. I wonder who he passed that trait on to?

He also did security jobs and was a bouncer at clubs in the West End on Friday and Saturday nights. He went out a lot with his brothers and had plenty of other mates to keep him entertained.

He was into clubs and music in a big way, just like me. He loved Marvin Gaye and old reggae. There was always reggae playing in our flat when he was there. Mum would be cooking and cleaning and the reggae would be playing on the pirate radio stations.

There were no CDs or iPods back then. Dad taped stuff off the radio and had shelves full of records and tapes in the front room. Whenever he went out I'd put his records on and dress up in his clothes. My favourite was his blazer with a waistcoat stitched inside. Then I'd put on his brogues and pose round the flat, listening to the songs.

I guess my parents splitting up means I come from a broken home, but it didn't feel like it. Dad made a conscious decision to live near us and only moved across the road to the Yellow Brick Estate. He thought about going back to St Lucia, but realised he couldn't be apart from his sons.

I worshipped Dad, but discussing our feelings was not a big thing in our house. When he was home I'd just sit and watch TV with him. I have a picture of me and him on the couch – a shocking couch by the way – and I'm sitting snuggled into him. That was me spending time with my dad.

For some kids, time with their parents means talking and sharing emotions, but my dad was more reserved. You never knew what he was thinking, when he was going out or when he was coming back. He often wouldn't get back to the house till I was in bed and would be out the next morning before I got up. But if I was awake and heard him come in and make himself some rice or something I'd get up and share some with him.

He seemed like an old man to me when he was younger. He had a full beard, his rocking chair and a pipe. Now he's like a young bloke and has become my best mate.

Maybe he didn't know how to talk to us back then. He came from a background where his parents would often hit him. He was living by himself and working by the age of 14.

I'm sure his dad, my granddad, loved him, but he probably didn't know how to show it. So perhaps Dad didn't know how to show it to us until he moved out and could look at things from a different angle.

My relationship with Dad – and I think Anton's as well – grew from that moment he moved out. I've often wondered why him not being at home with us made such a difference but I haven't really come up with an answer – from our point of view or his.

I see him now with my sisters Chloe, Anya and Remi by his fiancée Lisa and he's so relaxed and comfortable with them, whatever tricks they're getting up to. I'll say to him, 'If I had done that when I was a kid I'd have had a clip round the ear.'

My sisters will refuse to do something and my dad will go, 'Do I have to ask you again to do it?' There weren't no asking again when I was a kid. I would have been slapped straight away. If Mum told me to do something and I said, 'In a minute,' she'd just say, 'I'm going to tell Dad,' and that was it, it was either done or I got clouted.

One time, Dad was on the warpath, walking through the estate looking for me. I raced past him and straight upstairs, he didn't have to say anything. He's always been a fit bloke. He was into kung fu, did a lot of weights and had a quiet authority. You didn't mess with him.

In my last year at secondary school he said that if I didn't get at least five GCSEs at grades A to C I couldn't play football the next year and would have to go to college. He may have moved out, but he still played the proper father's role. He was a big influence on me. I've never worked so hard in my life. I revised like never before and got the results I needed.

When I was ten and started playing football for Bloomfield

Athletic, Dad got into the game. He'd never been interested before, but he became the team fitness coach. These days he thinks he knows everything about football.

Once or twice a week he and I would go running up Old Kent Road to a big play area and do sprints, press ups and sit ups, to be fit for football. Dad was very athletic and quicker than me until I was about 15.

We also used to play tennis in Burgess Park or go out on our BMXs and we'd drive to football practice together in his yellow Beetle, with his reggae tapes blasting away. I remember being in the car coming back from football once when someone in another car shouted some remark. Dad jumped out and swore at this geezer while I stayed in the car, bricking it.

There were about six of them in the other vehicle but, when he got back in, Dad was cool as you like and nothing was said. He could 'have it', as we would say. He could look after himself.

Yet he's very mild mannered. You wouldn't think he was hard. He even sounds quite posh sometimes.

Mum met Peter a couple of years after Dad moved out and, if I'm honest, I didn't like talking to him at first. I just decided I didn't like him. He was from Peckham and lived in a flat nearby, but I didn't know him and I didn't want to know him. I just thought, 'Aargh, my mum's with him!'

I would ask Dad why he wasn't with Mum any more and he used to say, 'Ask your mum. Your mum doesn't want me.' In my eyes back then, Peter was an obstacle to Mum and Dad getting back together, even though I can see now it was never going to happen.

My auntie Janine, who was a social worker, came round to find out why I was behaving the way I was to Mum and Peter and I screamed at her, 'She's my mum! She should be with my dad! Why isn't she with my dad?' I was crying, everyone in the house was crying, and I shouted at Mum, 'You should be with Dad! Dad wants you to be with him. Why don't you be with him? It's all 'cause of you that my dad doesn't live here any more.' I kept this going for ages until Mum broke down and said, 'I can't live like this. Peter's the only man that I've met after your dad.' It was a right scene.

Then, one day, Dad took me into his flat and introduced me to Lisa and almost immediately I felt everything was all right. Weird, innit? I don't know why. I can't work it out.

At Mum's wedding to Peter I made a speech and said, 'Peter, as long as you look after my mum then I'll be happy.' And I have been. He's a top bloke and we get on really well now.

We all moved in together at 81 Latona Road, a bigger three-bedroom flat, when they had my sister Sian. I was about fourteen, Anton seven and it was fine.

Dad's happy and is still working. He's got his own factory which makes clothes for places like Topshop and Miss Selfridge. He doesn't need to work. I could look after him, but he doesn't want that. He's his own man.

I'll speak to him and ask, 'How's it going?' and he goes, 'Oh murder. It's murder. These people in Romania, the stuff they've sent. The quality of it is not right. I've got to go out there.' I think to myself, 'Why are you doing this, man? You could be sitting at home chilling.' But he's still relatively young and I know I wouldn't be able to sit on my backside doing nothing either, so I understand where he's coming from. I respect him for that, he's a hard-working man.

Dad's too proud to let me look after him for the rest of his life, but I've bought both him and Mum houses. He told me not to, but I just said, 'Shut up.' He was already moving anyway and I took over the mortgage. He lives not far from Mum and they still talk to each other. They weren't on speaking terms for a few years, but now they've realised that it's best for all parties, especially the children, if they do.

I'm close to both Mum and Dad and look back on my childhood fondly. Last Christmas Mum wrapped up my very first teddy bear, Loopy Loo, and gave it to me as a present. I couldn't believe it. It's got a seventies type of jumper, coloured greeny-blue and cream, with a bit of brown thrown in. It brought back loads of memories and now he takes pride of place in my house, in the dressing room. I'm not embarrassed to have it on show. It was a favourite toy and gives me a happy feeling.

Mum and Lisa have become good friends, they get on like a house on fire, so everything's worked out very nicely.

It's all part of how I became the Rio of today, what shaped and moulded me into the person I am – and I haven't even touched on football yet.

Falling in Love with Maradona

Whenever we picked teams on the field at the Friary I always wanted to be Maradona or John Barnes, but I was so young I ended up getting Steve Nicol, the Liverpool defender.

My first clear football memories are of lying on the couch at 18 Gisburn House mesmerised by Maradona at the 1986 World Cup.

He scored a wicked second goal for Argentina against England and I went mad. It didn't matter to me at the time that England lost or that he applied the Hand of God for the first one, because I loved his second solo goal so much. Seeing quality football has always got me even if it isn't my team playing.

Nowadays I'd want to rip his head off, but at the time I was only seven and I just kept replaying that individual goal over and over in my mind and ran outside to recreate it, pretending to be him.

Gabriel Heinze, the Argentine defender at Manchester United, tells me that when he met Maradona for the first time he cried because he felt so emotional. The geezer was a legend, the best individual footballer ever.

I used to adore all the showmen – John Barnes, Ian Wright, Paul Gascoigne, Paul Ince, Marco Van Basten and Frank Rijkaard – but Maradona was the guv'nor, a genius. I'm proud to say I have one of his signed shirts on my wall at home.

The 1986 World Cup was one of those events which makes you go, 'God, I'd love to be a footballer,' and I'll always remember the atmosphere on the telly – if that doesn't sound double-Dutch. The commentator was going nuts.

There wasn't the sound quality or picture clarity you get nowadays, which somehow made it more magical because it highlighted the fact that it was all going on a long way from England.

Whenever we picked teams on the field at the Friary I always wanted to be Maradona or John Barnes, but I was so young I ended up getting Steve Nicol, the Liverpool defender. It always pissed me off that. Nothing against Nicol, but he was hardly Maradona or Barnes.

Whenever I watched domestic football on the TV, Barnes was the man. There was a goal he scored against Brazil which was just amazing. He beat I don't know how many players before scoring.

I used to video all his games and learn the commentaries of the goals he scored. 'Will it be Barnes? It is now' was one commentary for a goal against Everton. I can still hear it.

I remember him setting up a goal for Gary Lineker in the World Cup and laying on two for David Speedie at Old Trafford. To score the number of goals he did from left wing was astonishing. I couldn't understand it when he used to get criticised in some of the papers for his England performances. I don't care what anyone says, he's one of the best players ever.

While I enjoyed football as an eight-year-old, I didn't play it much. I preferred 'runouts' which was a game where one team had a minute to run round the estate and hide and then had to get back to base without being caught.

All the older kids played football and kept asking me to join them until eventually I gave in. I wasn't the best because they were at least three years older which makes a lot of difference at that age. But it was good for my development because it meant I had to use skills to get past them rather than brute force. I didn't think I was particularly good and that I was going to take on the world. It was just cool playing with the older boys.

We didn't have a primary school team but we used to have a youth worker called Everton – yes, seriously – who was a semi-pro and coached us at our play centre after school. He was the first person who ever said to me, 'You're good, man, you should play for a team.'

My uncle, David Raynor, my mum's sister's husband, persuaded me to join his side, Bloomfield Athletic. I've still got that very first kit framed on the wall next to one of Maradona's shirts. You might say those shirts represent both ends of the football spectrum.

I've got all sorts of shirts on my wall at home now. There's one from the famous basketball player Michael Jordan, a T-shirt from Usher. I've got one of Gazza's shirts and others from Roberto Baggio, Del Piero, Rivaldo, Roberto Carlos, Raul, Figo and Ronaldo. I'm quite a collector. But I don't bother swapping with an opponent if they don't have their name on the back of the shirt. You've got to have the name. Argentina didn't have their names on their shirts when we beat them in a friendly in Geneva. I was gutted.

My cousin Ben, David's son, used to play in goal for Bloomfields and all the team were a year older than me. We played on a full-sized pitch with big goals, which seemed absolutely massive to me at the time. When I was growing up nobody played seven-a-side on little pitches like they do now.

I can still remember my first ever game for Bloomfields. It was against Gallians on a soggy, rainy Sunday. I realised on the Friday night before the game that I'd have to get some football boots, but Mum said she couldn't afford to buy me any. She asked around and finally discovered some at a friend's place.

I rummaged through this filthy cupboard and pulled out a pair of Hi-Tec Strikers. They were rock hard, two sizes too big and hadn't been used for years. But Dad said there was no way I was getting a pair of my own until he and Mum knew I was taking football seriously.

About two months later, when I'd convinced them I was interested, Mum and Dad bought me a pair of Mitre Scorpions. They were the business – black with white stripes and a brown outline round the stripe. Wouldn't be seen dead in them now of course, but back then, wow!

I worshipped those boots. Every day after training I washed

them carefully and put them underneath the radiator to dry out. Then I used dubbin to polish them up. I would wake up early just to check they were still there. They were like my pets.

Bloomfields' big rivals were Red Lion from Bermondsey, whose star player was Nigel Quashie who went on to play for the likes of QPR, Southampton, Portsmouth and West Brom.

Everyone knew about Nigel, he was *the* player in our area, the golden child, and we always had hard games against his team. Me and Nigel were on nodding terms. His mum and my dad were old friends from the same area. He went to school with my cousin Bernard and my big mate Gavin Rose played for Red Lion in the age group one year above him. He actually went on to play for the England Under-21s around the same time as me, although we were never in the same team.

Glenn Hoddle talked about Nigel as a possible for the 1998 World Cup, but it didn't happen for him with England and he ended up being capped by Scotland. Dunno how that happened! I never had him down as a Jock.

Bloomfields were in the Mercury League which was like a pub league compared to other leagues like the Echo. But we punched above our weight and played in the London Youth Cup against a team called Long Lane, which was known as one of the best around, and beat them 3–1.

I was 11 years old and a well-known local QPR scout called Sandy was watching that day and took four of us to Rangers. There was me, Ben, my mate Gavin Williams and a kid called Said Youseff, who was a wicked player who went on to play badminton for England.

It was my first flirtation with big-time football. Nigel was already at QPR and we trained together at 'the big one' which was the Barclays Bank ground at Hanger Lane. I was a school year below Nigel and trained on the pitch next to him.

Even though I was at QPR I carried on playing for Bloomfields for two years before joining Eltham Town who were in the best local league. I'd been playing a year above my age for Bloomfields, but now I was joining boys of my own age at a higher standard. Uncle Dave didn't want me to leave, but he understood.

I'd played in defence for Bloomfields, but I moved into midfield at Eltham. I scored 30-odd goals a season for two years and we won the title.

The secondary school I went to, Blackheath Bluecoat, wasn't a sporting school, but we used to play football at break and had the occasional game against other schools. The PE teacher, Mr Delaney, was a good bloke and used to cram us all into his VW camper van to take us to games. I'm sure it was illegal, but we didn't mind. His missus used to come to the matches as well. We all fancied her, so being squashed in the van next to those delightful curves was no hardship.

Mr Delaney entered us for the Metropolitan five-a-sides and we won the area competition to qualify for the All England finals. We had some good players. One of them, Tony Russell, played at Charlton for a while. But as a proper school team we were a joke. We asked Mr Owen, the head of Lower School, if he could get us a football coach so we could start playing in the cup competitions. He just kept saying it couldn't be done. We didn't even have our own playing field.

To compensate for this, Mr Delaney found out when the trials were for the district side and we went along to them instead. It took place over an entire day. We started with about 60 players and got whittled down to two teams playing each other.

The manager was Dave Goodwin, who was destined to become a massive influence on my career. I was in midfield and he picked me out and said, 'I'm going to call you Pelé, son, I like the way you play.' After that he took me under his wing.

Dave became like a second dad to me and I used to be

round at his house all the time. Dave, his wife Kate and daughter Danielle became like family. He worked part-time for Middlesbrough, doing reports on the opposition for their manager Lennie Lawrence. He would go to all the big grounds like Highbury and White Hart Lane and take me with him.

We would also go up country, to places like Coventry and Preston, on the train. It was one of the best bits of education for my football career.

We went to Wolves to see Middlesbrough get promoted. Their striker, Paul Wilkinson, was in the bar afterwards and gave me his cycling shorts, which he wore under his football kit. I was made up!

On the way home Dave used to test me, asking what formation the teams had played and where the goals had come from. And at the games I'd have to write down how the corners and throw-ins were taken.

Although Dave's team was a representative one it became the team I played for on a regular basis. We played every other week and for the All England Cup we would go all over the country. We went to Durham and the Isle of Wight, which was pretty exciting for a youngster who was normally never allowed off the estate.

I regularly used to have dinner round at Dave's and would even stay over on a Saturday night. Even now I still speak to him before and after games and I've always valued his opinion. He works at Newcastle now, but he worked at West Ham for ages, as well as Charlton and Middlesbrough. He knows his football. I'll always be grateful to him for what he did for me. I cannot thank him enough.

It was my choice to go to Blackheath Bluecoat secondary school. It was a half-hour bus journey from home, but I wanted to spread my wings and meet new people.

There was a sense of freedom about getting off the estate, although, typically, Mum insisted on coming with me on the bus for the first week. How embarrassing was that?

Bluecoats was academically better than the schools nearer to us, so Mum was pleased about my choice. But in Blackheath they thought Peckham boys were roughnecks and bad boys. Admittedly we liked messing about and having little fights but it was never anything serious.

We didn't have to wear a blazer, which was a plus, but on the downside we had to wear a blue jumper with an emblem and a tie. I've always hated uniforms. Later in life I had to wear the official suit to go to the 1998 World Cup with England and it was an absolute horror – a sort of washed-out green.

You weren't allowed to wear trainers in class, which also used to do my head in. I didn't like shoes. I had big feet and shoes looked funny on me.

But secondary school was wicked. I didn't like some of the lessons, but, just like at Camelot, I loved the banter and messing about in class with my mates. All my school reports said the same: 'Capable and very intelligent, but easily distracted, distracts others, talks too much.'

I couldn't help it. If my mates were talking and having a laugh I had to be involved. It's the same in the dressing room; it's like my classroom.

I enjoyed reading, though. One of my favourite books, perhaps not surprisingly, was *The Twits* by Roald Dahl, which is about a couple who like larking about. Another Roald Dahl book, *The BFG*, was also a favourite of mine. I also got hooked on a book about Jimmy Greaves which I found in the school library. It gave me a real insight into the highs and the lows of the game.

I got the nickname 'Bart Simpson' after the character in *The Simpsons* because my hair stood straight up. I was also known as 'The Fresh Prince' because I was really into the programme *The Fresh Prince of Bel Air*. Will Smith, who was the star, was a really cool dude, so it was no bad thing being compared to him, I can tell you. I watched *Fresh Prince* all the time. It was one of the best programmes on TV when we were kids. But it still didn't beat *EastEnders* which I'm still obsessed with today. Maybe it's because I live away and it reminds me of home.

Bluecoat was a mixed school which meant there were plenty of good-looking birds in the class and they loved me. It's true – well that's the way I remember it. I never had a girl-friend though. The closest I came was with Kelly Martin for a little while, but I didn't want a regular on my arm because I used to hate people knowing my business. That's never changed. If it got to me then, you can imagine how much it annoys me now.

If I ever kissed any birds I'd always insist they didn't tell anyone. Most kids would have bragged about it, but I didn't. After we'd had a kiss, a girl would say, 'Let me hold your hand. Let's walk back to class together,' and I would be like, 'Hold hands? No way!' If anyone put me on the spot about it I'd say, 'What are you talking about? Do you think I would do anything with her? No chance.' I tell you, I used to be weird in that way.

I went to France once with Leyton Square and me and my mate ended up pulling a couple of 13-year-old French birds. We were in this barn and I was kissing one of them, trying to get her top off and then I felt something furry and realised she had hairy armpits. I've never shit myself so much in my life. I just jumped up and left.

As I've said, I never missed many days at school, but I would go missing when I was there. I would occasionally hide in the toilets with my mates if there was a lesson coming up we didn't like. Science, maybe, or RE because I'm not very religious.

I had my chance though. My school was Church of England and I used to go to Sunday school now and again. My mum's right into religion. She's a born-again Christian and her husband Peter is a deacon.

But, while I believe there is a superior being up there, I can't work out why he would let people die in car crashes and natural disasters. If he's as powerful as everyone says why do innocent people die in Iraq? Why do people die in Palestine and Israel? Religion seems to be at the root of a lot of trouble.

At the same time, I'm fascinated by different religions. I've got friends who are Muslims and I wanted to understand their faith. School should have helped me with that, but it didn't. I believe things happen for a reason and I'm interested in why.

One of the reasons I struggle to understand why God acts in the way he does is when things happen like the death of Stephen Lawrence, who went to my school. He was four years older than me, but I knew him quite well. He was a quiet lad, a nice kid who loved art.

One day, in April 1993, whispers went round school saying he'd been stabbed. No one believed it until the headteacher told everyone he'd been killed at a bus stop in Eltham. The school shut down immediately and everyone had to go home.

Stephen had been with a boy called Duwayne Brooks, who I remember was a good footballer. Duwayne was meant to have carried Stephen, trying to get help. Everyone thought they knew who the kids were that did it and the same names kept cropping up. The *Daily Mail* even named the five who were supposed to be involved.

No one knew what Stephen, who was a black lad, was doing in the area where he'd been stabbed. It was an especially dangerous place late at night and if you were black you just wouldn't be seen walking round there.

Stephen's parents, Neville and Doreen, fought a big

campaign to obtain justice for their son. They went all the way through the courts and had meetings with MPs, but still there has been no result. They need closure but they haven't got it.

I went to one of the dinners for Stephen's campaign a few years ago and donated some gear. I know that's not much, compared to what the Lawrences and others have put themselves through, but I was proud to be involved.

Just when it seemed the campaign had gone off the boil, a BBC programme, *The Boys Who Killed Stephen Lawrence*, was aired in July 2006. I couldn't believe some of the stuff in it. All sorts of allegations and claims about what was going on. If there is a God up there, I pray that justice is done some day for the Lawrences.

Some of the lads at school smoked, but I didn't like it. It made me feel sick. I would only take a couple of drags to be part of the crowd, but I even stopped doing that. It wouldn't have been very good for my football either.

There were subjects I liked, such as PE, English, maths and drama. I was lucky; I had good teachers who made those subjects interesting.

I was one of the stars of our school production of *Bugsy Malone*. I played that wicked geezer Fizzy, the cleaner in the club, and I sang 'Tomorrow'. The audience gave me a standing ovation, as I remember it. Or maybe were they just getting up to leave! I had a thing for acting then and I used to go to the classes when the drama club came to our estate.

I got a B in drama in my GCSE. It should have been an A, but my written coursework let me down. I couldn't be arsed. I liked acting, not writing about it. I used to fudge my way through school copying coursework. I'd chat all lesson, then I'd get a kid to give me his book and I'd go and copy bits and pieces on the bus, but put it in my own words. It wasn't that I couldn't do it; it was just easier that way.

I only started working hard in school in the last year when my dad gave me that ultimatum that I couldn't play football unless I got five GCSEs at A to C grade. Fortunately I did.

I've had two chances to join Chelsea in my life. Some reckon it was three, after I was seen talking to their chief executive Peter Kenyon last season, but I can assure them it wasn't. I've never been interested in going there.

The first time they tried to sign me was when I was 14 and the other was when I was about to make my £18 million move from West Ham to Leeds in November 2000.

Although I was training at QPR as a youngster and enjoying it, I was interested to see what other clubs were like. When I turned 14, I didn't sign for any club as a schoolboy. I could have done, but I didn't want to commit myself.

Chelsea had been trying to get me to train with them, so I thought I'd have a look, but I hated it. For a start, they trained miles away at Battersea Park and when you did get there, it wasn't worth the bother.

One day with Chelsea our team won a game 10–6 and our reward was to do six laps of the Astroturf pitch. Anyone who's ever been there will tell you it's massive. I was only a young lad and already did plenty of running all day at school and on the estate. The reason I went to training was to learn about football, not be a cross-country runner, so I didn't bother going back.

I then went to Charlton where a kid called me a 'black bastard'. The kid got chucked out and I got told I could stay, but I didn't like the atmosphere so I left.

My mum had always supported Millwall and, even though the club and the surrounding area had a reputation for being racist, I decided to give it a go. I went for a week in the summer holidays and trained with the likes of Ben Thatcher, Mark Kennedy and Jermaine Wright. The coach, Tom Walley, was highly respected and put on some wicked sessions.

For all that Millwall had a poor reputation, you didn't sense it inside the club. I quite liked it and the manager, Mick McCarthy, tried really hard to get me to stay, but I still wanted to look at other options. I was enjoying life and I didn't want to be tied down anywhere. I liked travelling to different clubs during the holidays and at weekends to find out what each one had to offer.

My nomadic existence took me to Norwich for a while. It was there that I ran into the formidable Ade Akinbiyi, who is now at newly promoted Premiership side Sheffield United. He was four years older than me, but took part in our practice games. He's always remembered me from those days and every time I see him play we have a little natter.

I went to Middlesbrough because of Dave Goodwin's connections with the club and I loved it there. I went for nearly a year, every school holiday, with my mate Anthony McFarlane. We stayed in a bed and breakfast in Stockton.

They used to give us loads of stuff to take home, like tracksuits, new boots and kit bags. The give-aways were all designed to create a good impression of the club and I loved getting free gear.

Graham Kavanagh, the Republic of Ireland midfielder who now plays for Sunderland, stayed in the same digs and looked after us. We thought he was the greatest player in the world.

He took me out a few times in his car and I used to think, 'I'd love to be like Graham Kavanagh. Oh God, I'd love to be like him.' I was a skinny string bean and Graham looked really big. I feared that I wouldn't grow up to be as big as him and consequently wouldn't make the grade. I've filled out since, of course, and grown a bit. I've played against Graham in the Premiership and he's only about 5ft 10in, whereas I'm 6ft 3in.

While I was commuting up and down to Middlesbrough in the holidays, and still training at QPR, Frank Lampard's dad, Frank Snr, was scouting for West Ham and kept pestering Dave Goodwin to take me along there.

Although Dave worked for Boro, he never stood in my way when I wanted to try other places and he reckoned we might as well go along, just to shut Frank up if nothing else.

It was a disaster. Everything went wrong that could go wrong.

We got completely lost, it took over two hours to get there and we were more than an hour late. I was knackered before I'd even started. And, without thinking, all I'd brought with me was my QPR kit, which didn't go down too well.

The other lads were a bit bolshie, taking the piss out of me for wearing a QPR shirt and they plainly didn't think much of kids from south London, so they just kicked me. Joe Keith, who went on to Leyton Orient, remembers me coming that day and still laughs about it now.

Needless to say, I didn't enjoy myself and didn't go back for a couple of months until Frank rang my home and persuaded me to give it another go. He made life easier by coming round to pick me up in his Mercedes to take me to a game.

It was the first time I'd ever been in a really nice car. He pulled up outside our council flat and didn't half look out of place. My mates saw me getting in the car and asked whose it was. I said, cool as you like, 'It's just Frank Lampard from West Ham. He's giving me a lift.'

I'd never been to east London before I started training at West Ham. Those who don't know the capital could be forgiven for thinking south-east London and east London are very much the same, but they are worlds apart.

Billy Bonds was the manager and used to practise with us sometimes. He was a hard man, a well-respected former player who took no shit. But I wasn't scared of him and, after he came through the back of me in training one time, I refused to be phased by it and gave as good as I got in the next challenge.

Billy wasn't angry, far from it. 'I like that, son,' he said with a grin on his face. From then on West Ham cranked up the pressure to get me to sign and it was clear I was going to have to make a decision.

I was now 15 and all the clubs I'd been to were offering me a schoolboy contract and suggesting that if I signed they would give me two years as a YTS trainee and then another year as a pro. If I'd pushed it, Charlton would probably have offered me two years as a pro, taking me up to the age 20.

I thought about going to Millwall and Mum was really impressed with Mick McCarthy. I also came close to joining Middlesbrough because I liked the training there best, but, even with my desire for adventure, I knew at that age that I would miss my family and my mates. It was just too far away.

In the space of a 45-minute discussion with Mum and Dad, and Dave Goodwin over the phone, I opted for Boro, then Millwall, then Charlton, back to Millwall, then Boro again before eventually settling for West Ham.

In January 1994 I signed on the pitch at Upton Park, watched by Mum, Anton and Frank Lampard Snr. The photograph taken that afternoon is one of my proudest possessions.

I was a Hammer and desperate to make it all the way as a pro, but I chanced my arm over the next few years and could easily have ended up on the scrapheap.

Me and Frank

I'd still like to go out on a Saturday, have a mental night out, then do it all over again on a Sunday and not have to worry. The popstar lifestyle has always appealed to me. They work hard and play hard and it doesn't have an effect on their work. Unfortunately, it has a detrimental effect on footballers.

West Ham's Chadwell Heath training ground was a long old hike from school. You had to get the bus to New Cross, which took 20 minutes, then you went from New Cross to Bank station and at Bank you had to change lines and walk through to Embankment. From Embankment you got a train to Mile End and then another from Mile End to Dagenham. Then it was another bus and when you got off there was still a ten-minute walk.

There were three of us from Peckham who trained with West Ham – me, Anthony McFarlane and Justin Bowen – and we would meet up as soon as school finished. As ever, we'd have a good laugh on the way and I got to quite like the journey in the end. As I've said, I loved mucking about and the best fun used to be had when we went for trials for the England Schoolboys side. It was a long, drawn-out process, involving quite a few trips, and it was possible to make a right few quid.

The boys from the Inner London district side, who included Jody Morris, the best local player in the capital, always travelled together on the train and it was a riot. We'd have a game of cards, mess about and play knuckles. Some of the kids would be screaming because their knuckles would bleed, but Jody and I always made sure we didn't lose.

We had to go to Keele in Staffordshire one time and reckoned we could make about £60 on the trip – a lot of money when you are 15 – if we kept our wits about us. We watched out for the ticket man and when he came past some lads pretended to be asleep while others ran into the toilet. The geezer went by, we didn't have to pay and we claimed the fare for the journey. It was a breeze.

Another time I tried it, we got caught and an official complaint was made. We got the third degree and escaped with a severe warning, but at that age you shit yourself and think the police are going to turn up and throw you in jail.

I never did as well as I should have in those trials and didn't make it on to any of the England Schoolboys teams. I got too nervous and froze. I started thinking about it all too deeply and didn't play my natural game.

I only ever made the last 40 of the England Schoolboys squad. I never got any further. I know there are England and West Ham scouts at that time who thought I would never make it.

I also suffered a partial tear in the anterior cruciate ligament of my knee which I'm told could have wrecked my career. Fortunately the best physio in the world, John Green, repaired the damage. He was the West Ham first-team physio but took time out to look after me and I'll always be grateful to him for that.

Six months after joining West Ham, I had a growth spurt. I shot up about four inches and lost all co-ordination. I couldn't kick, couldn't pass, couldn't tackle, nothing. It was embarrassing.

Frank Lampard's son, Frank Jnr, who became one of my best mates at the club, was killing himself laughing as I stumbled about like Bambi on ice. It might have been funny to him, but it was serious for me. I knew if I went on like that my career could be over before it had begun.

I was being made sub for the club's schoolboys side and, as statistics prove very few make the grade as a pro anyway, it wasn't looking good.

Dave Goodwin was coming to our games and on the train on the way home he would hammer me, telling me I was a disgrace and that I had to sort myself out. Nearly every club in the land had wanted to sign me and suddenly I was absolutely shocking.

I didn't like the schoolboys coach Paul Heffer at first. He

would mimic my relaxed style in front of the other lads and I thought he was taking the piss. But when I moved up to YTS he told me that he'd got on my case because he knew I was a good player and he felt I had more to give. I appreciated that and I'm grateful for what he did. He made me more determined. A few years later Peter Taylor was another coach who got on my case, when I was with the England Under-21s. He was good for me too. Both of them brought out the best in me.

Anyway, the turning point for me at West Ham came in May 1995 in the South East Counties League Cup final. I was only picked for the second leg against Chelsea because half the usual team were injured or away with the first team in Australia and, as we'd already lost the first leg 5–2 at home, nobody was expecting much in the return at Stamford Bridge. I was 16 and still at school. I had to get the bus and the tube to Stamford Bridge, which was miles away.

We were up against some of the best young players in the country. A kid called Junior Mendes was playing for Chelsea that night who was a hot player back then. He was at Notts County last I heard.

Me and Frank played together in central midfield and I scored our first goal after six minutes, running through and shooting past the keeper. Then I set up another two and we won 4–1 to take the final to penalties. I scored one in the shoot-out and Frank fired home the decider to cap an amazing comeback. To top it all, I was named Man of the Match. I fitted into my own body at last.

People who say I don't appreciate football don't know me at all. They don't understand my feelings for the game and how much desire I have to play. That final was possibly the most significant game of my career. I should have the medal mounted in a glass case.

The manager Harry Redknapp, who had taken over from Bill Bonds, sent his dad, Harry Snr, to watch the game. He apparently gave his son three guesses who the best player was on the pitch and Harry Jnr didn't get it. When he found out it was me he was quite surprised. I'm sure he expected it to be one of the older lads.

That game made me realise I could mix it with the best of them and I was no longer worried about my future. My confidence rocketed and a couple of months later I signed for the Hammers as a YTS apprentice on £29 a week.

On my very first day as a YTS player I was given the job of cleaning Harry's and Tony Cottee's boots for the year. I'd done the job when I got a shout from Cottee. He was standing there fuming, asking why his kit, training tops and boots hadn't all been put together by his peg.

I told him I'd cleaned his boots and that he had to get his kit and stuff from the kit man. He wasn't having none of that. He told me he expected me to get his kit and put it all together with his boots in the changing room. That wasn't part of the YTS agreement, but I did what I was told. And at Christmas all I got was a £40 tip. Dicksy gave Frank £100 for doing his boots!

Growing up with my mates, I had always said I would die happy if I played just one minute of league football. I'd even said it when I started out at West Ham. But now I knew I could do more and set my sights higher. I had the potential to be a proper footballer.

We had a cracking youth team, one of the best West Ham have ever had. There was me, Frank, Lee Hodges, who went on to play for Scunthorpe and Bristol Rovers, and Manny Omoyinmi, who made it into the first team for West Ham but was bombed out when he forgot to tell Harry he was cup-tied for a League Cup game and the match had to be replayed. He went on to Scunthorpe and Oxford and I last heard of him at Gravesend.

There was also David Partridge, who years later played against me for Wales in a World Cup qualifier, Danny Shipp, who went to Dagenham and has been around the non-league scene for years, and Joe Keith, who I mentioned earlier.

While I was doing my Bambi impression in the early days, Frank had problems of his own. He was struck down by glandular fever and struggled with it for a while. He had no energy and couldn't get going. But once he got over it, there was no stopping him. After the strikers Lee Boylan and Danny Shipp, he was one of our top scorers. He must have scored 20 goals a year from midfield for two years, just like he has for Chelsea.

We won the South East Counties League, which was a big breakthrough because before then it had always been won by Spurs or Arsenal, who we always reckoned were a bit flash. They all had lovely pristine boots and silky skills, but we turned the usual order on its head.

Those days were the best of my life in terms of pure enjoyment.

After a game we'd all go to McDonald's on the way home for a burger. Then we'd go have a sleep and go back out to a club, usually 5th Avenue in Ilford. It was a carefree life and there are times when I really miss it.

Although Mum was worried that I was burning the candle at both ends, I persuaded her I was fine and didn't let on when I'd been drinking.

I'd still like to go out on a Saturday, have a mental night out, then do it all over again on a Sunday and not have to worry. The popstar lifestyle has always appealed to me. They work hard and play hard and it doesn't have an effect on their work. If anything, it enhances it. Unfortunately, it has a detrimental effect on footballers.

I've always enjoyed clubbing, but I have to curb my enthusiasm for those big nights out these days because there is so much more pressure to be successful. I'm not complaining – it's the way it is and the rewards are fantastic. Football is big business, with millions of fans watching and millions of pounds riding on results.

Even doing all the menial jobs we had to do at West Ham, like cleaning up the dressing rooms and polishing the boots or scrubbing out the toilets, could be a laugh. We were all mucking in together and it helped with team spirit.

We had to be at Chadwell Heath at 9a.m., which meant getting up at 7a.m., and we might not leave until 5p.m. if the jobs weren't done properly. If there was so much as one ball missing we'd all be sent back out to look for it. West Ham couldn't afford to lose any!

I don't want to sound like an old fossil, but the kids coming into the professional game now would benefit from some hard graft. If you asked a trainee to clean your boots today, he'd wonder what the hell you were talking about. These days the kit men do it.

When 14-year-olds turn up at Premiership clubs they come chauffeur-driven by their agents and are wearing their Ralph Lauren tops or Armani suits. They already have the best gear from Nike or adidas and are signing for £500 a week. You shouldn't even be thinking about a wage when you're so young.

In my day, which wasn't too long ago, you might have a moody Ralph Lauren shirt if you were lucky, but you also had a shitty old tracksuit, a pair of trainers half beat up, and you got the bus to training.

The West Ham youth boss, Tony Carr, was a big influence in my early career and when he did a book on coaching I was delighted to be asked to write the foreword to it.

Jimmy Hamson and Jimmy Neighbour used to help Tony, as did a bloke called Ronnie Boyce, who wasn't really a coach, but took part in the sessions. Even at 50 he was a brilliant player. Later on, the reserve team coach, Frank Burrows, and another coach, Roger Cross, were a big help to me too.

We were taught all the right habits. 'Pass and move' was the mantra and the quality of the touch was everything. It was part of West Ham history, playing the beautiful game which had been part of the fabric of the place since the days of Moore, Hurst and Peters, if not before.

Frank's dad, who became Harry's assistant, gave me one of the best pieces of advice ever, yet it was so simple. He told me to always have a picture in my head and for a week I didn't know what he was talking about. Then he explained that, as the ball comes to you, you should have a picture of where your team-mates are and where you're going to play it. It's always stayed with me that one, and it works.

We used to play a game called Ds where you would volley the ball from one end of the gym to the other and it had to bounce in the semi-circle shaped like a D. If you drilled the ball straight into the goal at the other end without it bouncing anywhere else or the other boys touching it you would get two goals. If it didn't go straight in, the other team were allowed two touches, one teeing it up, the other volleying it back. It was great for your control.

Me, Frank, Joe Keith and Lee Hodges would play it till the cows came home. Tony put on brilliant sessions, but was also a hard taskmaster and very disciplined. He always drilled into us that we should use what we called 'the third man run'. That is, when you play a ball into a player it comes back and a third man goes on a run and is released with a pass.

Every Monday he would make us run a mile before training started. It was hard and had to be done at full pelt, but I always won. I loved doing all the fitness work and still do today. Those days spent racing round the estate in my socks served me well.

Me and Frank came from totally different backgrounds. His dad made a good living as a player, then as a coach at West Ham and could afford to send Frank to public school.

I would stay at his house after youth games on a Saturday or before a Sunday kick-off. It was a mansion, the biggest house I'd ever been in. Beautiful. Their kitchen seemed the size of a five-a-side football pitch and there was a huge garden with a golf hole in the middle.

I couldn't believe how many tellys they had. They were everywhere. Frank had Ralph Lauren jumpers and shirts piled high in his wardrobe, a different one for every day of the week. I used to think, 'You lucky boy.'

What with his dad, his uncle Harry Redknapp and Harry's son Jamie, a pin-up boy who had just joined Liverpool, professional football had always been very much part of Frank's life. His knowledge of the game was beyond that of most other kids. And because of his background his work ethic in training was up there with the best of them. He knew the whole football scene; I was green as grass.

He was older than me and when he got into the reserves first and then the first team it spurred me on. If I stayed out for extra training, he would do the same and vice versa. If he was in the gym, I'd go in the gym. Neither of us wanted to be left behind. We were competitive in a positive, friendly way, yet we never spoke about it.

Frank announced one day that we were going on a night out to the West End with Jamie and a few other Liverpool players. I was only 17 and shitting myself about going with them, worrying how I should dress and how to behave. I wore my old school trousers with a shocking shirt and the whole

outfit must have cost about as much as Jamie's boxer shorts.

Here's how bad it was: I'd actually sewn a Dolce & Gabbana logo on to my shirt to make it look cool. But it actually looked crap. Fortunately, I decided at the last minute that it wasn't right and ripped it off. God knows what they'd have thought if they'd seen it. Frank, of course, was in a trendy shirt and trousers which probably came from Armani. He looked the nuts.

Jamie was 'the face' at the time, the bloke to be seen with. He had everything going for him and had just started getting into the England squad. He was where I wanted to be. He arrived with his brother Mark, Phil Babb and Jason McAteer and we went to one of the best clubs in the capital – the Emporium.

When we arrived there was a queue about 100 yards long. We walked straight past the lot of them and were in through the front door in ten seconds flat. I didn't know that was possible. I'd always had to queue before, sometimes for hours, and here we were, at this top place, going straight to the front.

When we got in there were loads of other footballers, all really smart dressers, and I felt so inadequate. I was just in awe.

What a club too. They played funky house in the main room, which had a big bar and dance-floor, and in the back there was an R&B area, which is where I ended up going religiously for the next four years. I had my own spot in there. I used to stand at the bar and lift the shelf, which the barman raised to get in and out, so I had more space to dance.

Even for Frank this was a bit of an occasion and we sat in that club telling each other that if we played well we could go on and play for England and be like Jamie. We were going, 'We want to make it, man. We have to make it, we have to make it.' I wasn't really aiming for England at that time – I wasn't even in the West Ham first team – but I had come to realise what was possible. And that night, for the first time, it really hit home what the fringe benefits of being a top footballer were.

People were buying the players drink after drink and there were birds crawling all over them.

Jamie's a good-looking lad, of course, but I soon learned that if you're a footballer it doesn't matter how pig-ugly you are, you will always get attention from the fittest birds.

When I first dreamed of becoming a footballer, fame, birds and wealth didn't come into it. As a kid on the estate, sitting with my mates at the bottom of the stairs leading to our third-floor flat and shuffling aside for the old lady to walk past, we just talked about the game.

But the money was important to me when it came. Not that I was very sensible with it. From the moment I started getting my £29 a week I would blow the lot in one go and I'd have to borrow money off my mum. It was the same every week.

At 17, I got a new contract which paid me £400 a week and I felt like a millionaire. I immediately passed my driving test and went out to get a car. Dave Goodwin came along to help and we decided to go round a few dealerships and see if they'd sponsor me. Clearly I'd got carried away with my own importance. I was only in West Ham's reserves and no one gave a fuck.

When the realisation dawned that I wasn't going to get a free car, I settled on a two-door Ford Fiesta Freestyle which cost £3,999. It was blue with a Freestyle sign on the back and mudguards and it was a little bit different to the basic build.

I'd got a signing-on fee of £4,000 for agreeing the new contract so the whole lot was going on the car. I was made up with it.

Just as I was about to sign the papers, the salesman asked about my insurance. I sat there puzzled. I'd never heard of it.

I don't think anyone insured cars on our estate! He explained that I had to have insurance to drive and if I didn't I would be breaking the law. I thought he was having me on. I told him to get things signed because I was driving out of the showroom.

He wouldn't let me, so I asked him to phone someone to get the insurance sorted. I couldn't believe it when he came back and told me the cost – £2,000 a year! Bloody hell, it was half the price of the car. Apparently, teenage footballers were high risk. I couldn't imagine why!

One minute I'd been happy as a bunny with my new wheels and now I was slumped in a chair, stunned. I had to ask Mum to lend me the money and took out a loan to pay her back.

That Fiesta was the dog's bollocks. Julian Dicks had the most expensive car at the club, a Porsche, but I wasn't a Porsche fan, I honestly preferred the Fiesta. Frank had a Fiesta too, but his was an SI, which was the top of the range, and I couldn't afford that.

I wasn't a boy-racer, honestly, not someone who did handbrake turns all over the estate. But me and my mates would go out driving for hours round south London.

We'd cruise to a little bar, sit around and chill, seeing if there were any birds about, and then trying to pull 'em. I'm sure they were looking at me as if to say, 'Who does he think he is in that Fiesta?' but I wasn't bothered. I was living my dream.

One day, I'd driven round to the Acorn Estate in my pride and joy to see my cousin Bernard and a few of his mates. We were sitting outside the video shop when two meat wagons screeched round the corner and out jumped a load of coppers who shouted at us, 'Don't move!'

They told me they had to search my Fiesta and asked how

I could afford to buy it and what I was doing round there. So I told them I was visiting Bernard and that I played for West Ham. 'Never heard of you,' said this copper and asked for proof.

You tend not to carry ID saying 'West Ham United footballer' and short of finding a ball and doing 500 keepie-uppies it was going to be difficult to prove it on the spot. But I said, 'West Ham pay me enough and I've bought this car with my own money.'

They started searching the car and, to my embarrassment, found a few porno mags in the boot which I'd forgotten about. This policewoman held them up for everyone to see and laughed. I was going, 'They're my mate's, they're not mine.'

Meanwhile, Bernard was shouting his mouth off, as he always does, saying, 'Just fucking leave him alone. What's wrong with you? There's nothing in his car. He don't do drugs. He doesn't do nothing like that. He plays football. He don't do no mad shit,' which wasn't exactly calming the situation.

Suddenly, one of the other lads in our group, someone I'd gone to primary school with, ran off. The police caught him, which was impressive because he was a quick lad, and found drugs in his pocket. He got a year in prison.

When they weren't being banged up, my mates were proud of the fact that I had the Fiesta and played for West Ham. They wanted to know every detail about training, the games, what other players were like, how the manager was, who the best youngster was, who was playing well, who was crap. They couldn't get enough of it.

Football was our lives and they were so pleased that their friend from Peckham had made it, just like I would have been if it had been one of them.

My first experience of playing centre-half as a West Ham player was at Chadwell Heath against Charlton Under-16s

because we didn't have anyone else. If we were losing or drawing they'd send me up front and I usually scored. But a lot of my younger days had been spent in midfield and now I was being used as a defender. To be honest, I had a strop on about it. I was worried I would be considered a utility player who wasn't good enough for one particular position.

I needn't have worried though. The coaches had obviously seen something. Sometimes the gaffer would ask me and Frank to join the first team for a game in training if they were a couple of players short. We'd get the chance to get stuck in with Marc Rieper, Iain Dowie, John Moncur, Julian Dicks, Ian Bishop, Steve Potts, Tony Cottee and Alvin Martin and I wanted more of it. This was an unbelievable experience for a first-year YTS like me – something to report back to the lads on the estate. But I wasn't overawed.

When I was a YTS boy there was more to do than just training. I had to go to Kingsway College as part of the YTS scheme, which would have been fine if I'd been given a choice of course. I was told I had to do an NVQ in Travel and Tourism and I couldn't see the point. I wanted to do something in sport. When Anton went a few years later he asked to study music and they found a course for him.

There was no such flexibility in my time and I would sit there during lessons staring out of the window. It was shit, but at least they had an amusement arcade and a pool table.

I was in the same class as Harvey, who was on Barnet's books at the time and later became part of the band So Solid Crew. He was not a bad footballer, although he talked a better game than he played.

I didn't have to suffer the course long though. Harry told me not to go any more because he needed me to train with the first team full-time. I was ecstatic. I was still only 17, but I was in the big boys' world now.

West Ham was a crazy place. At the training ground ticket touts were always coming in for cups of tea and a bit of lunch. Then there would be geezers selling everything you could imagine: jewellery, clothes, all sorts spread out on the tables. It was like the local market.

They'd just open the front door and all these geezers would pile in and we'd come and have a look at what they had to offer. They were harmless blokes and we trusted them. They didn't go running to the press with stories. At least I don't think they did!

Harry's a great bloke. He comes from a wide boy kind of background, and a lot of those who came down to the training ground were his mates. He loved a deal, whether it was in the transfer market or off the back of a lorry. All legitimate, of course. And we loved the whole scene, lapping it all up.

One day, he called me into his office and told me I had to do a deal with Mizuno. Jamie had a deal with Mizuno as well – Harry said they wanted me to wear their boots and I was to go to the Sports Cafe in London, where they were having a launch, and I would get loads of free gear. He was right as well – I couldn't carry it all home.

Another time, Harry sat me down and said he'd improve my contract by £100 a week if I added another year on. There were no agents there, just me and Harry, and I told him I was worth more than an extra £100 a week. Harry was not impressed. He said, 'Son, you've got a nice little car outside and now you'll be able to go out and buy your mum a new sofa. This is a great deal. You might even be able to buy her a coat as well. When did you ever think you'd be able to do that? Not long ago you didn't have a pot to piss in and now you're asking me for more money than your dad's ever earned.'

He was going redder and redder. 'What's your dad on? He won't be on that, I can tell you, so be happy with it.'

I was really mad when I walked out and thought he was out of order to imply we should be grateful because we'd never had any money before. But in the end I signed it. I had no choice. The young players who come through the system always get treated differently to those who come in from outside.

I've come to realise it was just the manager trying to get a good deal for the club. It's the same at any club.

When the gaffer told me he was putting me on the bench against Sheffield Wednesday for the last game of the 1995–96 season it was the greatest feeling. Frank had made his debut a few months earlier and I'd been desperate for my turn. There had been a lot of talk about me in the press and now it was the chance for the fans to see what I was about. I wasn't nervous like I had been in those England trials. I was ready for the step up.

I came on as a sub, at the age of 17 years and 6 months, for Tony Cottee. As I aimed to play the ball down the line with my first touch, I sliced it straight into the stands. I got a big cheer and smiled with a sort of fixed grin, but it was an embarrassing start. Fans who were there that day still talk about it, but fortunately my game picked up the longer I was on the pitch.

At one point, their striker, David Hirst, tried to elbow my head off, but I got the ball off him and we started wrestling on the floor. He seemed to want to kill me and the fans were loving it. Then I went up for a corner and crashed into him and the ref had a go at us.

It was great stuff. After years of dreaming about this day, going right back to the time lying on the couch watching the 1986 World Cup, I'd done it. I'd tasted the real thing. But that minute of play I'd dreamed about was certainly no longer enough for me now. I wanted more.

The end to that season was mad because my debut was

sandwiched in between the two legs of the FA Youth Cup final against Liverpool.

There was a lot more press interest than normal, because much had already been written about me and Frank, and also Michael Owen, who was Liverpool's red-hot 16-year-old striker. Jamie Carragher was also in the Liverpool team and we knew each other because by then me and Carra were playing for England Youth. Yes, I'd finally made it into an England team.

Michael had scored in every round of the competition up to the final, including two hat-tricks, and, typically, got one in the final as well. We lost the first leg 2–0 at home in front of 15,000 fans and there were 20,000 at the second leg at Anfield, where we lost 2–1. I played central midfield with Frank, who scored our goal.

I got Man of the Match but we'd lost 4–1 on aggregate. Little did I know there was an incredible consolation prize waiting for me that summer.

A Boy Among Men

I was sat there, swinging on a chair in the hotel, wondering what my friends would think if they could see me now, with the best footballers in the country. It couldn't get any better than this.

When a letter came through the door from the FA at the end of the season I didn't open it immediately because I thought it was travel itinerary details for the European Youth Championships that summer. When I eventually got round to reading it, I couldn't believe my eyes. I was being invited to train with England's Euro 96 squad.

I thought someone had to be taking the piss, although even by my mates' standards this was a good wind-up.

I rang Harry Redknapp who told me the letter was genuine. He explained that England manager Terry Venables, a friend of his, thought it was a good idea for promising youngsters to get a taste of life with the senior squad.

Frank got chosen too, along with Jamie Cassidy from Liverpool and Andy Ducros, who was at Coventry. I knew Andy a little from the England youth scene. He was a nice lad and a good player, but a tad on the small side and, unfortunately for his career, he never grew any bigger.

There was so much hype around Euro 96 because it was being staged at home. The country was in a complete frenzy and I was going to be part of it. I couldn't get back to Chadwell quick enough to get my boots.

Man, was I excited. The FA sent this big black Mercedes to pick me up and I was driven to the training camp at the start of the week leading up to the match against Scotland.

I was like a kid in a sweet shop. There were stacks of free gear and Robbie Fowler gave me a pair of his boots which I've still got to this day. You always get loads of stuff when you are picked for any England squad. Even with England Youth you got a huge Umbro bag full of T-shirts, shorts, jerseys and tracksuits. I got so much that I kitted out all my mates on our estate. People must have thought the entire England youth team lived in Peckham!

Paul Ince, Jamie Redknapp, Robbie Fowler and Les

Ferdinand all took me under their wing at Euro 96. Les especially, because by then we'd discovered that he and my dad were cousins. Gary Neville tells me he was there as well, but I don't remember him. Funny that, considering he's such a quiet and unassuming sort of bloke!

I was sat there, swinging on a chair in the hotel, wondering what my friends would think if they could see me now, with the best footballers in the country. It couldn't get any better than this.

I got myself noticed by hammering everyone at table tennis, which I'd always played at Leyton Square. I doubt there's a footballer who can beat me at the game. I'll challenge anyone. Cristiano Ronaldo has a go at United, but he ain't in my league yet.

We got free phone calls, so I reported back to my mates every day with all the details. I was going, 'I've just had dinner with Paul Ince and Gazza, then I was playing computer games against Gazza, and I took the ball off him in training and did a bit of skill, and Terry Venables said, "Well done, son" to me. I'm killing it here, killing it.' And they'd be going, 'Oh my God, seriously?'

Because a lot of them were Liverpool supporters, going back to our days on the estate when we used to idolise the likes of John Barnes, they wanted to know all about Fowler. They'd say, 'Has he got skills? Tell me he's got skills. Tell me he's doing shit to people.' It was mad. I was like a reporter at the very heart of the story.

Gazza did tricks in training I never imagined possible. I was dumbstruck watching him and wondered how the hell I was ever going to be as good. One time, he got the ball on the halfway line, turned, went past two players and, while he was still in the centre-circle, he smashed this shot past David Seaman. Venables couldn't stop clapping and my mouth just stayed dropped open in amazement. Gazza was frightening.

I didn't see the likes of that again until Wayne Rooney was selected for the England squad for a Euro 2004 qualifier against Turkey and he scored a wonder goal past Paul Robinson in training. It reminded me so much of that Gazza moment.

Practice games were unbelievable, but I didn't feel nervous or that I didn't belong. I was enjoying myself too much. All the players were brilliant to me. They didn't treat me like an outsider. Terry Venables would say to me, 'Just relax, son. Enjoy it. You wouldn't be here if you didn't deserve to be.'

I admired Venables as a coach and liked him as a bloke as well. That's why, later in my career, it became so much harder to leave Leeds for Manchester United when he took over as manager just as I was making my mind up to go. I had a lot of respect for him. He gave the lads loads of confidence and there was a good atmosphere at training. Serious when it had to be, but fun as well.

At West Ham you could get away with making a few mistakes in training, but with England you had to concentrate and make sure that you didn't make any mistakes at all.

Incey was brilliant in training, as was Nicky Barmby, who had a lot of skill. Alan Shearer, on the other hand, wasn't my type of player. He was a great footballer and goalscorer, which is no bad thing of course, but I preferred the silky, skilled performers. Gazza was the man.

England won the game against Scotland 2–0, of course, with Gazza scoring that unbelievable goal which he celebrated by doing his dentist's chair impression, where he lay on the ground while the boys poured water in his mouth. They'd all been slaughtered for their exploits in Hong Kong prior to the tournament, when they went to this club and sat in what was called 'the dentist's chair' while shots were poured down their necks.

This was the sweetest of answers to those who'd dismissed

the players as no-hope piss-heads. The squad was absolutely buzzing and it was a blinding experience for a kid like me.

When they asked me to stay on for the next game against Holland, something which hadn't been part of the original plan, I was in heaven.

It was amazing, sitting on the coach, being in the changing room beforehand, hearing Tony Adams leading and encouraging all the boys, seeing Stuart Pearce psyching himself up, watching Shearer, who was concentration personified, and seeing Gazza just being Gazza.

Standing in the Wembley tunnel before the Holland game, watching the Dutch players run out into a banging atmosphere, was awesome. I wondered what it would be like to play against them one day.

They had world-class stars like Edwin van der Sar, who became the keeper at Manchester United, Ronald de Boer, Patrick Kluivert and Dennis Bergkamp. But England thumped them 4–1 on one of Wembley's greatest ever nights.

I had to leave after that and was absolutely gutted when we lost to the Germans on penalties in the semi-final. It really hurt because I'd been part of it all.

As I've said, I was never involved with England as a schoolboy, but once at West Ham I was picked for the England Under-18s against France, where I came on as sub.

Their forward line comprised Thierry Henry, David Trezeguet and Nicolas Anelka. I think they may even have had William Gallas and Mikael Silvestre at the back. Henry and Trezeguet were a year older than me and everyone who knew their European football had heard of them, especially Henry.

Thierry used to play on the left of a front three and inspired them to win the European Youth Championships in that summer of 96. We'd been knocked out by then and watched their final against Spain, when Thierry scored the only goal in a 1–0 win.

There was this gala dinner at the end of the tournament and John Curtis of Manchester United spoke on behalf of the England team and got plenty of stick off the lads for being a goody two-shoes. John came out with words no one had ever heard of. He was the brightest footballer by a mile and the best player of our age group. Italian clubs were after him and West Ham were desperate to sign him. He was brilliant at that age, as was a boy called Marlon Broomes. Marlon was tipped to be the next Des Walker and John the next Tony Adams.

I don't know what happened with John. He couldn't get in the first team at United for a while, then, when he did, he came up against an on-form Marc Overmars at Arsenal, who could skip past the best defenders in the world, let alone an aspiring youngster. Perhaps that knocked the stuffing out of him, who knows. All sorts can happen to you at that age. I've mentioned how I lost my co-ordination for a while and might have gone out of the game.

John had Gary Neville in front of him, who'd been playing for England at Euro 96, and I told him a move would benefit him because it looked like Gary would play for United for 20 years. I might be proved right – he's already been there for 13.

John argued that he wanted to play for the best club in the world and, because he was so confident in his ability at that time, he believed he'd make the breakthrough. He was so talented he could play anywhere in defence and all across midfield, but it never worked out for him at United.

In our England Under-18 squad were Emile Heskey, David Thompson, Jamie Carragher, Stephen Clemence and Richard Wright. Stephen was my room-mate and made the fatal mistake of letting the lads mess my bed up, which everyone knew I hated. I'd happily fuck about in someone else's room, but if anyone did it to me I was devastated.

My gear was all over the place and my bed was wrecked, while Stephen's was untouched, so it was pretty obvious he was behind it. I couldn't let him get away with it. Stephen used to have a 'curtains' hairstyle and he loved his hair as much as he loved himself. He would be looking in the mirror all the time, just like his dad Ray, the England goalkeeping coach, does!

So, when Stephen came in some of the lads held him down and I got my hair clippers out and went for him. I only meant to scare him by whizzing the clippers close to his barnet, but I misjudged it ever so slightly and he got a big bald patch right across his head. Stephen had an absolute fit – he was worried he'd lost his looks.

The other lads heard all the commotion and came to see what was happening. David Thompson, who had long hair at the time and was a bit of a nutter, started shaving his own hair off and told Stephen he was being a baby. It was all going off and we went looking for another victim.

Richard Wright, our goalkeeper, who also had the curtains hairstyle, seemed the best target. He's a good lad Richard, but rather quiet and he crapped himself as we ran into his room and plugged the shears in. He jumped off the bed and went for the door, only to be met by Emile, who caught him midair and slam-dunked him back on to the bed. I'm desperately trying to get the shears to Richard's head, but the lead wasn't long enough. I've never seen someone so scared in my life.

The manager, Ted Powell, heard the racket and kicked us all out of Richard's room and he was saved by a hair's breadth. These sort of antics are all part of being in a squad, especially when you are away for long periods.

*   *   *

I came back for the new season full of enthusiasm and brimming with confidence after training with the Euro 96 boys.

I travelled with the West Ham squad for the first game of the season at Arsenal and was gutted when I didn't get named on the bench. As I wasn't involved, I headed for the bar and had a couple of Jack Daniels and Coke before kick-off. I was still only 17 and drinking under-age, but I managed to get myself served all the same.

Suddenly I got a call telling me to hurry downstairs immediately because I was going to be sub after all.

It turned out our new Portuguese superstar Paulo Futre, a legend in his homeland, although not quite Eusebio level, had stormed out in a huff because Harry had given him the number 16 shirt.

Futre's name was synonymous with the number 10 and he said that without it he wouldn't be playing and buggered off. I got on late in the game and we lost 2–0 and Ian Wright had a right go at me.

He was in my face saying, 'Who are you, you piece of shit?' then he tried to put his finger in my face before laughing and jogging off. I had always admired Wrighty, but I found that a bit strange.

I met him later, on England duty, and pulled him about it, but he just said that was part of being a footballer. Michael Duberry told me the same thing had happened to him with Wrighty.

Anyway, Harry averted a diplomatic incident in the following game by persuading John Moncur, who had been given the number 10 shirt for the season, to give it up to Paulo. God knows how Harry managed that. Knowing Moncs, he would have driven a hard bargain.

I only made three sub appearances in the first few months and my career hit the buffers. In a reserve game at Luton I had a shocker, giving two goals away, and Frank, who was playing as well, was going, 'What the fuck's happened to you?' I was playing shit in training and in games and it was a similar experience to when I had lost my co-ordination as a schoolboy.

We played a team from Thailand in a friendly and, unbeknown to me, Mel Machin, the Bournemouth manager, was there and asked Harry if he could take me on loan. It was my eighteenth birthday, 7 November 1996, when Harry rang and told me he thought I should go.

Harry was an ex-Bournemouth manager and knew the set-up there. He insisted it would be good for my career, that Mel was a good mate of his and his team played good football which would bring out the best in me.

The worry for me was that if I went and didn't play well, no one would want me and West Ham would just get rid of me. But Harry reassured me that I had a big future at West Ham. 'It'll make you into a man. It will be brilliant for you, son,' he said.

Harry could talk the socks off anyone and that night, after talking it over with my parents and Dave Goodwin, a man I could always rely on, I was on my way to the south coast instead of having an eighteenth birthday party.

We trained in a park and the next morning went to Blackpool, where I started my first ever professional game. I was up against James Quinn and was really pissed off when he scored but fortunately we equalised. Nine years later, Quinn came back to haunt me when England lost in Belfast against Northern Ireland in the World Cup qualifier and he was up front again. He's been a bit of a nuisance, him.

Mel Machin was a real motivator. He made you feel ten feet tall. I'd walk past him when he was doing an interview with the press and he'd say to me, 'All right, Class?' That's what he called me 'Class'. How good a nickname is that to get from your manager?

I stayed in a B&B called the Matchester Hotel where I had to wash my own kit in the laundry room and the food wasn't my favourite. I would get a Chinese from the takeaway round the corner most nights, which wasn't the healthiest way to live.

It was the first time I had spent a long time away from home and I decided to explore. I went to this club and Dale Gordon, a former West Ham player, was there. He was now Bournemouth's reserve team manager and was holding court at the bar.

I joined his crowd, which included one of the players, John Bailey, and the chat got round to Michael Duberry, who had been on loan at the club before me and had done really well before going back to Chelsea. Dubes was being talked about as the next England centre-half. Bailey reckoned I could be as good as him and maybe go on to play for England myself. It might have been a load of old bull at the time, but it sounded good, I can tell you.

I'd go out with another player, Jason Brissett, in his car on the Friday night before games and we'd just sit outside clubs waiting for birds to come out. He had a BMW M3 and I thought I was the top man. We just kept bibbing at girls to come over and talk to us and they did it in droves. This was life as a proper first-team footballer. I had the attention of the girls, I'm not denying it, and was being a bit of a lad, but it was fun.

The players were gods round there and it was a lively town. There was this kicking place called the Zoo & Cage where I often went. Every night seemed to be student night, which is just the job when you're 18.

Bournemouth had everything you could want on the social side and the playing side. I couldn't have asked for more.

I went from a player with a youth-team mentality to feeling like a senior player, playing for points, playing in front of big crowds of around 6,000 every week. Luke Young's brother Neil played for them and Steve Fletcher, who is as legendary as the pier, was up front.

Mel was always arguing with Brissett. He'd say, 'You've got to do more for me,' and Brissett would just go into one and argue back. But it wasn't wise to cross Mel. He was similar to Harry in that he was relaxed most of the time, but he could also lose it big style.

It was traditional to get smashed on a few drinks over the weekend after playing on a Saturday and the management knew we did it. So on a Monday morning we had to go down to the beach and run from one pier to the other. Waiting for you at the other end was a bacon butty and a hot chocolate which made the hard work worthwhile. You had to do it in a good time as well because if you didn't, you got no bacon butty.

In the ten games I played I was only on the losing side twice. I'd been playing shit when I arrived, but now I'd started playing well and it boosted me no end. Harry was dead right. Bournemouth was the making of me as a professional foot-baller.

When Harry rang to say I had to go back to West Ham I argued that I wanted to stay. But then he told me he wanted me to play against Wrexham in a third-round FA Cup replay and I couldn't get back fast enough. It was going to be my first start for the club.

To be honest, I almost I wish I hadn't bothered. It was not a day to remember, as we lost 1–0 to a world-class goal from some bald-headed geezer. Don't know who he was but it was a great goal.

It was a sickener, but at least I was being considered for selection now and two games later I scored my first goal, at Blackburn Rovers.

I came on as a striker, playing off the front man, and

terrorised Colin Hendry and Graeme Le Saux. When a ball came out of the sky over my shoulder on the left-hand side I steadied myself and volleyed from 15 yards.

I knew it was in the moment I hit it and it flew past England keeper Tim Flowers. What a moment. I felt like my head was going to explode.

I was flying and did a few tricks and crossed into the box for Marc Rieper, who should have scored to make it 2–2. In the end we lost 2–1. I got some good headlines in the papers which gave Mum some cuttings for her scrapbook.

When I got back that night I raced straight round to Dave Goodwin's house to ask his wife Kate if she'd videoed the goal. She had and I kept rewinding it for an hour, acting it out in front of the TV set again and again.

I had a whole lot more confidence about me when we faced Wimbledon, and I was going down the tunnel at half-time shouting, 'Well done boys! Come on!' when their resident hardman Vinnie Jones eyeballs me and goes, 'You little fucking squirt. Who do you fucking think you are? You've only been playing fucking football ten minutes.'

Vinnie was not a man to mess with and I stood there, rooted to the spot, wondering if he was going to punch a skinny rake like me. To my relief, Johnny Hartson and Iain Dowie jumped in front of me.

Vinnie might have been hard, but you wouldn't want to meet Hartson or Dowie in a back alley and they told him in no uncertain terms to fuck off. He did.

In the next game, I scored again against Coventry when I chested the ball down and toe-poked it in. This time it was more satisfying because we won. Mine was the second in a 3–1 win.

I'd been no stranger to goalscoring in the youth team and the reserves. I knew where the net was, but I then went four bloody years without a goal and it would later take me 140 games before I scored my first one for Man United. God knows why, I went up for enough corners and free kicks.

I never scored at Upton Park for the West Ham first team, although, ironically, later in my career I did score there for Leeds during a staggeringly fertile run of three goals in five games.

On the final day of the season, West Ham lost 2–0 at Manchester United and I remember it vividly for the moment when I tried to run past Eric Cantona with the ball.

I got it just outside my own area and ran towards the halfway line as Eric ran back with me. Then I kicked it about 10 yards in front of us, thinking I'd outpace him. As I did so, Cantona moved his arm across me and goes, 'Stay where you are,' then ran past me and got the ball. He showed all his experience and it taught me not to let myself be shoved around, whatever a player's reputation.

It turned out it was his last ever game. He made the shock announcement that he was retiring the following week. Maybe he thought the game was too easy or maybe my skill frightened him. Probably the former I would guess. And, would you believe it, John Moncur had swapped shirts with him at the end. When he found out Eric had retired he sold it for about £25,000.

I'd made my Under-21 debut against Switzerland a month before at Swindon and it was not a memorable occasion. It was 0–0, it rained a lot, it was a generally crap game and I came off injured to be replaced, bizarrely, by my old sparring partner Jody Morris.

I only made five Under-21 appearances and, as I got more games for West Ham under my belt, my thoughts turned to the full England team. After all, I'd trained with them at Euro 96, which felt like a bigger achievement than getting into the Under-21s to me, and I hadn't felt out of place.

But my approach to the game needed a few adjustments.

In those days all I thought about was skill. I based my whole game on it. If I did a neat turn on someone with a trick I thought I'd had a good game even if we lost 3–0. That's what me and my mates always loved, the skills. But that's not enough.

Mind you, Harry never stopped me. He would just say, 'Go out there and play,' and was always very positive about me in the papers.

Harry could be a hard man when he wanted to be. He'd muller the team and he'd muller players personally. I've seen trays of sandwiches and coffee cups fly across the room count-less times. Sir Alex is not a patch on Harry in that department. Defeat hurt him badly and he would show it straight away; he couldn't hold it in. With Sir Alex, he sometimes leaves the bollocking until the next day rather than immediately after the game.

For me, Harry could have been an even better manager than he is. When we were playing Liverpool, Arsenal and Man United, that week's training would be the best you would see anywhere. Harry would be out there every day, working on the shape of the team and getting everybody in the zone. But for the other, so-called lesser games maybe the atmosphere at the training ground became a bit more relaxed. If he had employed the big-game approach to every match he could have been the best manager in the world. Just look at what he did when every match mattered for Portsmouth in order for them to stay up at the end of the 2005–06 season.

Maybe it was a West Ham thing. Not enough belief in how far we could go. Much as I loved the place, it was frustrating that the club seemed to have such limited ambition.

They still have dinners for a group of players called 'the boys of 86' because they finished third in the league in 1986. That's West Ham for you.

We finished fifth once and it was like we'd won the World

Cup. We did win something, mind you – the Intertoto Cup that summer. We had the players to compete at the very top – men like Paolo Di Canio, Trevor Sinclair, Slaven Bilic, Frank, Nigel Winterburn, me and later Stuart Pearce. Ian Pearce was brilliant to play with, as were Steve Lomas and Steve Potts, and we could have achieved more.

Being England manager would suit Harry because he would have to be up there for every match and that was when he was at his best.

West Ham was like a comedy club, there were so many characters. Dale Gordon, Neil Ruddock, Dowie, Moncur, Bishop, Lomas and Paul Kitson were all players who had something to say for themselves, as did Ian Wright – big surprise, eh? – when he joined us towards the end of his career.

It was a large squad, so there would always be one or two not involved on a Saturday and, later in his career, one of the regular fall guys was John Moncur. On a match day, Harry would tell the players in his office if they weren't going to be playing and, because his office was right next door to the changing room, you could hear everything.

Moncs would be going, 'Fucking joke. For fuck's sake. Fucking out of order. Fucking not playing in this team. It's a fucking joke,' and Harry would be going, 'I'm the manager. I've told you you're not playing, now deal with it.'

After five minutes of arguing Moncs would walk back in, put his coat on and go and Harry would walk in with the reddest face ever and a cheery, 'All right lads?', acting like nothing had happened.

Moncs was an absolute legend at West Ham. We used to have a sweep on how long it would take him to get a yellow card after coming on as sub. If you had anything over five minutes you had no chance.

He's one of the funniest blokes I've ever met. He reckons

they called him the White Pelé at Spurs and it was just the fact that Paul Gascoigne was in his position which held him back. Yeah! In all truth, Moncs was a quality player but being behind Gazza and a few of the others, he just wasn't able to shine.

He boasted he had the record for the most appearances in reserve team football and that he'd won more trophies in the stiffs – as we referred to the reserve sides – than any other pro. If England had had an international reserve team, Moncs would have been captain. No question about it in his eyes.

His finest moment was on the coldest morning ever at Chadwell Heath when everyone was scrambling for extra kit to keep warm. You had to get in sharpish if it was cold because there wasn't enough stuff like long tracksuit bottoms to go round. We used to moan at Eddie, the kit man, that a Premier League club should be able to afford enough kit but it made no difference. Moncs, who was never the earliest into training, used to go bananas muttering, 'Fucking young kids get all the good gear and I'm a fucking experienced player and get the fucking dregs.'

On this particular morning we were running round doing our laps, wondering where Moncs was, when he came charging out of the dressing rooms stark naked apart from a pair of underpants and his boots.

He was going, 'No gear, boys. There's no fucking gear. Fuck it,' and he threw himself headlong into a puddle. We were in tears. It was one of the funniest thing I'd ever seen. Harry went mental.

Harry's reaction to things like that depended on how he was feeling on the day. Sometimes he'd laugh, other days he'd give the offender a bollocking, send him back in and tell him to stop taking the piss. The lads' theory was that it depended on what horse he'd backed the previous afternoon and whether it had won or not.

We'd watch him coming on to the training field, trying to assess the mood. We'd be going, 'Look at his face. He's not happy, boys. The cloud's coming out. It's going to be a running session all day today. The horse must have gone backwards.'

Training had its lively moments, that's for sure. Anything could happen. Like when Johnny Hartson booted Eyal Berkovic in the head and it was replayed on TV for days and days. Now that *was* lively.

Bust-ups happen a lot in training at all clubs, but this one was something else. Eyal was one of the best trainers I've ever seen and incredibly skilful. You always wanted him on your five-a-side team because it was a guaranteed win. On this day, his team was winning 8–1 and the tackles started flying in. Wrighty was going, 'Stop the game. Someone's going to get fucking hurt.' Eyal nicked the ball from John and was running away and laughing, so John came in from behind and took him down.

Eyal was on the floor and Johnny went, 'Get up. I've not even touched you.' Eyal sort of half-slapped John's leg and the big man snapped and kicked Eyal in the head. It was lucky it was Johnny's left foot and not his right or Eyal's head would have been off.

Time stood still for a few seconds, then Eyal walked off to the changing rooms. The whole thing went out on Sky TV and it looked terrible.

It was gloomy at training for the next few days. Eyal was a good lad, all the lads liked him, and Johnny was just devastated and really apologetic. Everyone knew that he had a temper and could flip, but not quite like that. The pair of them made it up eventually.

John was actually a funny geezer, an example being when we went to Scotland for a few days and the gaffer said we couldn't go out. The lads weren't having it and Iain Dowie decided they were going out anyway, so Frank and I thought we might as well sneak out too.

Everyone was drinking and getting smashed and someone pinched a bird's backside. This bloke came over and said, 'Listen, don't pinch the bird's arse.' Paul Kitson, who I reckon enjoyed doing weights more than playing football, was as hard as they come, and he's gone, 'All right, mate,' and the geezer's said something again and it's all about to kick off.

Johnny gets up and I'm thinking, 'Here we go,' and he says, 'I've got to leave. I can't stay in here otherwise I'll go to prison. I'll hurt someone.' His leaving certainly defused the situation.

Johnny walked out the door then bounded back in later and jumped on stage with Dowie, Moncs and Kitson and they pretended to be a band. They had no instruments, they just used bins and chairs and the whole pub erupted. Don't know what happened to the bird or the geezer though.

While West Ham gave me a magnificent football education, some of the players were the worst influence a young lad could ever have. Smoking, drinking, gambling, clubbing – they did it all.

Bernard Lama, a French keeper, Slaven Bilic and Dicksy all smoked on the team coach. The smoke filled the coach and you had to walk through a fog before you could see your way clear to get off.

At the back of the coach there was a semi-circular settee and a table which was always the hive of activity. Dicksy and Moncs and the like would say to me and Frank, 'Come and sit back here. See what it's like to be a real footballer.'

We went to Man City one Friday and the lads stocked up with booze. When we arrived Ian Bishop was so pissed he fell off the bus! He was supposed to be playing the next day.

Me and Frank didn't think it was bad. We just looked at

each other and thought, 'Is this what it's like? It's blinding!' We didn't drink on the bus, though, we left that to the older ones. We just watched.

Harry didn't seem to notice most of the time. Apparently he's got no sense of smell since a bad car crash in Italy when he was over there watching the 1990 World Cup. On the way back from games the lads would have cartons of wine, spirits and beers and Harry would be sat at the front, totally oblivious. The lads hid it well.

Lama was at the back of the bus once when there was a dispute about his contract. I think we must have lost the match, because Harry didn't tolerate any noise on the coach if we'd lost. Bernard was smoking and having a laugh so Harry stormed up the aisle and said to him, 'Are you talking about me? Fucking sign the contract.'

Bernard just goes, 'Harry, pay me £1 million a year net and I stay,' and carried on smoking. I just sat there with my mouth gaping open. The lads were trying not to piss themselves in front of Harry.

The foreign players would go on about the drinking culture in England, telling us not to drink 20 pints in one night because it wasn't good for you. It didn't seem to register with them that smoking 20 Embassy wasn't either. It certainly wouldn't have helped me fulfil my big ambition, which was to pull on the full England jersey.

Banned by England

Off we went in the taxis to the airport, our careers as England players apparently over for ever. It seemed like a very long journey. We had a lot of time to think about our futures and the consequences of what had happened, although it was difficult to think straight, given how many beers we'd had.

When I was picked for the full England squad for a World Cup qualifier against Moldova at Wembley in September 1997 it should have been one of the proudest moments of my career. Instead, it became one of the most shameful.

We'd beaten Wimbledon 3–1 on the Saturday and went out celebrating in Kingston and, after my call-up, I decided to go out for a few more drinks on the Sunday. At some point a bird told me I shouldn't drive home because the coppers were really hot round there. I wish I'd listened to her, but I took no notice and anyway I thought I'd be all right because I'd only had a couple of alcopops. Trouble was I'd downed shedloads the night before and it was still in my system, so I suppose I must already have been over the limit when I drove to the pub. How stupid can you get?

I was giving Jody Morris and Jason Euell a lift home and was pulling out of a garage on to the main road when the police stopped me because I didn't have any lights on. They told me to get out of the car to take a breathalyser test. It turned orange then red and my heart sank. I'd failed it.

I remembered a tip, God knows where I'd got it from, that if you sucked on a 2p coin it could have an effect on the machine. So I sucked like hell on this coin, which tasted horrible, all the way to the station. But when I took the test again it made no difference.

It was bad enough that I'd been done having just been called up by England, but the country was in mourning for Princess Diana, who'd been killed earlier that same day, and there were rumours that her driver had been over the limit.

That made my actions look even more irresponsible than they already were. I had to pluck up the courage to tell Mum the news and didn't even want to think about admitting it to Dad. Predictably, they went mad and told me in no uncertain terms that I had to sort myself out. They had a point, but I didn't feel I was off the rails. I was just a young footballer who had been unlucky to get caught, in my eyes. Mum doesn't swear these days but she did then and called me a 'fucking idiot'.

When I joined up with the England squad at the Burnham Beeches Hotel a couple of days later I already felt shit and then the manager, Glenn Hoddle, told me I was being dropped from the squad but would still stay and train with the team.

It was a decision which provoked a ferocious debate in the media and among the players, comments being made that Hoddle was being unfair making a public show of me and that I should be allowed to go home. Every day I was there to be photographed by the press on the training field and a lot of people thought that was wrong.

But I wasn't so bothered. I reasoned that if I was there, cocooned in that environment, with my phone switched off and the press not able to hound me – apart from the photos they were taking from the side of the training pitch – it might be a blessing.

Diana's death was obviously dominating the news, but there was plenty about me on the back pages and some of the columnists were having a go, saying I was in danger of blowing my career.

I didn't feel that was the case. It was just a stupid mistake and it didn't stop me from going out. But it did make me stop drink-driving. I was banned for a year for a start and when I got my licence back I never did it again.

I've got nothing against Hoddle for how he dealt with me that week. His idea was to show me what I'd missed out on. He wanted to make me feel as bad as possible and, just to twist the knife in a bit more, he told me I would have played. I doubt that. It was a World Cup qualifier, I was still only 18 and this was the first time I'd been called up.

Harry was raging when I returned to West Ham and he pulled me in for a dressing down. He pointed to the picture of his friend, the late Bobby Moore, hanging behind him, and said, 'He wouldn't have done that. He used to have a drink, but at the right time. Look at him, he was a great player. You've got to aspire to be like that.'

I wasn't very popular with the boys either because Harry banned alcohol from the players' bar after that.

I can still see the headline in the *Sun*: 'Redknapp Hammers Boozers'. In the article he said, 'Rio has learned his lesson the hard way and will be all the better for it. He has been a silly boy, made a big mistake and must now take his punishment. The days when players poured crates of lager down their necks have long gone.'

Harry had a good few chats with me about my lifestyle, but it went in one ear and out the other. I was a young lad who enjoyed going out and I wasn't prepared to change my habits, especially as I was in the first team and doing well. If I'd been playing badly and not getting picked then maybe I'd have taken stock.

Johnny Hartson actually wrote an article in which he said all footballers had been drink-driving at some time and I was just unlucky to get caught. I appreciated him sticking up for me, but I don't think that was the message Harry was looking to get across!

I wasn't picked for the World Cup qualifier against Italy in Rome, which came a month after the Moldova game. I went to Italy with the Under-21s instead.

We travelled out with the first team and then went on to Rieti, just outside the capital, to play a European qualifier which we won in great style, despite the fact that we were left with ten men after Ben Thatcher got sent off. Kieron Dyer smashed in the only goal of the game on the volley two minutes from time.

We were on a high after the game and naturally had a few drinks in the hotel bar before heading next door to a pizza place for a few more. When that shut we came back to the hotel bar again. To be honest, it probably got too rowdy. We were in high spirits, dancing around the room, and eventually we had to go to bed because we'd drunk the hotel dry.

Next day, the manager, Peter Taylor, was okay with it. He accepted that we were bouncing after a great win and told us we could go round town to do some shopping and have a coffee and some lunch, but that we had to be back for 5 o'clock to get the coach to go and watch the seniors' game.

His final words were, 'Don't go in any bars!' It was good advice, but it wasn't going to stop us going on the drink again. Frank Lampard, my drinking buddy at the time, Jamie Carragher, Ben Thatcher, Danny Murphy and I led the way and most of the other lads came too.

We settled down in the corner of a bar at about midday, ready for a right good session. It was like the naughty-boys' club. We never needed much excuse for a celebration at any time, but we felt this was thoroughly justified. The pints kept coming and no one bothered to look at their watches.

As the time approached for us to get the coach, I thought I'd run down to the shops. I had a look around, but didn't buy anything and jogged back. I didn't think I was pissed, but I probably was and, as I walked up the stairs back to the bar, Taylor was in there going bonkers, reading the boys the riot act. If I'd been sharp and noticed a couple of seconds earlier I would have been able to turn round and not get caught, but I walked straight into it.

Taylor clocked me and I was done for. He ripped into me, Jamie and Ben. He was going, 'You're a disgrace. You're never playing for England again, ever. You've let the country down, you've let me down, you've let yourselves down and you've let your team-mates down. You're going home now. You're not coming to the game. Get your bags.'

There was one bloke missing – Frank, who had chosen just the right time to go to the toilet. When he came out he was quick enough, certainly quicker than me, that's for sure, to spot Taylor and nipped back into the toilets to hide.

Taylor kept ranting on, manhandling us out of the bar. Unbelievably, Thatcher said, 'Hang on, let me finish my beer.' He must have had a screw loose. Maybe he'd already decided to go and play for Wales, as he subsequently did.

Meanwhile, I'm pleading my defence, with my fingers crossed behind my back, saying to Taylor, 'I wasn't even here. What you talking about? I've just turned up and seen you here.'

He wasn't fooled. 'Don't lie to me. I can see it in your eyes. You are totally out of order. All of you are pissed. You've been in here all afternoon.' Which was true enough, of course.

Then once more he goes, 'You'll never play for England again.' The first time he said it I hadn't paid much attention, but when he said it again I started to shit myself, thinking my England career was finished. After all, it was only a month since the drink-driving episode. Not smart, Rio, not smart at all.

When we got back to the hotel he told us to get packed, that we were going straight to the airport without seeing the seniors' game and if he couldn't get us on a flight we'd have to sit around at the airport until the seniors had finished and we could go back on the team plane.

We were waiting for the taxis to take us to the airport while the rest of the Under-21 team were settling down in the coach to go to Rome. Frank and the other boys thought it was hilarious and were laughing at us and pulling faces.

Then Thatcher, who was having an absolute blinder and was completely bladdered, piped up again and says, 'Can't believe Frank got away with it. How did he do that?'

Taylor's ears were like radar. He dragged Frank off the coach and told him he wouldn't play for England ever again either.

Frank's face was a picture as he protested to Taylor, going, 'What do you mean? I weren't there, I swear I weren't.' Taylor wasn't interested, and he repeated, 'You're all finished with England.'

Frank was gutted and especially pissed off when he found out Ben had unwittingly grassed him up. A few minutes ago he had been taking the piss and now he was landed in it. It was quite funny, actually. I have to be honest and admit I was pleased in a way that Frank got pulled as well and I wouldn't be the only one going back to West Ham to face the music. At least I had someone to share the mullering with.

So off we went in the taxis to the airport, our careers as England players apparently over for ever. It seemed like a very long journey. We had a lot of time to think about our futures and the consequences of what had happened, although it was difficult to think straight, given how many beers we'd had. When we arrived, a couple of the lads were so hammered that as soon as they fell out of the taxi they had a piss up against the airport wall. There were police just yards away with guns and dogs and I thought they were going to kill us.

There was no early flight home, so we had to sit there for hours, waiting for the senior team. We were put on the plane first and then everyone else came on. They were all staring at us. They were buzzing, having got the draw to go to the World Cup, while we were in disgrace. We couldn't complain really; it was what we deserved.

Hoddle had obviously already been told because he gave us the dirtiest look ever. It was one of the most embarrassing incidents I've ever been involved in and it was all over the papers. I got butchered by the columnists, but Taylor tried to save us, which was good of him, all things considered. He told the press the reason we were disciplined wasn't drink-related, but no one believed him and me and Frank got bollocked by Harry.

Frank, of course, got it double because he also had to face the assistant manager – his dad.

I didn't feel like I'd let the country down as Taylor had said. I'd let the manager down, yes, but not the whole of England. It was Taylor's way of making sure we learned our lesson.

I had to go home and talk to my mum and dad about it and they laid into me for being an idiot once again.

Staggeringly, given my list of indiscretions, I was picked for the England senior squad a month later, for a friendly against Cameroon. It was a week after my nineteenth birthday and this time I managed to keep my nose clean.

Dave Goodwin and his wife Kate came to watch with my mum, my dad and Anton. Kate and Mum were crying and getting all emotional.

I was only among the subs, but as I warmed up on the touch-line the crowd started singing, 'Rio, Rio!' It was brilliant. I just wanted to stay out there exercising. I didn't want to sit down on the bench. Years later, when Theo Walcott was warming up for the England B team against Belarus just before the World Cup, the crowd started chanting, 'Theo, Theo!' I was in the stands watching and it reminded me of my Cameroon experience.

Gareth Southgate got injured and I got the call to go on. It was a moment I will never forget. And if Robbie Fowler hadn't been so greedy and had passed to me, I might have scored as well.

I intercepted a ball and knocked it to Gazza. It was a dream come true in itself to be in the same team as him. Gazza passed it back and I played it through to Robbie and carried on running into the box for the return.

Me and Mum. I'm two. In a photo booth.

First kit. Thre

That's Anton.

Me and Dad. I'm seven by now.

Cool! Callum, Aaron, Anton, Max, Me and Bernard.

RIO Ferdinand
MAKING A NAME FOR HIMSELF

Exciting loan signing Rio Ferdinand is always asked the same question, "What's it like being Les Ferdinand's cousin?" So to start this piece off, I asked him, are you fed up with always being asked the same question!? "Not really, it's a bonus having someone like that in your family. In some ways it helps and in some ways it's a drawback. People tend to want to look at you because of the name but it can nag me a bit when people keep asking me about him. It's one of those things you just have to live with."

FULL DEBUT
Rio needs no-one else's name when it comes to being singled out with his man of the match performances and I asked him how he feels he has done since arriving from West Ham? "I think I've done all right, I've had a few good games and a few average games, but I feel that I've worked hard and enjoyed it". His Cherries debut at Blackpool certainly turned heads with an assured performance and it was a game that was memorable for Rio, "It was my first start in the Football League, I have made substitute appearances for West Ham this season, but the match at Blackpool was my first start and a good experience and we didn't lose. I'd already played at Dean Court earlier this season for West Ham in Sean O'Driscoll's testimonial match and that was a good game. It was my first game of the season as I'd been away playing for England Under-18s in France."

FULL LEAGUE DEBUT
Coming down from a Premiership club, it really opened his eyes to life outside the top flight, "It's nice to see the other side of the coin. It's a good set-up down here, though obviously it's a lot different at West Ham. It really is nice to be here, it's a good club and very friendly. It has certainly lived up to the expectations that Harry had given me. The team are doing reasonably well now. I'm gaining a great deal of experience being here and I'm in a side that do play good football so it hasn't been much of a change for me being here. There's a young set of lads here and I reckon in a year or so, this side will be that much better. All they need here is confidence and a good run."

SET FOR THE TOP?
There is no doubt that Rio has been reminded on many occasions that Michael Duberry came here on loan last season as a virtual unknown, and within months was a Chelsea regular and is now rated in the £3 million bracket, so does Rio look at that and take heart? "A lot of people have spoken to me about that, but I try to keep it our of my mind and concentrate on my own game. Of course I would like to achieve what he's done in a short space of time, but I'm a different player and a different person. He may have had that bit of luck that I might not get."

TRUE COMMITMENT
Despite Rio's future lying away from Dean Court, there is no denying that whilst he is here, he has only one aim, to do well for AFC Bournemouth, typified by his after match reactions when the side have won, "I appreciate Bournemouth giving me the chance to have the experience, and if I've put in some good performances then it's good for everyone. I just want to do the best for the club and myself. If you don't have any commitment for the team you're playing for, even if you're not there permanently, then you're not going to do as well as you can do. Some people show it in different ways. Some show it emotionally and other won't let it come out and I think I'm one of those people who just let's it known where my loyalty lies while I'm here. There will always be a place for Bournemouth in me now. I like it down here, it's a lovely town, full of friendly people. Everyone's been good to me here, the fans, the staff and the players. If West Ham don't want me back, I'd love to spend another month here."

TREMENDOUS SUPPORT
It has taken the Cherries faithful no time at all to take to Rio, and he has certainly appreciated the support, "The crowd are quality here. There may not be the biggest crowds here, but you get really good support. For the distances, the away support is brilliant. In my first game at Blackpool, there may not have been many there, but you certainly knew where they were. The fans have certainly helped me enjoy my time here and I want to keep giving good performances and that the team does well."

BURNING AMBITIONS
Rio has undoubtedly got a very bright future in front of him in the game, and he certainly has got a burning ambition to succeed, "I have aspirations the same as anybody to play for England in a full international, but first and foremost I want to get in to the West Ham first team, claim a regular place and then go on to bigger and better things. That's all down to me now to work hard and show commitment. I have to be dedicated and make sure that other distractions don't get in the way. People might be saying that I have the potential, but I've got to prove it - keep striving on."

GOOD BANTER
Finally, I asked Rio if he's found it easier at Dean Court due to the fact that everyone speaks English in the changing room! "Yes it does make it easier! We've got an interpreter at West Ham. The atmosphere is good at both clubs and the lads are more my age group here. There's good banter here because we all talk the same language!"

Bournemouth v Bristol programme, 26 December 1996

Harry telling me what to do, again.

My second, and last goal for West Ham...

...and this time we won

At Mum's. Anton, Sian, Mum,
Peter, Jeremiah and me.

Chloe, Remi,
Anya

At Dad's.
Lisa, Dad
and Chloe.

Rebecca, Chloe, Liberty,
Me, Jeremiah, Sian and
Goofy. Wait, might have
that wrong...

Me and Frank and the boys. Ayia Napa.

On the boat in the South of France. Justin, Gavin, Bernard and Anthony.

Wicked holiday. That's our boat in the background.

White Chalk finalists.

Usher!

The Man!

I was in loads of space, but Robbie shot wide from a disgusting angle when, if he'd given it to me, I had a shot on goal. That's strikers for you, always thinking of themselves.

We won 2–0, although I'm told it was a boring game. Not for me it wasn't. If there is one match I'd like to have on a DVD at home it's that England debut. I'm sure a recording must exist somewhere.

West Ham were knocked out of the 1998 FA Cup after a quarter-final replay against Arsenal, which went to penalties, and we finished eighth in the Premiership.

I'd done okay in my first full season, but didn't think I had much chance of going to the World Cup. I was up against Tony Adams, Gareth Southgate, Martin Keown and Sol Campbell for a centre-back spot and I knew I was on the fringes. But I was one of the 28 players Hoddle picked to go to the La Manga training camp, from where he was going to choose his squad.

It turned out to be a very eventful tournament indeed.

We played a couple of friendlies and I came on against Belgium in the second one, but it was difficult to judge whether I'd done enough.

I would be on the sun lounger most days, next to Paul Merson, and we'd go over and over the different scenarios that could happen. We'd be saying, 'I know he's going, he's going and he's going, so that means we're not.'

The day before the squad was announced me and Merson were thinking about going on holiday the following week, because we couldn't see how we would be in the squad. I'd done well in training, but there had been no feedback from Hoddle. His assistant, John Gorman, might say, 'Well done today, son,' but that wasn't much of a clue. Gorman was a good bloke, he was always there for the players, but Hoddle made his own decisions.

What I hadn't reckoned on was my big hero Gazza being dropped.

He was wearing a black bin bag in training because he had to lose weight. It was an old-school thing that pros used to do to sweat out the drink. Harry Redknapp used to tell us about it at West Ham. It doesn't really happen these days because there is not the same drinking culture in the game.

Despite Gazza's battle with the extra pounds, when we had a few sessions one-on-one he was excellent. Unbelievable, in fact. I reported back to my mates that he was ripping it out of some of the best defenders in the squad. Then again, he was going out on the golf course drinking cans of lager, which did not seem the wisest move.

The papers were tentatively suggesting that Gazza could be left out, but they didn't seem to believe it was actually going to happen, and neither did I. He could do things no one else could do.

The night before Hoddle picked the squad we were all drinking in the Piano Bar which has attracted a notoriety in football for various incidents over the years. Stan Collymore allegedly set off a fire extinguisher in there, for one.

Gazza was a touch the worse for wear, singing his heart out on the karaoke machine. Mind you, a lot of the lads had put away a few. Gazza was just showing it more than the rest. Me, I was a good boy, I was drinking Coke! We were all having a laugh, chucking peanuts at each other. Just mucking around really.

When I went to the toilet Hoddle followed me and said, 'Where are you going, son?' I told him I was just going to the toilet. 'Okay and then make sure you go straight on to bed,' he said.

I had been playing cards with Paul Ince, Steve McManaman and a couple of others and was up about £800. All I could think about at that moment was what would happen to my money. I was not a happy boy. It didn't cross my mind that sending me to bed was a little clue that I might be in the squad.

I sneaked out of my room later to see if they were still playing cards somewhere else, but couldn't find them. Incey cracked up laughing the next morning and I never got my money. I can't remember exactly what I was earning at the time, but £800 was a shit-load of money, I know that.

Hoddle put a list on a whiteboard telling us when we had to go and see him to find out if we were in the squad. It went something like Sol Campbell at 2.05, Phil Neville at 2.10, Gary Neville at 2.15, then Andy Hinchcliffe, Gazza and me.

A queue started building up in the corridor because the times had overrun and Gazza was just ahead of me. Glenn Roeder, one of Hoddle's assistants, was there as well and he was a mate of Gazza's going back to Newcastle days. He'd even acted as Gazza's chaperone for a while when he joined Lazio in Italy.

Gazza's going, 'Glenn, tell me whether I'm in the squad or not. For God's sake, tell me, I want to know now.' He was getting more and more heated and poor Glenn was saying, 'Gazza I can't tell you. I can't tell you nothing.' Gazza wouldn't take that so he tried again, saying, 'Just give me a nod. Am I in or not?'

It was getting very uncomfortable for everyone and it was gradually dawning on us that he wasn't going to be in the squad. I was thinking, 'He's going to go nuts' and I wasn't wrong. Gazza stormed into Hoddle's room while Andy Hinchcliffe, who was being told he was out of the squad, was still in there.

There were sounds of crashing and screaming and the lads in the corridor were standing there stunned, because of the scene going on, and also because Gazza wasn't going to the World Cup.

When I went in, certain pieces of furniture were not where they should have been. There was a table overturned and a broken lamp on the floor and the gaffer looked flustered. He apologised for the mess and told me to take a seat.

It felt like the time when I was waiting for the results of my GCSE exams, after Dad had given me that ultimatum. I had sweaty palms and was shaking.

I can hear Hoddle's next sentence like it was yesterday, 'I'm going to take you to the World Cup for experience. You're a quality player with a lot of potential and this will do you good. Make sure you take it all in and learn from it.'

I was gobsmacked. I was going to the World Cup and I wasn't even 20 yet. I must confess I wasn't too worried about Gazza right at that moment, but when I came down from the clouds I was gutted for him – and for myself. I would have loved to have gone to a World Cup with Gazza.

For me personally, Hoddle was one of the best coaches I've ever had, though his man-to-man skills could have been better. He had a tendency to treat players like kids in some ways.

At Burnham Beeches, where we often stayed before home games, there was a shop about ten minutes away, but you had to ask permission to go. Getting a pass out to the shop was like being given permission to play out when you were a child after you'd been grounded for a week. Anything you wanted to do you had to go through Hoddle. It was completely regimented. That was why he needed John Gorman as an antidote. John was always upbeat and kept the ambiance going whereas Hoddle was really serious.

But his training sessions were superb. He'd see a weakness in the other team, say their full-backs, and we'd do a whole session based on getting the ball to our wingers in all sorts of different ways. He really analysed other teams and we knew everything about them by the time we played the game. He would tell you all you needed to know and more about your direct opponent. Nothing would be left out and you had no excuses.

Sven-Göran Eriksson was not as in-depth. He'd go through the team and say who was good at what, but he was a lot more relaxed about the opposition.

I would love to have had an hour just to sit down and talk football with Hoddle – the players he played with and against, what he thought of them, who were the best.

He has often been criticised for being a show-off, but I used to love training with him. He was still one of the best passers there. When we played two-touch and one-touch he was brilliant. He was usually the best player in training. His prime as a player was before my time, but in training you could see in an instant how good he must have been.

One time, he was talking to me and the ball came over behind him and he just brought it out of the sky. I didn't even know he'd seen it, I thought it was going to smack him on the back of the head.

It did make me laugh, though, how he used to make a swooshing noise with his mouth as he connected with the ball. It was louder or quieter depending on how hard he struck it. I suppose that was the kid in me, analysing everything about someone I admired.

He could put incredible back-spin on the ball, so that it landed perfectly. His touch was amazing and that's probably why he got frustrated at times because he could do things other players couldn't.

There were rumours that he showed Becks how to take free kicks because he felt he could do better, but I never saw that happen myself. Becks seems to have a fair amount of ability in that department as it is . . .

I headed off to the World Cup in France knowing I was unlikely to play much, but hoping I would get on at some point. That old line from my days on the estate came into my head again: 'If I play for only one minute, I'll be happy.'

Me and Michael Owen, who were 19 and 18, were the babies of the squad and knocked around together the whole time, playing the amusements, pool and table tennis. We got on really well. He used to batter me at pool and I would do the same to him at table tennis. I think I've already boasted about my prowess there, haven't I?

We would talk about football, but Michael's not a lover of the game in the crazy way I am. He would tell you that himself. I can watch any match, from school games to Sunday League through to the World Cup.

I realised what a serious business the World Cup was when we were out on the training pitch in France and Hoddle was doing free kicks and corners with the starting eleven and all the subs were behind the goal.

He was walking us through all the different signals, telling us that one arm means it's going near post, two arms means far post, one arm halfway up means on the penalty spot. On and on it went. Touching the ball means this, bouncing the ball that, hand on the head, hand on your hip.

Me, Michael, Merse, Les, Martin Keown, McManaman, plus a few others, were chatting behind the goal when Hoddle went to us, 'Now, you lot, come and do it.'

I didn't have a clue and neither did any of the other subs. Hoddle's gone, 'Les, what does one arm mean?' and Les has given him an answer and he's gone, 'No.' Then he's asked me what two arms mean and I've said something like 'edge of the area'. Wrong. By this stage he's not happy and he's asked a couple of the other lads who also couldn't give the right answer. Hoddle just looked at us all and shook his head in despair.

So he made us stay out there till we knew all the drills. He absolutely hammered us and told us we could be going on at any time so had to know all the signals otherwise it could cost the team the game. He was right, of course. I was there to learn how to be part of a squad and those lessons have never left me.

It was a lovely warm day when we played our first game against Tunisia in Marseille. I looked around and thought, 'Bloody hell, this is it.' I saw the Kiss 100 radio DJ Steve Jackson and a girl who worked for Nike shouting and waving at me.

I soaked in the whole thing. That feeling changes with age, of course. I'm more used to big occasions now. I don't walk out at Old Trafford with 70,000 people screaming and take in every ounce of the atmosphere and go, 'Woah!' That's the time when you should be concentrating on the game. But being a sub, I could do it in Marseille.

The atmosphere did get to me four years later, though, when we played in the quarter-final against Brazil in 2002. I almost cried when the national anthem was being played. I realise now I mustn't get emotional. It affects your game.

We beat Tunisia easily, although it wasn't until Paul Scholes scored a cracker in injury time that it was safe.

In the next game against Romania we went one down. I was sat on the bench next to Michael and Merse. Michael told us, 'If I get on, I'll score. I feel like I'm going to score,' and ten minutes after replacing Teddy Sheringham he did. Me and Merse were giving it high fives, but we lost the match in the last minute.

We won our final group game against Colombia 2–0 to go through and it's a game I'll never forget, even though I didn't play.

With ten minutes left, Hoddle told me to warm up because I was going on. I was stretching on the touchline, stripped and ready to grace the World Cup. My moment of glory had come. But then Incey started limping about and Hoddle told me to sit back down and put David Batty on instead to replace him in midfield.

There are few things more embarrassing for a footballer than being stripped and bursting to get into the action, only to be told to put your tracksuit back on again. Incey wasn't even injured, he just wanted a rest before the next game because we were two up. Afterwards I collared him when he was on the massage table and I was steaming. 'Incey, I was going on, man. You're not even injured!' He said, 'I know. If I'd known you were coming on I wouldn't have done it.' I was so pissed off with him and went, 'Fucking hell, Incey, you've ruined my chances of playing in the World Cup.' He'd done me twice – made off with my £800 and stopped me playing in the World Cup!

I couldn't hold any grudges though. Incey was a senior pro and a nice guy who always had time for me. Anyway, we all had to concentrate on the big one coming up – Argentina in the second round.

The whole end behind the goal in St Etienne was full of Argentina fans jumping up and down and singing. I stood there watching them for a good five minutes and knew it was going to be a wicked atmosphere.

They scored a penalty, then we scored a penalty in an amazing start and then came that goal from Michael which was to change his life.

It is one of the great World Cup goals. I never get tired of seeing it.

When Michael first got the ball on the halfway line there was nothing much going on. Then, all of a sudden, he took off, carving his way through their half, and the nearer he got to goal the closer we got to the edge of our seats on the subs bench.

Then – bang! – it hit the roof of the net and everyone went berserk.

Me and Merse were going, 'He's a joke, he is. There's nothing like him. There's never going to be anything like him ever again.'

Michael's game was heavily based on pace back then, getting a yard on the defender who couldn't get back at him. He was lightning. I'd watched him kick the ball beyond Gareth Southgate, who wasn't slow, and breeze past him like he wasn't there in one of his very first training sessions with England.

When Michael first came on the scene Jamie Redknapp told me he could be as good as or better than Robbie Fowler. He was never a skills man, Michael. He knew where to put the ball and his legs would carry him past anyone, he was that quick.

Because of his hamstring problems he's maybe not as fast as he was, but his all-round game has developed and he links the play more than he used to. He's still a poacher in the box, he's never lost the knack of scoring goals. He's reinvented himself and all credit to him for that. His injury at the World Cup in Germany, when he damaged knee ligaments, must have been a real sickener for him. But, injuries permitting, I still think he will become the leading England goalscorer of all time.

Argentina equalised to make it 2–2 on the stroke of half-time and then David Beckham famously got sent off in the second half. I didn't even know how. From where I was sat, I didn't see him flick out a boot at Diego Simeone and having seen it on TV since I don't think it was that big a deal. But he was off and eventually we lost on penalties, just for a change, when David Batty's kick was saved.

Fast forward eight years and I would be going through it all over again at the 2006 World Cup when we lost the quarter-final to Portugal on pens.

Batts didn't seem too bothered about missing the penalty. Football didn't get to him like that. He was a great competitor on the field, but he never appeared to think about it afterwards. I'd have been devastated and in tears, but that's Batts for you. The gaffer said something afterwards to Becks about being irresponsible, but nobody in the squad was blaming him.

Then, with the dressing room in silence and Hoddle about to address us before we packed up for home, my bloody phone rang in my trousers, which were hanging on my peg above me. I could have died. It went on for what seemed like forever and I prayed no one would realise it was mine. Luckily, Hoddle blanked it out, but it put the icing on the cake for me.

We went back to the hotel for the last time, feeling totally dejected. We weren't ready to sleep so we played pool till the early hours of the morning. It was just Michael and me at first, then Gary Neville and Becks came in.

We were all gutted, of course, but I was saying to Michael, 'You're going to be massive when we go back. Do you realise how big you'll be? You won't be able to go anywhere. You're the golden child, man.'

I knew people would be talking about that goal for years and they have. It was being replayed over and over on the telly and we were saying, 'What you going to buy, what you going to buy? Are you gonna go get a Ferrari?' as youngsters do.

It hadn't crossed our minds what was in store for Becks. Becks said he was gutted and that the manager had said a few things. We just told him to go and have a holiday and he went straight off to America to join Victoria on tour with the Spice Girls. I realised what he'd be coming back to when I saw a picture in the paper of his dummy hanging outside a pub. It was mad.

I am a passionate person about football, as a fan and a player, but a bad result would never lead me into wanting to make someone else's life a misery. You can be upset, but what was directed at Becks was bang out of order.

Even though I didn't play at all in that World Cup, thanks

to Incey, it was an important experience and stood me in good stead for Japan in 2002. I learned how to prepare properly for games and that everything had to be spot on and nothing could be left to chance.

Hoddle got all the tactical stuff right, which was his way of getting the best out of players. He didn't always make players believe they were capable. One of the arts of management is to make players believe they are ten feet tall. He did that with me even though I didn't need much boosting, but perhaps others needed more. Hoddle had some strange ways. Not least when he urged everyone to see his favourite faith healer, Eileen Drewery. I went to see her after my drink-driving ban because he told me to. In all honesty it did nothing for me.

I was sat in a chair in the middle of a room and she said I had eight temple points in my body and that if I drank, smoked or took drugs it would open up a temple or something like that and then all the good things would leave my body. Er . . . right. Hoddle said that if I wanted to see her again he'd sort it, but I gave it the swerve.

We all had to see her. Ray Parlour asked for a short back and sides when he sat down and she put her hands on his shoulders. Quality. He told us the story at dinner one night and we couldn't stop laughing.

Hoddle probably didn't like the fact that the lads weren't into the faith healing, but he had a lot of good ideas and in some respects was ahead of his time. He got a doctor in to explain the value of certain tablets and vitamins, ones we take for granted now.

I will always stand by Hoddle. He was a fantastic coach. He took me to the World Cup when I was young and inexperienced and wanted me to play the way I love playing, coming out from the back with the ball.

I've never run with the ball as much as I did under him.

He would tell me to go out there and express myself and he would have taken my game even further had he remained as England manager. He might even have played 3–5–2 with me either one of the back three or sitting in front.

Hoddle got the sack because of comments he made about disabled people. He said they were paying for their sins in a past life. Even though I didn't agree with what he said, I thought it was shocking that he was sacked. I felt there were certain elements out to get him.

Religious beliefs can be very strange. Some people feel their religion allows them to walk into a restaurant or on to a bus and blow themselves up and everyone else in there. I don't know the whole truth about what Hoddle believes or what exactly was said, I just remember being so disappointed when he went.

I was even more disappointed when I started working with his replacement, Kevin Keegan.

Getting Hammered

The truth is some women will do anything to crack on with footballers and, let's be fair, which young players would pass up the opportunity to take them up on some of their offers?

RIO MY STORY

If you had a pair of boots you could get a trial at West Ham. Harry was a chancer and would let all sorts have a go just in case one turned out to be a world-beater. Some of them were absolute shockers and wouldn't get into your pub side.

Harry always put the defenders up against our Italian striker Paolo Di Canio to test them out. One of them kicked lumps out of Paolo and he just walked off. Harry pleaded with Paolo to come back out, but he wasn't having any of it. Paolo was a law unto himself.

He once told the press I wasn't good enough to play for England. I pulled him about it and he said he'd been misinterpreted. But I don't know, you were never quite sure with Paolo.

At times he was potty. When we played against Bradford we had three stonewall penalties turned down before winning 5–4. Paolo wasn't happy, so he sat down on the pitch when he got fouled and wouldn't get up. He was going to Harry, 'I'm coming off. Bring me off.' Harry told him to get up and stop being silly, but it was ages before he moved. Then he had an argument with Frank about taking a penalty and they were both tugging at the ball before Paolo eventually claimed it.

There were pictures taken of him making what looked like fascist salutes when he went back to play for Roma, which makes him an absolute idiot in my book.

And his mood could change with the wind. For two weeks he would be top drawer and one of the lads, then he would just erupt and walk out of training because something wasn't going his way.

He showed his passion more than any player I've ever played with. He'd regularly scream his head off and you would wonder what on earth he was doing. But it was his way and you had to accept it.

Paolo's not the easiest person to work out, but he was a top professional and a superb player.

Harry could spot a talented player, no doubt about it. Whether his acquisitions had the necessary commitment was another matter. For instance, we signed a great player called Dani from Portugal towards the end of the 1995–96 season who could do things in training which took your breath away. I couldn't understand why he wasn't the star of the best team in the world. He had a great left foot, he could pass, dribble, shoot: the make-up of a great player.

For the first two weeks he trained every day and was brilliant, then one day he wasn't in and we thought, 'Where the hell is Dani?' He turned up at 12 o'clock, walked on to the training pitch and Harry goes, 'Where the hell have you been?' He says, 'Modelling at a photo shoot.' Harry didn't know what to say. He hadn't heard that one before.

Dani wasn't bothered one bit. At QPR he didn't get on the bench and neither had I, so I walked up to the bar where I found him downing Budweisers and chain-smoking.

I've never seen fan mail like he got. Birds would send him photos of themselves completely naked or wearing naughty lingerie. The boys would be gagging, asking if he was going to ring them and he would just shrug his shoulders.

Carlos Queiroz, our coach at Manchester United, knew him and said he was unbelievably talented, but sometimes his attitude to the game might let him down. He's only 30 and now works on Portuguese TV when he could still be playing top-flight football. It was a real waste of football talent.

Dani might not have worked hard, but he was good and Harry had spotted that. Not that he wasn't occasionally fooled by flashy skills.

Marco Boogers, who Harry signed from Dutch football, has been rated the worst West Ham player ever, but in his first training session he did some impressive stepovers. I don't know what happened, but suddenly he was shocking and

Harry got rid of him. The story goes he ended up living in a caravan.

Then there was the Romanian striker Florin Raducioiu. He was missing from the team bus one day and, when Harry rang him up to find out where he was, Florin said he was out shopping in London!

Joey Beauchamp was a strange one as well. One day he signed and the next day he'd gone. Apparently he'd decided it was too far away from his home in Oxford.

Neil 'Razor' Ruddock was a good lad, but, like a few others, was maybe not a good influence on a young 'un like me. Razor organised the defence when he played and also organised the all-day drinking sessions and entertainment.

Once, when I was injured, he said, 'Ree, we'll go and have a spot of lunch.' We went to a pub called Chequers, about 15 minutes from the training ground, had about four pints, then had to go back for afternoon treatment. Fortunately, Harry never found out – he'd gone home by the time we got back.

Me, Frank, Razor and Trevor Sinclair used to go out a lot together and me and Frank would be out every Saturday and Sunday night without fail.

After a big Saturday night, I'd meet up with Frank again at about four on the Sunday afternoon and we'd go drinking until the early hours. We'd still be on time for training on the Monday though. We felt like we could do anything. We never wanted to go to bed.

If there was a party on Monday I'd go to that and I'd be out at least two nights out of the next four. I would be drinking alcopops and Jack Daniels four days a week minimum.

I never thought, 'Jesus, I'm pissed a lot.' I was enjoying it. It was part of the culture and I was locked into it. But me and Frank could hide what we'd been up to because we were always on time for training and our general fitness was so good. When you're young you can usually get away with it. It doesn't show. I couldn't do it now.

One time though, when I was 18, I did get caught. I'd been on an all-night bender and gone straight to training. I thought I was hiding the effects pretty well until I was put clean through on goal and it was like a sniper had been in the bushes and shot me in my leg. I didn't even connect with the ball, I just fell over. The effects of the night before had obviously taken their toll. Harry sent me inside, mullered me and I got fined. I couldn't really complain.

More often than not, though, me and Frank would be first into training and last out. It was never a chore for either of us. Frank's dad would have us doing doggies – shuttle runs – after training and we never complained. We always had a good work ethic – it was instilled into us.

When I wasn't out with the West Ham lads I'd be in all different parts of London and was never spotted by anyone who would tell on me to the gaffer. Frank would say, 'Have you been out, Ree?' and I'd go, 'No, man, I've been nowhere.' Then about a month later he'd find out I'd gone somewhere and tell me what a liar I was.

Frank got a flat in Buckhurst Hill and if I was going out in Essex I'd stay there. Like all kids he wanted his independence. With his dad being assistant manager it was difficult for him. When he started getting picked for the team, there was an unhealthy vibe around. Other players felt he was only picked because of his old man. The fans thought it too. Yet he deserved his place.

While the West Ham supporters have always been great to me, they have been out of order in the way they've treated Frank over the years. When he was there they thought he shouldn't be playing and were calling him 'Fat Frank'. But he can't have been that bad because Chelsea bought him for £11 million and he's gone on to win Premiership titles and become an integral part of the England team. They got a bargain.

Whenever he goes back they still give him hassle. It's not right. He and his dad did so much for West Ham. They deserve to be appreciated. I've never understood it. Frank was a great midfield player and scored goals for fun.

I wouldn't change anything about my West Ham days. I've got so many great memories. But I was lucky I didn't go off the rails completely and ruin my career.

I was always in denial about the amount of socialising we did. My mum would say, 'You've been out a lot,' or 'Why are you coming in so late?' and I would say, 'I've only been round my mate's house watching videos.' That was often true, but we'd be watching them till three in the morning.

When you're young you don't worry about the drinking, the partying and staying up till all hours, but when I reached 22 I hit the wall and couldn't do it any more. If I have a night out now it takes me days to recover.

Harry had publicly called me the new Bobby Moore when I was in the youth team. It was a big thing for him to say and it meant I had a lot to live up to but I never felt it put pressure on me.

It seemed like every question from the press was, 'What do you think about being called the next Bobby Moore?' The simple answer is that to be mentioned in the same breath as such a distinguished footballer is a great compliment.

I didn't mind Harry saying it, but I decided to just keep playing my own game and not let it go to my head. I never actually met Bobby Moore. People assume I must have done, but I didn't. I was only 14 when, sadly, he died of cancer. But I've been involved with the charity set up by his wife and have donated signed shirts to raise money for the cause.

Whenever I needed advice from someone in the game I

went to Iain Dowie and Ian Wright. They were my biggest shoulders to lean on and still are. Whenever I've needed someone to talk to – when I've moved clubs, when I've been playing well, when I've been playing badly – they are the two I've turned to.

Dowie would try to bully me in training, which he says was his way of toughening me up because I was really skinny.

In the early days, I was guilty of jogging to the ball because I had the time, but Dowie would hustle me and say, 'Get there quick, because it gives you more time to look around and play it where you want.' I make sure I always do that now and I tell Anton to do the same.

I knew Dowie would become a manager. He could read a game better than anyone. He got a job at Oldham and turned their season around. When he took over at Crystal Palace they looked favourites for relegation and he got them promoted to the Premiership. They subsequently went down again, but he belongs in the Premiership and I was delighted for him when he got the Charlton job.

It took him a little time to make the breakthrough, but some clubs, like QPR, where he worked for a while, don't realise what they missed. He's got so many great ideas about football. When we go for lunch we sit and talk about the game for hours.

They say management is not rocket science, but Iain's background suggests it is. He has a master's degree in mechanical engineering and worked for British Aerospace testing missiles! He is so intelligent it's frightening. He's very different to your ordinary football person. He has an open mind and it shows in his training methods.

Before I'd even celebrated my nineteenth birthday I was earning around £4,000 a week. I'd long since stopped looking at the price of petrol and worrying about whether I could afford to put a tenner's worth in. My dad sometimes paid for his petrol with coins, we had to be so careful. I always remember that and it's made me more appreciative of what I've got now.

My biggest vice was that I was spending a fortune in the shops. Before I became a pro I would go up to the West End with my mates just to look, but the guys on the doors would not let us in. When I went back as a footballer with a bit of money those same dudes would be opening doors for me and asking if I wanted a glass of orange while they went to Customer Services to get someone to look after me. I told the security guys in Versace how they used to lock the door on me and now I could see all their teeth because they were smiling so much. I thought it should be pointed out.

I would go to Bobbies in Soho, which sold quality gear, and come back with bags full of clothes. I had to hide the prices from my mum. I was a shopaholic, buying things for all my mates as well.

Mum had to arrange for me to get a financial advisor so I'd start saving and not waste it all. But I loved spending.

I went to Park Lane with Jody Morris and Emile Heskey to pick up a new car, a light-blue BMW convertible. It was blinding and had a nice set of wheels on it. I drove it off the forecourt – I knew all about insurance by then – feeling the absolute business until I stalled after going about ten yards. I felt a right fool.

I've always had a thing for cars. They are a hobby of mine. I like cars that are a bit different from what everyone else has. I've had all sorts. After the BMW I got a Jaguar XK8 which was light green with a dark-green hood – very nice.

Then I took a shine to Jamie Redknapp's Mercedes 500 SL, which was a limited edition with a glass roof. My dad's got that one now. I followed that with an Aston Martin DB7 which was the best car I've ever had. I should have kept it, it was the business.

I had a Ferrari Spider at Leeds, but didn't like it. It was a manual and I've always preferred automatics because you don't have to do too much work. I've had a couple of Bentleys and other Aston Martins. I've currently got the Aston Martin Vanquish which is a real classy machine. And I've kept an Aston Martin Vantage from the eighties.

The daft thing about having the BMW convertible was that I was still living in a little council flat with my mum, Peter, Anton and my sister Sian and my shiny BMW was parked outside. Dad pointed out that the car was worth more than the flat and he was probably right. It laid a seed in my head. Dad has a way of doing that sometimes.

I resolved to buy Mum a new house so me and Dave Goodwin went looking round different areas and bought one. Mum was reluctant to move at first, but in the end she agreed, happy that it was only 20 minutes down the road and not too far from her friends.

I wanted to get her new furniture and stuff as well, but it was hard to persuade her. She's been so used to making ends meet she finds it hard to adapt now we don't have to worry about the finances. My dad's even more proud than her about accepting anything off me.

I don't like giving Mum money because she will spend it on everyone else but herself. I used to enjoy getting clothes for her, but what I like and what she likes are two different things. So I just get her vouchers from Monsoon, Marks & Spencer or John Lewis, so at least she has to get something for herself.

There was a big buzz around West Ham about a player called Joe Cole. I'd heard he did a trick or two and I loved tricks so I went to watch him play in a schoolboy game against Southend when he was 13. I wanted to see exactly what this boy had. He didn't disappoint me. He flicked the ball over his head, then

over another player, ran round the other side and collected it. The only time I'd seen anyone do that was when Ossie Ardiles did it in the film *Escape to Victory* and I bet he didn't do it in one take. I was screaming on the touchline, going mad. It was brilliant. I was screaming again when he scored his 30-yard volley against Sweden at the 2006 World Cup. His finishing has come on a bit.

Every time I saw Joe at the training ground I'd say hello and when he signed on I had a picture taken of me and him in the tunnel before a game.

When he was 15 he trained with the first team. I was 19 and had established myself, but he was the best player out there. We did two-touch and he scored three goals. It was magnificent. Harry Redknapp was raving over him.

I would shout, 'Come on, Joe, show me something, show me something.' He had the ability to get away from anyone. In the one-on-ones, when I was up against him, it would be a good little tussle.

John Moncur nicknamed him the Conjurer. It made me chuckle when Michael Carrick called him the Conj when we were training at the 2006 World Cup. I hadn't heard it for years.

I always wanted to see Joe performing his latest trick. Jose Mourinho would have hated it. I love seeing skills from any player – as long as it isn't against my team.

Razor Ruddock wasn't keen on facing Joe. He wouldn't try to tackle him. Instead he would either kick him or jockey him all the way towards the goal and allow Joe to shoot so he didn't look a mug by being nutmegged.

What was missing for a long time with Joe was the end product. You can have all the skill in the world, but if you don't do anything with the ball at the end, like produce a good cross, a defence-splitting pass or a goal, there's no point to any of it. He could beat players with his eyes closed, but when you step up to a higher level it's not just tricks that get you past people, you need physical prowess as well. Now Joe uses both. He's a strong little bugger for his size.

I used to say to Joe the same as I do to Cristiano Ronaldo at United, 'Assists, goals. Assists, goals.' Everything else is natural to players like them, but it's the assists and goals which will determine their careers, not the fact they could beat three men and disappear up a cul-de-sac. Now they are consistently producing the goods. It comes with maturity.

That's why Ryan Giggs is top class. Giggsy's got the balance right. His assists record is up there with the best of them and his goalscoring record from the wing is good as well.

He is a living legend and will probably be appreciated a lot more when he retires than he is now. It is unfair that he is not revered the same way as Thierry Henry is at Arsenal. For over a decade at United, Giggsy's been doing what Thierry does for the Gunners.

West Ham had a never-ending production line of good young players. There was Frank, Michael Carrick, Joe, Jermain Defoe, Glen Johnson and Anton. Lee Hodges might have been another one. He was hailed as the next Gazza, but suffered some shocking injuries. He did his cartilage three times within the space of about 18 months and had no luck at all.

When you consider how few kids make it, West Ham's record with youngsters is exceptional. Many have gone on to make a living in the game, even if it hasn't been at Upton Park.

There are probably a dozen lads in the leagues who were at West Ham between my year and Joe's, like Welsh international David Partridge, and Chris Coyne, who went to Luton Town. Tony Carr has the magic touch.

Howard Wilkinson took over as England caretaker manager in place of the sacked Hoddle for the friendly against France at Wembley in February 1999 and I didn't enjoy one minute of it.

To me, Wilkinson was like a school teacher. All he seemed to care about was set-pieces. He kind of bypassed actually playing the game as far as I could see. He would read out statistics about how half or more goals are scored from dead balls and that was the way to the promised land. He was right in that dead balls are very important, but they are not the be-all and end-all of a football match, which is the impression we got from him.

The morning of the match, Wilkinson got everyone in a great mood by making us stand outside the Burnham Beeches Hotel in some field, in what felt like a temperature of about minus five, doing set-pieces for 45 minutes.

I was the youngster and did what I was told, but the senior players like Adams and Shearer were looking at each other as if to say, 'Fucking hell, what's going on here!'

Then we go out and we get beaten 2–0. I came on and I was rubbish.

I felt I had been getting somewhere under Hoddle, who showed a lot of faith in me, and I was praying Wilkinson didn't get the job full-time because it was like being in the army. I couldn't see the team progressing, or myself. Hoddle was strict, but his training sessions were enjoyable and we played good football the way it was meant to be played.

So when Kevin Keegan got the job and not Wilkinson, I was initially pleased. It turned out it was not really good news for me at all.

Keegan didn't fancy me. It was obvious and I was pretty much cast into the international wilderness. There was an occasional appearance here and there, but nothing to get excited about.

Meanwhile, West Ham were comfortably plodding along

in the Premiership and I fell into a strange sort of comfort zone, which didn't make me feel fulfilled, but equally didn't cause me too much anxiety either.

Then, on 1 April 2000, West Ham lost 7–1 at Man United and we were exposed as real April Fools. It's a result the Neville brothers have never let me forget. If I ever did anything wrong on the pitch or in training Phil would say, 'That's you at West Ham.' The daft thing was Phil didn't even play in that game. He was sub.

I played right wing-back that day and Giggsy led me a merry dance. I just thought, 'Get me off this pitch.' I was getting absolutely slaughtered.

United were too good. They were on another planet to any team I'd ever played against and went on to win the league by 18 points. It made me realise how hard I'd have to work to get to that level.

Before that game, I believed I was going to be a good player, whatever Keegan felt. Afterwards, I thought, 'I'm hopeless compared to these guys. They're proper players.'

In just over a month the England squad for Euro 2000 would be announced and, what with that defeat and playing wing-back, it didn't look good for my chances.

With hindsight, I now realise I wasn't playing particularly well and couldn't expect to be in the England squad, let alone the team. I'd been going through the motions at West Ham and wasn't being pushed.

I need to be challenged. I've always been like that. It's why I left West Ham and why I later moved from Leeds to Manchester United. When Sven-Göran Eriksson dropped me after we lost to Northern Ireland in the 2006 World Cup qualifiers and I was getting criticised for my club performances I responded to that as well.

I had lost my edge. The burning desire to improve in every

game and be at my best had gone. My foot was off the gas and I wasn't playing to the maximum. I was coasting through games, which reflected the environment at West Ham. I knew I could do better. The club attitude was that they were happy to be in the Premier League, and that worked against me because my mentality went the same way.

But at the time I didn't really appreciate that. I was just thinking, 'Get rid of this Keegan geezer, please!' As a youngster that's your natural reaction, because you want to play. If the manager plays you regularly, regardless of how good a coach he is, you think he's half-decent.

Whenever I did get picked by Keegan I didn't enjoy it at all. He had Derek Fazackerley as a coach and I didn't gel with him, although I got on well with Keegan's assistant, Arthur Cox, even though he had a reputation for being dour.

When you feel someone hasn't got confidence in you, as I did with Keegan, it saps everything from you.

We had a friendly against the Ukraine on 31 May and Keegan said he would name his 23 for the finals on the afternoon of the game. The plan was that if he knocked on your door and came in that meant you weren't going and if he didn't come to your room you were going. Listening for that knock was agony, even though I was resigned to my fate.

I was lying on the bed with my bags already packed because of the game that night when the dreaded knock came. Keegan said, 'You know why I'm here. You're not in the squad, but I want you to play tonight.'

He then gave me some nonsense about how if I was French or Brazilian or Dutch I'd maybe have more caps. I thought to myself, 'Just tell me I'm not good enough or tell me why I'm not in the squad. Don't give me bollocks like that.'

It was bullshit, a throwaway line to appease me. I'd rather he'd just come in and said, 'Listen, Rio, you're not good enough and here's what you're missing.' I wanted something with more substance so I could go away and work on my deficiencies.

He told me I wasn't experienced enough, yet Gareth Barry was going and he wasn't experienced at all. He was a good young player but he didn't have a single cap when Keegan named the squad, while I had nine. Also, Gareth had not gone to the previous World Cup like I had.

When Keegan said he wanted me to play in the game that night I thought he was taking the piss. What was the point of that? I thought he should just play the lads who were going to the Euros. I wasn't good enough to go, yet I was good enough to get on the bench for this game? I sat there all night watching the match in a daze and didn't get on.

Then, at midnight, when he officially announced the squad, I had to talk to the press about being left out. Absolutely brilliant. Cracking day.

I couldn't understand why Keegan was making me go through all this. I shouldn't have had to answer to the press for his decision. But being dropped made me realise I had to buck my ideas up. I didn't like Keegan for what he'd done, but deep down I knew it was down to me. And, in a strange way, I'm thankful to him.

It was probably one of the best things that happened to me. It's fair to say, though, that I didn't really get Keegan's managerial approach, especially after someone like Hoddle, who was so precise on every single detail.

Keegan didn't seem big on the tactical side of things. He would go on about wearing your heart on your sleeve and that was it. To Scholesy he'd say that he wanted him to go and drop bombs all over the pitch, whatever that meant.

Maybe I'm more negative about Keegan than I should be because of the mindset I was in.

At the time, I thought I was right and the manager was

out of order. I was looking for any excuse going. But it was my own fault I didn't go. I knew I'd let things slip and was annoyed with myself. Playing football to the best of my ability means everything to me and I had let myself down and tried to blame everyone else for it.

I resolved to go back to pre-season, work extra hard, cut down on the partying and be more focused.

A few of us who weren't going to Euro 2000 got together and decided to hit Ayia Napa in Cyprus, a favourite place of mine, for a holiday.

There was me, Frank, Michael Duberry, Jonathan Woodgate, Kieron Dyer, Jody Morris, Jason Euell and quite a few other mates. There must have been 30 of us and we took over the place.

I loved Napa for the vibe. It played my kind of music. You got R&B, Hip Hop, House and Garage, which is what I used to listen to in London.

Frank wasn't bothered about the music. As long as there were birds and booze about he was up for it – just like most kids of our age.

We watched the England v Germany game in a bar in Napa. It was a lively night and we were dancing around like mad things when England won 1–0. If truth be told, I wanted England to win every game 4–3 to show that I should have been there in defence.

One of Frank's mates called Banger, a big fella, got up on stage wearing a Germany top after Frank dared him. He would do anything Frank told him to do. He stood on the stage, right in front of the screen, and got pelted with bottles. It was hilarious. When he came back down and sat with us I was crying with laughter.

Later we fell out of a bar at about 7a.m. and sat outside

by the main road with these two birds. We were having burgers and kebabs, as you do after a big session. It was one of those nights which run into the next day.

We told the birds that if they wanted to stay out with us they had to down a bottle of Bud in one. We were pretty cocky, I know. But they were having a good time and enjoying themselves.

One did it, but the other one couldn't, so we said that as a forfeit she had to go into the middle of the road and stop the traffic any way she could for 20 seconds. With cars going past to the left and right of her, she started stripping, and got her tits out. The traffic stopped all right and all the geezers were going, 'Yeahhhh!'

We all headed down to the beach with a load of beers, alcopops and WKDs from the local shop. We told the birds they had to down another bottle if they wanted to stay with us. Again, the first one does it and the other one can't. But I'm not going into what the forfeit was that time. Use your imagination . . .

The truth is some women will do anything to crack on with footballers and, let's be fair, which young players would pass up the opportunity to take them up on some of their offers?

Some birds will buy you drinks all night, strip for you, get shagged with other people in the room and do all sorts of tricks. Some of the stories you hear . . . I admit I got carried away with it at times but you get older, more responsible and leave that sort of thing behind.

You see it for what it's worth – that they aren't interested in you, just the notoriety and fame of being with a footballer, or anyone famous for that matter.

It is fun at the time though, no denying that.

On the same holiday, just after that incident with the girls and the forfeits, came a notorious episode involving a few birds and a videotape which all these years later is still used as a stick to beat me, Frank and Kieron with.

I can honestly say I did not take part in any orgy, even though that was how it was portrayed. I had sex with one girl, which was taped with her consent, and that was it. Okay, I played up to the camera a bit, but she knew it was on and it didn't bother her.

It was made out that the girl was unaware of the filming, but there were only two of us in the room and the camera was on top of the TV. It's not like it was hidden. It wasn't one of those tiny cameras you can get nowadays. It was a bloody huge thing, you couldn't miss it.

My performance was on the same tape as a recording of Kieron and Frank with a couple of birds, but it wasn't all at the same time. I didn't even know about what they had done. It was not one big orgy, as was reported.

Somehow, the camera got nicked. We suspected some English punters on the same floor of our hotel, but I don't know if they realised there was such juicy stuff on the tape. I've been asking myself those questions for years.

When we discovered the camera was missing everyone's room was turned upside down about ten times in the hope of finding it, but once I was back at home I forgot about it.

Then, about two weeks later, I was out shopping with my dad, buying stuff for my flat, when I got a call from a newspaper about a video of me shagging a bird. I could have fainted.

The bloke at the paper said I was abusing and degrading women, but I told him I'd never abused or degraded a woman in my life.

How could he say that? He didn't know anything about the circumstances. The girl had agreed to the video being on. I'm sure the girls with Frank and Kieron knew they were being taped too. It was not as if we had secretly set up the camera.

I didn't tell my dad about it. I just said I felt sick and went home straight away to ring Kieron and Frank. Kieron's people were trying to sort something out with the paper, but they were struggling.

It was highly embarrassing. It's not the best thing when pictures of you having sex are published in the papers, even though it was harmless and it was just young lads on holiday having fun.

We had not got into any trouble with any locals or any police. It was made out we were louts, but we hadn't been involved in drunken brawls, shouting the odds or making other people's lives a misery, which is what I would regard as loutish behaviour. But, as footballers, we had certain responsibilities that go with the job.

Mum went bananas and Dad said, 'I know kids do things like that all over the world, but you're not one of them. You're a footballer and you have to be responsible.'

Years later there was a Channel Four documentary drama about footballers supposedly preying on girls, with drugs and rape involved, and they used the Ayia Napa incident in the opening sequence. I was outraged that they could associate an incident involving consenting adults with something as serious as rape. Maybe that's the world of sensationalism we live in.

The hardest thing to get my head round was that I couldn't do what many other kids did, but that's the way it was. There are some who happily live the quiet life, but I was always outgoing and it was difficult to put a leash on me.

I never went back to Napa after that. It was never going to be the same again. What with the video, the drink-driving which saw me dropped from the England squad and being publicly shamed on the Under-21s trip, I was building up quite a crime sheet.

Yet the video to me was harmless, just part of growing up.

It is not realistic to expect young footballers to be perfect and never make any mistakes. I'd seen far more serious things – people getting shot, being hit with baseball bats and fights breaking out in clubs. Yet a shooting in Brixton will barely make the local news, let alone the national news, while I'm on the front page for shagging, which is something millions of people do every day of the week.

Strange world.

Keep out of Jail, Rio

I could have gone down the wrong path
had it not been for football. I imagine
I could have done the Del Boy bit, selling
what we called moody gear, fake clothing.
I had the patter for it.

RIO MY STORY

A good friend of mine went down for 12 years for murder and it was the biggest shock of my life.

I can't use his real name because, although he's out now, he's appealing to get his conviction overturned. We'll call him Kev. Kev was one of our mates from the estate who used to go to the Adventure playground. He had a lot going for him. He was a bright lad who did really well at school. He was also a good footballer and I believe he could have made it as a pro. He had the talent and was better than me.

But when he was 16 he got a moped and there were whispers that he was hanging out with a different set of boys. None of the rest of us had the money for a moped, which turned out to be a good thing because we might have got mixed up with them as well.

Kev stopped coming to the Adventure after getting banned for cheeking the youth worker, and, next thing we knew, he'd been arrested for murder.

The story goes that he was with this group who scuffled with a middle-aged man to nick his wallet. Kev said the bloke was on the ground and he was hurt but not dead. Later he learned he had died but did not know how.

He knew that he shouldn't have got involved. He got banged up in Feltham before going on to Wormwood Scrubs and various other institutions.

We used to get the train to visit him, or my mate Sava would drive us there.

Some of the stories Kev told us about life in prison made your hair stand on end. Guys would come into the prison playing the hard man and three days down the line you would hear them in the middle of the night crying to be let out because they couldn't deal with it. Kev would be woken up by the sound of screams.

He had an argument with a guy one time and later, when

he was cleaning out his cell, he felt an almighty whack on the back of the head. A warden had opened the door for this boy who came in and smacked Kev with a bottle. Kev beat the kid up and got put in solitary confinement.

For the first two years in prison he was fighting, arguing, and rebelling against any form of discipline. He said that sometimes he would be locked up for 22 hours a day. His whole life was over as far as I could see. I would have gone mad in those conditions.

He would say to me, 'Rio, don't get in trouble. Just play football, don't do anything else. If anyone says, "Come on, let's go and rob someone," don't do it, man, 'cause you'll end up in here like me.'

After a while he settled down and spent most of the day in the gym training other inmates and reading letters for them if they couldn't read themselves. He studied hard and got loads of qualifications.

I put him in touch with a friend of mine who does personal fitness work and was good enough to give him a job. Kev was delighted and grateful. He's earning decent money and has sorted himself out.

It's clichéd to say I could have gone down the wrong path had it not been for football. I imagine I could have done the Del Boy bit, selling what we called moody gear, fake clothing. I had the patter for it.

I did it at school. I had a mate from football who had well-off parents and I discovered why when he opened up his garage. It was full of boxes of clothes with Ralph Lauren and Versace labels. Normally with dodgy stuff the labels are on the wrong side or there's a fault in the design, but this looked like the real deal. Very convincing.

I asked my mate's dad if I could sell some at West Ham and at school and he had no problem with that. I took a few bits in which sold easily and I started taking in more and more. The orders were stacking up and I made a right few quid.

By the time I left school I had five-pound notes sticking out of all my pockets. Mum never knew though. It would have been curtains for me if she or Dad had found out.

I stopped selling the stuff when I left school. I knew you could go to prison for it and that could ruin your life. You go down for a petty crime, then you meet so and so who says his mate is outside earning ten grand a week doing credit card fraud. You think you could get away with that because it's not really bad and it's not high risk, but if you get caught you're knackered.

I could never have robbed anyone. I was in the Lazer Drome in Peckham when I was about 16 and a geezer came up to me and my cousin Bernard, showed us a gold chain in his hand and said, 'I've just popped it off a guy's neck.' I thought it was mad. I wasn't impressed. That wasn't my thing, thieving.

We would hear of men who would shoot others for the right price and I know people who've been kidnapped for their money.

Nothing got back to the police even though everyone knew who had done it. It's just the way it is. The criminals might not be doing it for vast amounts of cash. Many needed a couple of hundred pounds a day to feed a drug habit.

Yet I never felt threatened and always felt safe in my environment. If I walked through our estate at night, even though it was dark and eerie, I never feared I would get mugged or anything like that. I was more scared of the roaming dogs. It's hard to explain if you don't come from that kind of background.

Footballers like Jody Morris, Wes Brown, Wayne Rooney and Andy Impey grew up in tough areas and they have similar stories to tell. But they would all say they loved those days when they were kids.

My estate is not the same now, though. By the time I left

there had been a few stabbings and later guns became more common. Most of my friends have moved out now.

Where the politicians go wrong is they don't understand what's happening. You can't unless you've actually been there or talked to someone who has.

Kids need playgrounds and youth clubs and youth workers.

The Leyton Square Adventure Playground was a vital part of our existence. We need more and more of them in this country. But they must be properly run by trained youth workers who are paid a decent wage.

If the politicians went into Southwark and spoke to the youth leaders who work in the youth clubs in that area they would tell them the environment the kids are in is not a good one. They've got nothing to do, there's no money, there's no funding in the youth clubs so there's no trips out and there's no equipment.

Why would anyone want to work in a rundown youth club which has no money being put into it and have to deal with frustrated kids who can be violent and have behavioural problems which stem from boredom? They can go and work in a shoe shop, get better pay and have an easier life.

My good mates Gavin Rose and Leon Walters, who was the England karate champion, became youth workers at Leyton Square, but fought a losing battle because of a lack of funds.

What Gavin tells me about kids aged between 10 and 16 today is shocking. They seriously threaten to stab each other and there's a real problem with kids taking or selling drugs.

My mates used to fight occasionally. One might get knocked spark out and the next day those involved wouldn't be talking to each other, but then everyone laughed about it and they were mates again.

But there's no making up once someone's been stabbed.

There's an organisation called 'Kids Company' in south

London. It's run by a woman who deals with the rowdiest kids. She speaks to them on a level that they can understand and they have total respect for her. They look up to her like she's their mum.

People like that are hard to find and this country needs more of them.

It's expensive to keep kids entertained these days, but there is more money around. How many millions is the lottery raising? It's about time they concentrated on the youth clubs.

I once went looking for the chancellor, Gordon Brown, to tell him all this when Manchester United were staying at the Radisson in town before a home game and so was he. Brown was going to be making a speech about the distribution of money and I was hoping to see him, to get his thoughts on youth clubs and putting more money into activities for kids. Unfortunately, he had gone out for something to eat and I missed my chance.

It wouldn't cost a fortune to put money into after-school clubs and the government would reap the benefits. Between 3.30p.m. and 7p.m. kids roam around and get into trouble before their parents get home from work. Parents want somewhere their kids can go where they know they will be safe.

I want to join forces with the government and set up youth clubs like the one I went to. Hopefully, we'd also be able to get major companies involved as sponsors. David Beckham has his academies, I want youth clubs. There is a good chance I wouldn't be doing what I'm doing today if it hadn't been for Leyton Square.

Properly organised and funded youth clubs don't guarantee every kid will stay out of trouble, but they cut down the odds considerably.

I do quite a bit for the Prince's Trust. It funds young adults to do courses and gives them a second chance after they've messed up at school or college. Some get grants to start their own businesses.

Footballers are in a powerful position to influence young people. Kids look up to them and will listen to them more than they would any politician. It doesn't take much effort to speak out about things, but it can have a big impact.

I was involved in the Damilola Taylor Appeal to find who killed him. Damilola was a kid who was murdered on the North Peckham Estate near to where I used to live. He was only ten and was stabbed and left to die in a stairwell in November 2000. I made a nationwide appeal on TV to try to find his killers.

After six years and three trials teenage brothers Danny and Ricky Preddie were convicted of Damilola's manslaughter. We can only hope it brings some sort of comfort to his family. It won't bring him back though.

At Manchester United we set up an appeal to find the killer of Holly Wells and Jessica Chapman. There was a big reaction to that and eventually a local school caretaker, Ian Huntley, was jailed for their murder. I don't know if our appeal had any effect whatsoever in bringing him to justice, but it can't have done any harm.

Before heading off to Ayia Napa for that eventful holiday in the summer of 2000, I had approached the chairman at West Ham, Terry Brown, to ask where he saw West Ham's future going. I wanted to know what his plans were, who we could afford to buy and whether it was worth staying. I wasn't going behind Harry's back; he knew I was doing it and was perfectly happy about it because it added power to his argument for extra money in the transfer market.

Brown said he felt the team was solid and would get better, but that players would be signed to improve it even more. I wasn't convinced. I had a nagging feeling West Ham was standing still and, as I suspected, not much happened in the close season.

The chairman wanted me to sign another contract to show

my commitment, but I was already on a long deal and one of the top earners at the club. I didn't see how they could give me much more and felt it was just a PR exercise.

There had been rumours floating around that Leeds wanted me and they increased at the start of the 2000–01 season. Then, in the run-up to our game at Elland Road on 18 November, the speculation went into overdrive.

We won the match with a goal from Nigel Winterburn and I had the strange experience of hearing both Leeds and West Ham fans singing my name.

I didn't expect anything from their fans but the response to me was astonishing. It became a battle between the Hammers supporters and the Leeds ones about who could sing my name the loudest.

The lads had a good laugh about it afterwards but it's strange how football fans can be.

There I was being cheered by two different sets of supporters one day and a few years later I would be booed by my own fans while I was negotiating a new contract at Manchester United. Funny how things can change.

After the match, the Leeds chairman, Peter Ridsdale, put his money on the table and offered £15 million for me which, incredibly, Brown rejected.

The word was that Leeds would be back and the following week, when I was going out to meet my dad for dinner in the West End, I got a phone call from Paul Aldridge, the West Ham chief executive, saying he needed to see me urgently.

I told him I'd see him after training the next day but he went, 'No, I need to speak to you now. Leeds have made an offer for you of £18 million and we've accepted it.'

I went numb. I didn't know what to think. It was mad. I had mixed feelings about it. I was a Peckham boy from south-east London and Leeds was miles away from my family and mates. But there was a real buzz about Leeds at that time. They were the happening club and were expected to be the big rivals to Manchester United and Arsenal.

They were in the Champions League and had a lot of good players. I already knew Jonathan Woodgate, Lee Bowyer and Michael Bridges from England Youth and Under-21s and my friend Michael Duberry was playing for them as well.

I phoned my mum and dad to tell them what had happened and my dad went, 'Well, man, you've got to go. Just go. It will be good for you to get out of London. This is where the hard work really starts.' Mum agreed, but she didn't want me to leave. You know what mums are like when their little boy is going away.

My head was spinning. Silly things came into my mind like the fact that I had only just got my flat in Wapping looking like I wanted it. Not that I was there much. I only used it after I'd been clubbing or for entertaining friends. Most of the time I'd go back to Mum's new house in Mottingham. I'd go there after training, have lunch, go to sleep, get up, have dinner and go out. You could say that I hadn't yet let go of the apron strings. I'd stay at Mum's four nights a week. That wasn't going to happen if I moved to Leeds.

Aldridge told me in the lobby at the Tower Hotel in London that the decision was up to me and that if I stayed they'd sort out a new contract, but they were happy to let me go. I reckoned by the tone of his voice that they fancied the cash. If they needed the money more than they needed me then it was better to cut the ties. When it reaches that point the right thing to do is go.

Anyway, I felt it would be better for my career if I moved on. It was a new start. My dad was right. I needed to get out of London because I was in the comfort zone with my game and was going out too much. I never turned down an invite.

There was always something to go to, like the opening of a new bar, club or envelope. All the promoters and restaurant managers had my phone number. I'd get texts every night of the week saying there's an opening night here, there's a party on there with loads of birds, there's free drinks here, it's a birthday party tonight, it's our three-week anniversary. Any stupid occasion was good enough for me. If my mates were going somewhere, I couldn't miss out, whatever day of the week it was. It wasn't their fault, it was mine. I didn't need much encouragement. I couldn't say no. How I got away with it and managed to play any decent football, God knows.

It's no wonder I got a reputation as a party animal. But I'm not like that now. People judge me on my past rather than my present, which is frustrating but understandable. I can see how bad my lifestyle was, but at least I was sensible enough to realise it had to change.

If I wanted to make the step up from being a half-decent player on the periphery of the England squad to being an automatic choice I had to go.

I went back to Mum's house and then Dad came round. I said to Anton, 'I think I'm going to Leeds,' and he goes, 'You're going to have to live up there and you're not going to be here no more. When are we going to see you?' That upset me. Anton was at West Ham as a schoolboy at the time and probably thought I'd be there for ever looking after him. Then Mum joined in and said, 'Aren't there any clubs in London that want you?'

My agent Pini Zahavi, who has been a great support to me and is a shrewd operator, rang to say Ridsdale was coming down by private jet to sort out the deal. Then a well-known agent called Dennis Roach rang and said Chelsea wanted me and would match the offer from Leeds.

I told him I needed to move out of London for my career. Going to Chelsea would have been no good for me because I would have been around the same influences and the same bright lights. Mum would have preferred it but it wouldn't have been the right decision.

The way my lifestyle was going if I'd joined Chelsea it wouldn't have been long before they were giving me away to Leyton Orient. They had good players like Gianfranco Zola, Jimmy Floyd Hasselbaink and my mate Jody Morris, but I was more interested in getting myself right and I was looking forward to a new adventure. I turned Chelsea down.

I spoke to Michael Duberry who told me I would enjoy Leeds and, when me and my parents met Ridsdale at Pini's London flat, it took no longer than 45 minutes to make the decision.

The Leeds manager, David O'Leary, came on the phone while we were at Pini's saying he had high hopes for me and that he could bring me on as a player, especially as he was a central defender himself.

I said to him, 'Please just make sure you work me hard. Work me into the ground. I want to be a better player.' I knew I was a long way short of the finished article. I only had to think back to that Manchester United defeat to realise that.

O'Leary replied, 'Don't worry, son. I believe you can be one of the best. You coming here, working hard and playing with better players will point you in that direction.' He also told me he could improve me in terms of my concentration and positional sense. It was everything I wanted to hear.

When it came to the money side of things, Leeds didn't mess about, there wasn't much haggling. Anyone who went to Leeds at that time would confirm that you didn't have to fight very hard to get what you wanted.

I got a five-year contract worth £35,000 a week plus unbelievable bonuses. The most I could have earned at West Ham was £28,000 a week. On top of that I was getting a £300,000 signing-on fee, which was exactly what I'd paid for my flat. I'd only just had my twenty-second birthday and I couldn't believe it.

Yet, for all that, it has always been the football that has excited me most. Honestly if I hadn't made it as a pro, I would have continued playing at whatever level my ability allowed – money or no money. The next morning I enjoyed my first ever trip on a private jet as I joined Ridsdale on the flight up to Leeds. It was a class operation. We didn't do private jets at West Ham!

My medical must have been the longest in football history. I know I was costing a lot of money, but there wasn't a single part of my anatomy they did not examine.

It took seven hours – seven bloody hours! – and was conducted by the busiest physio in the world, Dave Hancock. I came to like Dave, although we had different opinions about how long players needed to stay in the physio's room. No wonder Dave was so busy. For him to be happy he'd want us there pretty much 9 to 5; not good news for footballers used to the strenuous 9.30 to 1.30 regime.

It didn't get off to the best of starts when he took me out on the training pitch just to kick the ball around and the enormity of the transfer fee suddenly hit me. For £18 million I reckoned they'd expect me to put the ball on a sixpence, but that morning I couldn't even keep it on a pitch 80 yards wide.

Players always say the transfer fee doesn't bother them, but at that moment it certainly bothered me.

Hancock was 30 yards away, pinging the ball to me, and I was kicking it to him half-heartedly so I didn't make a mistake. Then he shouts, 'Put your foot through it,' which I did and promptly shanked two in a row off my shin and they flew off at right angles.

The youth team were watching and I could hear them going, '£18 million? You're joking.'

I've never felt under so much pressure.

From that embarrassment I then went on the running machine and had to wear a mask while wires were attached all over me. I did two exercises where you had to run uphill on a treadmill to your absolute limit until you couldn't go on any more and fell off. I hadn't worked so hard since preseason.

I had to tell them about all the past injuries I'd had. There was a twisted ankle, a few back pains and that cruciate injury.

They did checks on everything at the hospital before coming back to me with a sheet of results. I was standing there all cool, waiting for them to tell me everything was okay, when one of them looked at me all serious and said, 'You've got an irregular heart.'

What? Had I heard that right? An irregular heart! Bloody hell, was I going to die? At the very least I thought I was going to have to give up football. All my dreams were shattered in that instant. Mum nearly passed out. She tried to calm down, but she was panicking.

They explained that one side of my heart was an abnormal size and that the blood was being pumped round in a different direction to most people's. It was four hours before they returned again, at 8 o'clock at night, and said it was not going to be a problem. That was a very, very long four hours.

They said it shouldn't affect me in life and so far it hasn't. I still think about it occasionally, but the subject was never even raised when I signed for Manchester United two years later.

What with the stress of the heart checks and the sheer physical exertion, the whole day completely took it out of me. I was knackered.

When I'd eventually passed the medical and signed all the papers, Ridsdale said, 'Come on then, cheer up!' Maybe it was all a bit much for me, the realisation that I was cutting the ties with home and embarking on a new adventure. Leaving a club which had been so much a part of my life was not an easy thing to do.

But Mum jumped in and told Ridsdale, 'Don't worry. He's happy, but you won't get him dancing all over the place and swinging from the chandeliers. That's the way Rio is.'

I wasn't registered in time to play the home game against Arsenal on the Sunday, which I was gutted about. But I was paraded in front of the fans who had chanted my name eight days earlier when I'd played at Elland Road for West Ham.

Ridsdale was keen to show me off and asked me to speak to the crowd, but I didn't fancy that. I just waved and they gave me a fantastic reception. Patrick Vieira and Thierry Henry went past and congratulated me. We won the game, so it was not a bad start, even though I'd not played.

The lads were brilliant helping me settle in and made me feel like one of them straight away. That night we went to the Bingley Arms, a pub near Linton, which was to become a regular haunt, though only in moderation, of course, what with my new determination to change my lifestyle.

At West Ham it had mainly been me and Frank who went out together, with maybe Razor and Trevor Sinclair joining us sometimes. At Leeds it was the whole team. Everyone was singing songs, with each player getting up and doing a turn. Michael Duberry, always up for a bit of fun, stood on a chair and belted out a Bob Marley classic. 'This is team spirit,' I thought. 'What a wicked club.' There were no little cliques, everyone was in it together.

Leeds were so professional. They had a relocation officer called Rosie who took me round looking at properties. She set up meetings with estate agents and arranged viewings. Any problems you had, Rosie was the woman to see.

I was only in a hotel a few nights before temporarily moving into a block of apartments where Robbie Keane, who joined a

KEEP OUT OF JAIL, RIO

short time after me, also ended up living. Robbie was a big help as he knew all the Irish lads at the club because they played for the Republic together. It made integrating easier and he became my room-mate on away trips.

It was all too good to be true, though, and I came down to earth with a mighty thud in my very first game against Leicester City at Filbert Street.

We lost 3–1 and were lucky to get away with that. We were absolute crap. The manager played three at the back, just to accommodate me, but it was something the team had never done before. I played alongside Woody and the Chief, Lucas Radebe, and we were three down after half an hour. I don't think I'd touched the ball.

O'Leary dragged Woody off, even though he wasn't the worst of the three of us. I don't suppose he could have hooked me having just paid £18 million for my services.

Woody was the scapegoat, but was also in the middle of a high-profile court case concerning an attack on an Asian student, of which more later, and may have been finding it hard to cope. But I felt embarrassed and a little guilty that he took all the flak.

Leicester played keep-ball and took the piss, frankly. What a way to start! The fact that West Ham won the same day against Middlesbrough made my performance look even worse. My old club had shown they could do without me and Leeds had shown they shouldn't have bought me!

We lost four of my first five games, only won two out of eight in the league and went out in the fourth round of the FA Cup to Liverpool. On the face of it, I was not a great investment.

Fortunately, the worm turned in the New Year and we went on a great run, including nearly making it all the way to the Champions League final.

*　　　*　　　*

I'd started going out with Rebecca Ellison a couple of months before Leeds came in for me. We met through one of her mates, who I'd known from knocking around in Romford and Ilford.

When I saw her with Rebecca in the Sugar Reef bar in London I asked her if she could sort me out. She goes, 'No, she don't like you. She don't like footballers or nothing like that.'

That was a challenge if ever I'd heard one, so I asked Rebecca to get a pen from behind the bar, write her number down and bring it back to me. She went, 'Pardon? No chance.'

But after I'd badgered her for a while we swapped numbers. I rang her the next day, which was a bit over the top for me because I tried to be a cool dude normally and leave it a few days.

Her mate answered and said, 'She's not here.' I rang back again later and this time I got Rebecca and asked her to come out for a meal. We went to an Italian in Knightsbridge called Scalinis. We had a good time, got on great and it went from there. But it wasn't like we rang each other all the time and met up every day. We were just seeing each other occasionally.

Rebecca's parents lived in Chingford. Her dad was a policeman and her mum worked as a hypnotherapist and reflexologist. Rebecca was the middle one of three kids, with an older sister and a younger brother.

They lived in a nice terraced house which was more upmarket than our old estate. The first time I went round I stayed outside and bibbed the horn. I wouldn't go in. I didn't see any point in meeting her parents if I didn't know her that well yet. We didn't know whether we'd still be going out the following week. So I bibbed again and then I rang her, but she didn't answer the phone.

Eventually, she came out, got in the car and asked, 'Why didn't you just come and knock on the door?' She didn't understand. I didn't go in the house until I'd seen Rebecca quite a few times. I explained to her that it was a bit hasty to be meeting the parents. I'd never met any girl's parents before.

But when I rang Rebecca to tell her I might be going to Leeds, I could tell by her voice that she was upset. I realised then that I didn't want to lose her. So when we next met up I asked her if she fancied moving to Leeds.

I didn't get an answer and when she drove past me to go home she was crying. I felt well bad. I'd never lived with her and I'd only known her a few months, but we were very comfortable together.

Rebecca decided she'd test the water and come up, but if it looked like it wasn't going to work out she would return to London. Her mum was upset because she was worried about Rebecca leaving her job and her mates.

Rebecca was an accountant in the City, had a good education and was very bright, not the media's stereotypical footballer's woman. Looks-wise I fancied her, of course, but I could tell there was more to her and we always had a laugh. She meant more to me than any girl I'd met before. She was the only girl I'd ever taken to my mum or dad's house so she must have been special.

Rebecca thinks I'm a mummy's boy because I'm always talking to Mum on the phone.

Mum deals with the bank for me and answers my fan mail, so if that makes me a mummy's boy then I am. But I'm close to my dad as well. I ask both my parents for advice and that will never change.

We decided Rebecca wouldn't come up until after Christmas because I needed to get a house. I wanted to be settled first. My mates were going, 'Ree, what's going on, man? Moving a chick up with you to Leeds. You are mad. Crazy. There's going to be new chicks up there. It'll be brilliant.' But, for the first time, I didn't care about other birds. I was happy Rebecca was moving up.

My mate Gavin, always the voice of reason, said, 'If you like her or you love her no one can say nothing to you, man.'

When we were younger at West Ham we used to slaughter

Anthony McFarlane for having a bird. He wouldn't go out with the lads on the pull any more because he was spending more time with her. He got a bit pissed off and fed up with us constantly having a go at him for being under the thumb. But I was never concerned about what others thought. I was going to do what I wanted to do.

I've always thought that if you get a girlfriend who is comfortable around your mates, even when you're not there, she's a good one. And if you can have a laugh with her when you're by yourself, so much the better. Rebecca was a perfect fit. I've been out on dates with girls who were pretty but had nothing else to offer and it was mind-numbingly boring.

I found a lovely converted barn next to a farm at the end of a country lane in Linton, which was near Wetherby, and Rebecca moved in. We picked furniture for the house and decorated it together. It felt totally natural.

I was no longer the single lad, another thing which helped curb my lifestyle! Rebecca did not become a substitute mum, however. She didn't try to change my life other than to take control of the bills. Well, she was a trained property accountant.

She was determined to live her own life and, as soon as she arrived, went straight out and got a job. I admired her for that. I despise birds who do nothing except spend their bloke's money on shopping, facials and lunch and shout about it from the rooftops.

Rebecca became pals with Gary Kelly's missus, Julianne, and got friendly with Stephen McPhail's now wife, Michelle. We went to Stephen's wedding. Rebecca also made lots of friends at work.

When I was away she would stay with Michelle because our place was so isolated. It wasn't till we left for Manchester that Rebecca told me how scared she'd been living in it on her own. She'd never complained once.

Marching on Together

I got my first Leeds goal, a header at the back post which went through the keeper's arms. As it hit the net, a photograph was taken which shows me jumping so high in celebration you think I'm about to go through the roof. That's adrenaline for you.

My **Leeds career** may have gotten off to a dodgy start, but I could see it was a top-class set-up. Everything was so professional and they had a magnificent training ground at Thorp Arch, near Wetherby.

Everyone made me welcome: the players, dinner ladies, laundry girls and the office staff. It was a real family-orientated club.

Leeds had outstanding young players such as Alan Smith, Woody, Harry Kewell and Paul Robinson. Many of them had been together for years and had come through the youth ranks together.

It was only a matter of time before everything clicked and after we beat Aston Villa at home towards the end of January we only lost one Premiership game until the end of the season. I just made the Villa game, having been ruled out for ten days with the most bizarre injury you can imagine. I was watching TV and reading a book with my leg up on a coffee table and must have been sat like that for a couple of hours. When I got up I could hardly walk. I'd strained my knee. It was the most stupid injury since the ex-Wimbledon keeper Dave Beasant dropped a bottle of salad cream on his foot, though perhaps not quite as bad as when Sunderland striker Kevin Kyle burned his privates with hot water. The manager was not impressed when I told him what I'd done. I never ever sit like that now!

In the Champions League we defied all the odds. Before I signed, the lads had got through the first stage by finishing second in a group which was won by AC Milan, while Barcelona and Besiktas finished below us.

In those days you went on to a second group phase and, when Leeds lost at home to Real Madrid a couple of days before I joined, the party seemed to be over.

I wasn't eligible for the next game against Sven-Göran Eriksson's Lazio, but we beat them 1–0 away, with Smithy scoring ten minutes from time. That was a right result. It was after that that Sven quit Lazio to take up the England job.

Anderlecht at home in February 2001 was my first game in Champions League football and they were no mugs. But we won 2–1 at home and absolutely battered them 4–1 at their place. Smithy and Mark Viduka were unbelievable.

Smithy impressed me most out of all the players. I didn't know him very well before I signed, but I discovered he had a great work ethic, a solid all-round technique and was an excellent target man. He was an out-and-out striker, not a midfielder as he became at Man United. His only flaw was he would get sent off for silly things and was a bit antagonistic. But he took no crap, I'll say that for him.

I got into a more organised routine than I was used to during my chaotic West Ham life. As soon as I finished training I'd go to bed and wouldn't do much more. Maybe I'd go out with the lads a couple of nights a week, but always at the right time and I was rarely out late.

They were a real bunch of characters. Our French midfielder, Olivier Dacourt, cracked me up. He was a funny geezer who acted like he was all sophisticated. He would only drink the finest champagne, Dom Perignon, or wines of the highest quality. None of your house white or a lager for him. He would shoo us away with his hand and in broken English would say, 'You boys have your drinks, I'll have mine.' He also thought he was the best dresser and listened to the best music. We used to call him Gandhi because he looked like Ben Kingsley, the actor who played him in the film.

When Jody Morris came up to visit, just after I'd joined, me and him went out with Dubes and had this hilarious exchange with a taxi driver. I was sat in the back and the driver goes to Dubes, 'Can you believe they've signed that wanker Ferdinand for £18 million?' Dubes couldn't help himself and goes, 'Yeah, I know. Shit, isn't he?' Then the driver tells him I'd been staying all week with a bird who lived next to his mate's house and that I was obviously going to be a disaster.

He told Dubes that he'd seen my car, a Mercedes, himself. But I didn't have a Merc, I had an American jeep at the time. He was talking so much rubbish.

I couldn't believe I was hearing this and the driver had no idea it was me in the back. Dubes thought it was hilarious and goes, 'You know what, mate? He's just an ignorant black twat.' I nearly choked, especially when the driver goes back to Dubes, who is black as well, of course, 'Blacks, they're all the same, mate.' Dubes goes, 'You're not wrong there.'

We were crying with laughter by the time the driver dropped us off. He never realised I was in the cab.

There was this brilliant laundry woman at Leeds called Mags who would always have a laugh with us. One day, she was walking past the dressing room when Jason Wilcox, one of the funniest blokes I've ever met, along with John Moncur, goes, 'Oi, Mags, get lost. You'll see me bits.'

Mags wearily replies, 'Seen it all before, Jason,' and walks off, at which point Jason dropped his pants, bent over, wiggled his bare arse towards the door and shouted, 'Bet you ain't seen this before.' Unknown to him, Mags had come back again and popped her head round the door just as Jason was exposing himself. I was lying on the floor in agony I was laughing so much.

We lost our next Champions League group game in Madrid, but drew with Lazio at home to make it through to the quarter-finals against Deportivo La Coruna of Spain who had earned a growing reputation across Europe.

We had been warned it would be a tough one, but we steamrollered them in the first leg. I got my first Leeds goal, a header at the back post which went through the keeper's arms.

As it hit the net, a photograph was taken which shows me jumping so high in celebration you think I'm about to go through the roof. That's adrenaline for you.

We were brilliant and won 3–0, my goal being the last one. I didn't know it at the time, but it was the winner. We lost 2–0 in the return leg over there and were hanging on for the final whistle.

They were like a different team. Their captain Fran, who'd been abysmal at Elland Road, turned into one of the best players I'd ever played against. We hung on for 17 minutes at two down and they had a couple more chances, but we crawled over the line. I'd never experienced a bigger contrast between how a team played at our ground and at their own. It was like they had 12 men over there.

After the away games in Europe, the Leeds fans would be kept back and would sing their hearts out till they left. That night we sang with them and both players and fans were completely hoarse.

That Deportivo goal was the start of my amazing run of three goals in five games. I also scored with a back-post header when we won 2–1 at Liverpool in the Premiership in what was a great performance. It gave us hope that we could pip them for a Champions League qualifying spot.

With West Ham, I'd always gone to Anfield, Arsenal and Manchester United more in hope than expectation. If you got a point it was the best result of your life. But I'd stepped up another level now. We believed we could beat anyone, home or away.

Incredibly, I went to West Ham and scored again which, ironically, was my first ever senior goal at Upton Park.

I didn't know what reception I was going to get going back for the first time, but the fans were unbelievable, just as they were when I returned with Manchester United a few years later. They sang my name as if I was still their player.

I scored the second goal with a looping header over the keeper and the lads jumped all over me. I jogged back to the halfway line without celebrating. I felt it wasn't right for me to go over the top because I loved West Ham too much. When the fans saw my reaction they sang my name even more.

I might have celebrated had I realised it would be another four and a half years before I scored another club goal!

Valencia came to town for the Champions League semi-final in May. We were so close to success we could taste it.

We should have won the first leg, but only drew 0–0. They didn't do anything to threaten us. They had obviously come for a draw and they got it, but we opened them up a couple of times.

No one had expected us to be in the last four, but we had performed so well in the competition that we went over there confident of winning.

As a bonding exercise we all had our heads shaved. Our philosophy was very much 'all for one, one for all'. The fans sing about marching on together and that's how it was. Whatever the supporters think of me for having later joined the enemy, Manchester United, I will always remember that passion they had for the team.

It was a thumping atmosphere at the Mestalla. It is one of the great European stadiums. It extends high up into the clouds, with the fans swinging from the rafters and firecrackers constantly going off. I love nights like those, although I do wonder why they are allowed to let off fireworks in many grounds in mainland Europe, yet if you so much as light a match in an English stadium there's hell to pay.

Valencia scored early on and, although we had a few chances, they were three ahead by the fifty-second minute, through Gaizka Mendieta who ran the game. Smithy was sent off near the end for a reckless challenge born out of frustration and it summed the night up. It was a bad end to a great adventure.

There was a huge picture in the *Yorkshire Post* of me bent down and the scoreboard behind showing 3–0. Mum gave me a print of it, which was nice of her!

It was a miserable flight home, but the gaffer told us that if you don't take your chances at that level you're going to get punished. He said that if we showed the same fight and determination we'd come back stronger the next year.

I liked O'Leary as a manager. He instilled confidence in me, which is vital for any player. He wasn't exceptional on the training field, but he had Roy Aitken and Eddie Gray by his side, who were both experienced heads, and later he had Brian Kidd.

They had all been great players in their day, knew the game inside out and the lads respected them. They would sit for hours talking about the game and you could ask them anything about old players and teams. I loved that. Me and Alan Smith could listen to them all day.

Kidd was a top man and a quality coach. No player had a bad word to say about him. And I enjoyed listening to Eddie, who joked that if he hadn't got injured he would have been better than George Best! He would go on about former Leeds legend Johnny Giles, who he worshipped.

I reckon Eddie was harshly treated by Leeds. He did every job imaginable at the club and then from what I can see they kicked him out. You always hear people harping on about players not being loyal – but what about the clubs themselves? There should always be a place for someone who's been such a good servant, but sadly football can be cold and hard.

O'Leary was calm, yet assertive and perceptive. An example of that came at Newcastle. Me and Woody were laughing in

the changing room before the match, kicking the ball at each other and messing about. I didn't play particularly well, nor did Woody, and after the game O'Leary told us, 'You two were messing about and your minds weren't right. You've got to prepare.' For the whole of the following week he was saying, 'Listen, son, you won't improve if your mind's not on the game. Don't mess about trying to be one of the lads. You've got to be focused.'

I was learning a lot of big lessons then – and that was one of them. I've never forgotten the things I learned. If any kids ask me for advice now I tell them that a lot of how you perform, at any level, is about preparation. It can mean the difference between winning and losing.

We'd lost 2–1 to Arsenal just before the second leg of the Valencia game and it was to prove costly – in all sorts of ways – for the club. It is not unfair to say that this was the beginning of the end for Leeds. Not that we knew it then.

Although we finished the season by thrashing Bradford 6–1 in our local derby and beat Leicester 3–1, we missed out on qualifying for the Champions League, and the riches that went with it, by one point and had to settle for a UEFA Cup place.

On a personal level, I was still pleased with how it was going for me at Leeds. I'd played in the Champions League semi-final, been to Anfield and won and scored a few goals. I also felt I'd improved as a player. But I was disappointed that we hadn't managed to pick up any silverware, which I'd thought had been well within our capabilities.

Before the next season started O'Leary made me captain.

I'd already done the job on a temporary basis when Lucas Radebe was injured, but the Chief was a man we all loved. He was one of the best defenders in the Premiership and he was our leader, whether he was on the pitch or not. But O'Leary decided it was time for a change and, one morning, I was in the physio room, where everyone went for a banter, when he called me into the corridor.

He said, 'I've spoken to Lucas and I'm going to make you captain.' I was speechless. I was delighted and happy, of course, but also embarrassed because the Chief was there, right in front of me.

It must have been hurting Lucas and I didn't feel at all comfortable, but he made it easy for me, he was a diamond geezer. He goes, 'Brilliant, Rio. I'm glad that you're captain. I think you deserve it.' I just mumbled, 'Sorry, man, sorry. Thanks, but I'm just sorry.'

When I walked back into the physio room there were Dubes, Woody, Bow and Gary Kelly and they'd obviously been listening. Dubes and Gary were winding me up going, 'He's not only took the Chief's armband, he'll be fucking taking his parking space as well. It's out of order.'

At the training ground the manager, the coach and the captain had their own parking spaces right outside the front door, while everyone else had to find one of their own, which could be up to 100 yards away.

When I came in the next day I didn't park in the captain's place. In fact, I don't think I parked there for a week. I said to the Chief, 'You keep your parking space, please. I can't do it, man. I feel bad enough as it is.' He said, 'Rio, you have to park there. I want you to park there.' It was bloody silly, really, but I felt terrible.

For a month the lads were hammering me. 'He's trying to finish off Lucas Radebe. He's trying to kill him. He's taking everything out of the geezer.'

It was a funny way for O'Leary to do things, telling me right in front of the Chief like that, but Lucas didn't seem to have a problem, so I got on with it – and, reluctantly, I took his parking space.

Before joining Leeds I'd heard about Lee Bowyer and Jonathan Woodgate facing trial over an assault on an Asian student called Sarfraz Najeib. There were claims the attack was racially motivated, but I knew both of them and wasn't rushing to make judgements because it was difficult to separate the facts from the fiction. When I moved to Leeds I got to know what the case was all about and how serious it was and realised they could go to prison if found guilty. But the way I heard it, there were a number of incidents, one of which involved a group which just happened to be made up of Asians.

Bow and Woody hardly talked about it at all. They dealt with it by themselves and got on with life as best they could.

But it was interesting to see how they both reacted differently to the situation. It seemed to me Bow obviously saw football as a release from the pressures and played out of his skin. He once came back from court in a helicopter to make a Champions League game and was fantastic, even though he'd done no training at all. He was amazing.

I reckon Woody, on the other hand, found it hard to cope and his game fell apart. He went very quiet. He wasn't the same Woody and the strain of going to court got to him. He lost a load of weight and we joked that he was fading away. At the training ground no one was wondering if they were racist. I never once considered that.

Me and Bow lived round the corner from each other and he'd pick me up for games and training and we'd go out for lunch. But we never had a deep conversation about the case. I knew he'd been involved in a previous incident in a McDonald's years before, but I take people as I see them and to me he was no racist.

Bow is not what you see on the football pitch. On the field he's aggressive, puts his foot in, gets up and down the field and runs all over the gaff, but off it he's a humble kind of guy. He doesn't take centre stage, shouting the odds. He stays in the background. He's got a reputation as a bad boy, but sit him down in a room with a group of players and he's one of the quietest.

Bow's the type who, rather than go on a big lads' holiday to Ayia Napa like me, would go fishing with a couple of mates who have no connection with football. People see him as arrogant, but he's not like that.

Michael Duberry got caught up in the whole case as a witness and life became just as difficult for him. I was closer to Dubes than to Bow or Woody and know how badly he was affected. His football suffered because he couldn't concentrate properly with everything that was going on. There wasn't much I could say to him except to keep his head up and tell the truth.

The first trial collapsed because of a story in the press which prejudiced the case and it went to a second trial. I thought it was never going to end. The verdict finally came nearly two years after the attack. Bow got off, but Woody was done for affray and got community service. There was no suggestion from the judge that racism had been involved.

The other Leeds players were delighted that their teammates weren't going to prison, but Bow and Woody didn't come back celebrating. They were very low key. Bow did say, 'Fucking hell, I was shitting it,' which was probably the most he'd said about it for a year. He's been tarnished for life, no doubt about it, but he wasn't found guilty of anything.

Woody had nothing to smile about, having been done for affray. One of his mates got six years.

What none of us knew was that O'Leary had written a book which came out a week after the case finished. I didn't have a clue and I was the captain. He lost a bit of respect for that, especially from Bow.

O'Leary said in the book: 'Those two players let Leeds

United down and the way they carried on in the streets of Leeds was disgraceful.'

A lot of us felt he should have left it alone and not aired his views in public. I don't know how David Walker, the press officer who wrote the book with O'Leary, could see it as being a good thing to do. I got on well with Walker, but in my view he should have advised the manager against going to print, or at the very least he could have run it by Woody and Bow.

As far as I could see there was no benefit to anyone, apart from a financial one. It just alienated the team. Bow and Woody had been under the microscope for nearly two years and the book added to the pressures already on them.

Looking back, I think I should have said something, but I didn't and I couldn't have stopped the book being published anyway. Ridsdale must have known about it. He was close to Walker and surely he should have told him to put a lid on it.

Relations between the manager and some of the players were never quite the same again.

We had made a good start that season and hadn't lost till mid November against Sunderland. Then, after the Woodgate–Bowyer verdict it all went downhill and the club started to unravel. There seemed to be no control.

Robbie Fowler, a legend who I looked up to, joined us for £11 million just before the end of the trial and, while I was delighted, I didn't see a striker as a necessity unless we were selling someone.

Smithy was doing really well and was in the England reckoning, Viduka was a regular scorer and Robbie Keane gave us something a bit different – goals and guile. I thought Fowler, undoubtedly one of the best goalscorers about, was going to make team selection more complicated for the manager rather than solve the problems which were elsewhere in the team.

That wasn't Robbie's fault though.

Although he was clearly disappointed to have left Liverpool he quickly got well in with the lads and brought a bit of fun with him too.

He told us about this game they had at Liverpool where a coin was passed around during the match. If a team-mate came up to you and offered you the coin you had to take it and the one left with it at the end had to do a forfeit. We scored a goal in one game and, while we were celebrating, Gary Kelly slapped a coin in my hand. You could see me on the replay going, 'Oh fuck.' According to Robbie, that was one of the best coin-passing games. It had gone round the whole team twice. We did it for five or six matches without the manager knowing. It didn't affect our play at all, but he'd still have gone bananas if he'd found out. We'd finish a game and the first thing on our mind was, 'Who has the coin?'

We all dressed in SAS or army gear for our Christmas party and a picture appeared in the local paper of Robbie asleep in his army outfit in the passenger seat of a car which was being filled up at a petrol station. It was so funny.

The Christmas parties at Leeds were sedate compared to what I'd known at West Ham, though. One year, Trevor Sinclair got pulled in by the police after jumping on top of a car to get out of the way of another one which had almost knocked him over. Those pictures made the papers as well.

The same night John Moncur climbed the Christmas tree in the middle of Romford High Street and couldn't get down so we left him there. And the senior players picked one of the young lads to go on stage with a stripper – she had some fun with him!

I was a hell of a lot better behaved at Leeds than I was at West Ham, but occasionally stumbled off the path of righteousness, like the time when me, Dubes and Robbie Keane had a big night out and got completely wrecked.

I phoned in and said me and Robbie had stomach aches

after eating something dodgy. But Dubes, the nutter, never rang in and went to training. He used to drink rum and blacks and everyone knew when Dubes had been out on a big one because his bottom lip would still be stained with blackcurrant the next morning. His lip was worse than usual that day and he got fined while we escaped.

We didn't win a league game from New Year's Day, when we beat West Ham, until a 2–0 win over Ipswich on 6 March. We were hammered 4–0 by Liverpool during that run, a game in which I scored an own-goal.

We were also beaten in the UEFA Cup by PSV Eindhoven and got knocked out in the third round of the FA Cup at Cardiff.

What a day that was. It was an intimidating, aggressive atmosphere, which I always enjoy – it doesn't scare me – but I went off injured early on with a twisted ankle. As I hobbled round the pitch to the changing room I got called every name under the sun. They were chucking little miniature bottles of spirits at me, which they must have had left over from Christmas.

Their chairman, Sam Hammam, did his walk around the pitch and it all went off. There was the predictable FA inquiry, but it couldn't change the fact that we'd lost.

Despite winning four of our last five Premiership matches, we failed to make the Champions League again, which the club had been banking on to keep its head above water.

Qualifying for the UEFA Cup was no consolation. Leeds were heading for financial meltdown.

The Rocky Road to Manchester

I loved Leeds and the fans and when I joined I did it thinking I would be there for years. But with the manager seemingly not being told the full story, no new players coming in which were necessary for success and Leeds needing the money, I knew I had to get away for my own good.

When Keegan quit after England lost at home to Germany in the opening qualifier for the 2002 World Cup I can't say I was crying. The only problem, however, was that Wilkinson took over for the next qualifier in Finland.

I was beginning to wonder if it was a sign that my England career was finished at the age of 21.

But, hallelujah, Wilkinson lasted for only one game and Peter Taylor was put in charge as a one-off appointment for a friendly in Italy.

Taylor had been brilliant with the Under-21s and had a fantastic record. I had a great relationship with him, despite the drinking incident in Rieti when he'd told me I'd never play for England again! All the players who worked under him had the utmost respect for the man as a coach and an all-round good bloke.

For some reason, the FA had temporarily allowed Wilkinson, who was their technical director, to take the Under-21 job off Taylor, but reinstated Taylor once Wilkinson had left.

In his one game in charge of the senior team, Taylor went for broke and bravely chose a side of under-30s, which I naturally thought was a good idea and a great opportunity to field a team the fans wanted to see. I was back.

No one could argue that the squad didn't need a shake-up. There were a few talented youngsters who hadn't been getting a deserved opportunity, being kept out by players who had been around for years. Keegan had invariably favoured experience over talent if there was a close call between two players. I think he reckoned that if a young 'un had a bad game he might never recover and you could understand where he was coming from. But sometimes chances have to be taken.

Taylor has never been given enough credit for the revolution. He had the balls to go for it and it was he who made

Becks captain that day, which was a big decision at the time and a good one in my opinion.

Although we lost 1–0 to a wonder-strike from Rino Gattuso, we should have got at least a draw. We played lovely football with great spirit and enthusiasm. The press were upbeat and there was a much happier mood in the camp ready for Sven-Göran Eriksson's arrival.

I'd heard of Sven, but didn't know much about him and I was on to Pini asking what he knew. Pini, who knows everybody, knew Sven well and told me how he had won the Italian title with Lazio and about the important jobs he'd had in Europe.

We found out just what Sven was like before his first game as England manager, against Spain. He had a simple straightforward philosophy, explained how he wanted the team to play and what he expected from each position.

He'd been coaching for years in Portugal and Italy and I thought he was going to have all these mad ideas. I expected the right-back to have to be able to do pirouettes and the left-back handstands. But he made football sound more simple than any manager I'd ever played under. There was nothing intricate about his approach.

Eriksson was a man who knew what he wanted and how he wanted it done. He stressed the basics. When the ball was on the right-hand side with Becks, he wanted the left winger coming in on the far post, not staying out on the left wing. He wanted one of the forwards to drop in a little bit behind the other one and, when the opposition had the ball, the midfield had to be quite narrow, not too wide. He didn't want big gaps in between the defenders, nor did he want us running out with the ball too much and taking risks.

If I took issue with anything, it was that I liked running with the ball. Always have done, it's one of my strengths. Sven preferred me to give it to a midfielder or a striker and let them get on with it. Mind you, given that I was back in the England reckoning again, I felt I could live with that.

We beat Spain 3–0 and you sensed the feel-good factor rippling around the country. That feeling had to be taken into the World Cup qualifiers, where there was some catching up to do.

We only had one point from two games, but we beat Finland at home and Albania and Greece away before one of the greatest nights in England's footballing history when we went to Germany in September of 2001 and won 5–1.

Our hotel was handily situated next to a huge bierkeller where they had oompah bands playing loudly and enthusiastically all night. That was good planning. There were people singing and shouting outside our windows till two in the morning and the Germans must have felt like they were 1–0 up before the game had even started.

We knew that if we lost we might blow our World Cup qualification chances altogether and maybe not even make the play-offs. Having beaten us at Wembley, the Germans were not expecting to lose and the pressure was on us.

When the big lump Carsten Jancker scored after six minutes it looked like curtains, but Michael Owen equalised and we were about to enjoy a night we would never forget.

Just before half-time, Stevie Gerrard smacked a beauty in the corner. At first, I thought he was lucky to have sneaked it in past a flat-footed keeper, but having watched the replays since, I can see it was a gem which curled back in at the last minute.

Owen always gets goals in the big games, even if he's been doing nothing. He's a machine and he scored two more before Emile Heskey added a fifth. We had smashed Germany in their own back yard.

Before the game, their fans and media in Munich's Olympic Stadium had given us loads of stick, telling us to book our holidays for the following summer because there would be no World

Cup for us. By the end, the ground was half-empty and it was a great feeling to walk round looking at the fans who'd stayed and seeing their miserable faces.

What made it even better was seeing the massive electronic scoreboard showing the score 1:5 in bright orange. What a sight that was. I've got a picture on my wall of the team in front of that board.

That win has to be one of my best moments in football, along with the victory over Argentina which was to follow in Japan.

We beat Albania again in Newcastle, which was actually harder than beating the Germans. We were expected to thrash them, but they shut up shop and took some breaking down before we eventually won 2–0.

It got to the point where a draw against Greece at Old Trafford in our final qualifier would see us through to the 2002 World Cup finals. Thank God for Becks, who got us there virtually single-handed.

I didn't have a good game. I could have closed their striker down better for one of the goals. Teddy Sheringham had scored for us, but we found it hard to shackle the Greeks, and they were leading 2–1 in injury time until Becks equalised with a wonder free kick.

It was a magnificent sight to see the ball arc away from the keeper into the top corner and I took off after him. I hurtled over to the corner flag near the tunnel and jumped on top of Becks, shouting to him, 'Thank you, thank you. Fucking beauty!' I felt it was my fault that we could have been facing a play-off had he not scored. Fortunately, my mediocre efforts were forgotten because of the sensational Becks show.

I was going to the World Cup again, but this time the little lad on the sofa who'd watched those hazy pictures of Maradona was going to play a real part.

Had the 2002 World Cup been played in a sauna I'm sure it would have been cooler than the temperatures we experienced in Japan and South Korea. We warmed up, if that's the right expression, at Jumeirah Beach in Dubai, which was a magnificent place. They were pushing the place as a tourist destination and we all got offered houses or flats at huge discounts, but I didn't bother. I wish I had. They are worth an absolute fortune now.

The heat there helped us to prepare, but we were not ready for the temperatures we faced when we got to Japan.

The two friendlies we played in Korea before the big kick-off gave us a taste of what was in store. We drew against both South Korea and Cameroon, but it was hard work.

We were lucky to get the draw against Cameroon and I was very happy we weren't in their group. They were pinging the ball from one side of the pitch to the other and it was too hot for us. The climate was clearly going to have a major influence on our chances.

Our team had a solid foundation, without being greatly pleasing to the eye. Steven Gerrard being injured and having to stay at home was also a loss and Becks wasn't properly fit, having suffered a broken metatarsal six weeks earlier. You might remember it. It was one of the first times that the word 'metatarsal' was on the nation's lips, but it wasn't to be the last.

I couldn't see us getting beat, but I couldn't see us beating many teams either. I had a feeling we might have to dig in for penalties once we reached the knockout stages because we were usually dying in the second half. The humidity was sapping our strength.

Funnily enough, I can't actually remember us practising penalties at that World Cup. But I fancied myself to score if I'd been asked to take one. I still do now, but I'm never on the list of the first five penalty-takers!

I stepped out for my first ever game in the World Cup finals against Sweden in Saitama. I wasn't particularly nervous. I'd been to the previous World Cup and though I hadn't played in France, I felt like I knew the scene and what was expected. We only managed a 1–1 draw, but then we beat Argentina 1–0 in the next match in Sapporo. It might have been decided by a Becks spot kick, but we were easily the better team. We played some great football that day.

The stadium was one of the best I've ever played in. It was an indoor arena and the atmosphere was trapped inside, with our fans at their loudest. I don't know where they'd all come from, but it could have been a home game.

I felt that if Argentina hadn't scored against us we could keep anybody out and I began to believe that we might actually pull it off and win the tournament. I'd never felt like that before about any competition, for club or country.

But the last group game against Nigeria was a renewed warning that there were more hurdles to overcome than just the opposition. It was the hottest game I have ever played in in my life, although the later quarter-final against Brazil and the Paraguay game at the 2006 World Cup were not far behind.

We drew 0–0, didn't over-exert ourselves and were delighted to get away with it. We were knackered.

Having qualified along with the Swedes and sent the Argies home in the process, which was an extra bonus, we faced our first knockout game against Denmark. The best news was that it was an evening match, no sunshine involved, and we came flying out of the blocks and annihilated them.

I scored my first England goal after five minutes. I saw the ball coming over all the way to the far post and knew I had a bit of space, but I didn't connect quite right. Fortunately my header went in off their keeper Thomas Sorensen. I was ecstatic. What a moment that was!

To this day, people think it should have gone down as an own-goal against Sorensen. Afterwards, the BBC interviewer, Garth Crooks, said to me, 'They're not going to give it to you, are they?' and I swore my head off saying, 'It's fucking my goal, man.'

Seeing my name up there in lights as a scorer in such an important game was unforgettable. I did a little dance to celebrate and every time I see it on video I get more embarrassed. I've got a picture of that moment, with a few of the players jumping on my back, and I look like a man possessed. The emotion in my face is a combination of joy, anger and relief.

Robbie Fowler came on in the second half, but it was the only time he featured in the finals. I don't think he was too impressed with Sven.

A couple of days before our quarter-final against Brazil, we sat in a room – me, Becks, Kieron, plus a few others – talking about what it would be like to win the World Cup. Whenever players tell you they take each game as it comes, don't believe them! It is only human to imagine what it would be like if you won a trophy like that.

Having done Denmark so easily, we couldn't help thinking, 'If we win this one, who knows?' The worry, though, was still the heat and while Denmark was exhilarating, Brazil was dehydrating.

When I drew the curtains that morning in Shizuoka, I've never felt so depressed to see a sunny day. There was not a cloud anywhere. We were kicking off at 3.30p.m. local time and I knew immediately the heat would make it an even tougher game.

We went out to warm up in the little patch of shade on the pitch and scampered straight back in again. It was stifling. We weren't wondering whether we'd win or lose, we were wondering whether we'd die. It was that hot.

But, as I lined up for the national anthems, I forgot all about the heat and was overwhelmed with emotion. I could hear my mate Dave Marshall shouting, 'Rio, Rio', but I wouldn't look because I wanted to concentrate on the game. Then he shouted, 'Your mum and dad are up there.' I spotted them in the second tier of the stand and tears welled up in my eyes. The whole occasion got to me.

I had a big lump in my throat because although as a kid Maradona was the player I worshipped, Brazil were the team I adored. Now here I was playing against them, with Rebecca, my mum and dad and my brothers and sisters in the stadium.

As a schoolboy, kicking a ball around on the Friary Estate, I could never have dreamed of this happening to me. Brazil were always the team we worshipped after England because of their skills and here I was playing against them.

When Michael scored to put us ahead I started believing even more that we were going to do it. A semi-final against Senegal or Turkey held no fears. We had a couple more half-chances and it was going well.

But then Ronaldo faced me up on the left-hand side of the box and played it into Rivaldo. Ronaldo then made a run past me to get the one-two and as I turned back to challenge he stepped inside again. I realised at that moment that this game was different from any I'd been in before. No one had ever done that to me.

While Ronaldo and Rivaldo were famous the world over, their team-mate Ronaldinho was not the famous superstar he is today. He was the young pretender and this was the game where he made his mark on the world stage. Just our luck.

Four minutes into added time at the end of the first half, he got the ball, did a stepover past Ashley Cole and gave it to Rivaldo, who cut back inside and shot low across David Seaman into the far corner.

You can't argue with the quality of that goal. You can beat yourself up about what you might have done better, but sometimes you have to accept the skill of the opposition as well, in this case the individual skills of Ronaldinho, drawing a couple of men to him, and the finishing of Rivaldo.

I'm proud of a photo I have in an album at home which shows me challenging Rivaldo. He is a great player. At the time he was probably the best in the world, but did not have the PR behind him to promote him in that way. He almost disappeared overnight after the 2002 final. In my opinion, you should do your talking on the pitch, but there's no doubt good PR helps.

Maybe we should have come out earlier to Ronaldinho to cut him off. Maybe the keeper could have done better, maybe the defenders should have done better. Maybe I could have done more. These are the questions you forever ask yourself after a goal goes in. You are always in search of perfection.

If we could have kept it to 1–0 at the interval, they would have had to come out against us in the second half and we could have caught them on the break.

At half-time there was disappointment at losing the goal, but despite claims I've heard that Eriksson sat there and did nothing, he did get up and speak and finished by saying, 'Go out and play and you'll get a goal out of it.'

The trouble was we didn't have the energy. No matter what the manager said there was nothing more he could have got out of us. Physically we were gone. It was just so hot. We wanted to attack them and make a game of it, but our bodies wouldn't let us. There was nothing left in the tank to help us go and win the ball back.

I thought if we were lucky we might take it to penalties, but that meant getting through another 45 minutes plus 30 minutes of extra-time. We dropped so deep we were camped in our own penalty area.

Then Ronaldinho scored that winning goal, which I'm convinced to this day was a cross to the far post which he mishit. Lucky sod! He was 35 yards out and, as he struck it, I thought he'd shanked it over the bar and a goal kick would give us a chance to get our breath back.

As it floated in, I realised it was not going over and waited for David Seaman to catch it under the bar. I reckoned at the time that David could have thrown his cap on it, which is what we usually say when a shot is easy for the keeper.

But it sailed over his head and in.

I was devastated. I knew we'd had it. We never looked like getting an equaliser, even when Ronaldinho was sent off and Brazil went down to ten men. The Brazilians can keep the ball for days if they want to and we couldn't get it. I'm not sure we even got in their half.

In the previous games against Argentina and Denmark, we'd played quick-passing football, but this time it wasn't physically possible. When the full-time whistle went and it was confirmed that our dream had died I could have sat on that pitch for the next hour. I couldn't move and didn't want to.

I'd had a good World Cup from a personal point of view and had enhanced my reputation as a player, but it didn't count for much just then. I was in it to win it and we'd come up short. Again, I was asking myself the same questions about whether I could have done more to stop the goals.

To make my day complete, I got picked out for the drugs test, which meant I had to go straight to drug control and didn't even go in the dressing room. I couldn't have forgotten that test, the officials grabbed hold of me the second I crossed the touchline!

Cafu and Ronaldinho were being tested as well and I told Cafu, who spoke a tiny bit of English, to ask Ronaldinho if he'd meant to score. Ronaldinho gave a thumbs up and a smile, which suggested he had meant it. I don't think so. I don't care how good you are, you don't shoot from where he was.

On the way back to the hotel all the players were pissed off, but we were also moaning about how knackered we were. The fact that we were out made us feel worse, but even if we had won, I wonder if we would have recovered well enough to do ourselves justice in the semi-final. Maybe adrenaline would have got us through, but I don't know.

Brazil deserved to beat us and were rightful winners in the end, after beating Germany in the final. There were times when I'd have been delighted about that. This wasn't one of them.

Pini had told me before I went to Japan that all was not well at Leeds and that they had financial problems. He's a sharp bloke, who has been around the block, and he said they would have to start selling players.

I later heard that the then Manchester United chief executive, Peter Kenyon, had told Ridsdale a month before the World Cup that if Leeds ever decided to sell me United wanted to be informed, but he was told I wasn't for sale.

Before the World Cup, a story had come out that I was already house-hunting in Manchester and a deal was imminent, which it certainly wasn't. Both Leeds and United issued a statement denying the story, but it was clear some discussions were going on between the clubs.

One night, I was in Sutra, a bar in Leeds which I co-owned at the time, and there were loads of Leeds fans in there with tattoos and big chains who were renowned around the city as being a bit tasty.

One of the biggest approached me, shook me firmly by the hand, looked me squarely in the eyes and said, 'If you ever leave this club, we'll find you and kill you.' I laughed and told him not to worry. But it was me who should have been worried. I'd had a preview of what could be in store if I did go.

Leeds had taken a step backwards, but it wasn't irreparable;

we were just unbalanced. We had Fowler, Keane, Viduka, Smith and Kewell in attack and couldn't keep them all happy, yet we were short in midfield.

I wondered what the future held and O'Leary's sacking on the eve of the World Cup finally gave me a clue when he said to the press, 'They wanted to take the cash for Rio and wanted me to take the stick.'

Leeds were obviously playing a poker game, hoping to hit the jackpot by selling me for the highest fee possible.

During the World Cup, Ridsdale admitted they would sell me at the right price. The likeliest payer appeared to be Manchester United. It was an exciting prospect, but I had to put it to the back of my mind. I was focusing on the World Cup.

When I returned, I went to see Ridsdale to find out what the score was and inquired whether we were bringing in any new players. I didn't get a very positive answer. He was talking round the issue rather than addressing it.

There had been loads of speculation about me moving either to Real Madrid or United, but I still wanted to know if Leeds were going to be a force. It was becoming clear they weren't. Everything Pini had told me was true. They had to sell or go under.

In Japan, I'd spoken to Nicky Butt and Becks about Manchester United. Butty said how different United was to anywhere else and how it was almost bigger than England, with supporters in every corner of the world.

Did I want a season pottering about or did I want to join a team which was going to chase trophies?

United were obviously very interested in getting me, but all the time I'd been at Leeds there'd been this voice in my head saying, 'Not them winning again, please.' In truth, I was just envious of how well they were doing, and the good players they had, people like Giggsy, Becks, Butty, Keano and Scholesy. They had them all. I thought about legends the likes of Charlton, Law, Best and Cantona and realised I'd be mad not to go to Old Trafford if the chance came.

I was reconciling myself to the fact that it was time to go and that Leeds would cash in, when a twist came that I hadn't foreseen - Terry Venables took over as manager. Anyone on earth could have become the new gaffer and I would have had no problem going. But this was different, this was Venables, the man who had brought me into the Euro 96 squad for that unbelievable experience and who had shown such faith in me at a young age.

He was brilliant. I loved him and knew this was an opportunity to work with a great coach, someone I really looked up to. He would make me a better player and I liked his philosophies on the game and how it should be played.

I met Venables at Pini's flat and he told me how much he wanted me to stay. I asked who we were going to buy and he said he couldn't lie to me and admitted that Leeds were not going to be able to purchase many players. But he also said that he wanted to play me and Woody together at the back and that only one player from the team would have to be sold. From what Pini had told me, I knew things were worse than that and I wondered whether Terry had had the wool pulled over his eyes to some extent.

Ridsdale knew Leeds had to sell me because they were flat broke, yet refused to do business with Manchester United. Fair play to him, he was driving up the price, but it was a hell of a bluff.

My opinion had always been that I wouldn't leave Leeds unless they wanted to sell me. That changed – even with Terry there – once I realised the mess they were in and that they had to sell me, but at the same time they were painting me as the bad guy, persuading the fans that it was me walking out on them.

I loved Leeds and the fans and when I joined I did it thinking I would be there for years.

But with the manager seemingly not being told the full story, no new players coming in which were necessary for success and Leeds needing the money, I knew I had to get away for my own good.

I had to put a transfer request in because Ridsdale wouldn't budge.

At first, Leeds turned down the request and Ridsdale told me I had to go on the club's Australian tour. I refused and told him, 'I'm not getting on that plane. I want to go to United.'

Later I was told that United informed Leeds that if I got on the plane the deal was off. Pini brought in his friend, the multi-millionaire businessman Philip Green, to try and sort it out.

Ridsdale had told the fans I would leave over his dead body. Two days later I was sold to United for £30 million and he was still alive!

I've seen Ridsdale since and we're okay now, but at the time I was furious about how things had been conducted. Ridsdale later claimed in the press that I'd only ever been bought as cover for Woody in the first place. What? Eighteen million quid for cover? If that was really true, no wonder Leeds nearly went out of business.

I could understand him wanting to sell me to the highest bidder, but I felt that if I had to leave I should go where I wanted to go and that was definitely Man United. I didn't want to move abroad to somewhere like Real Madrid without proving myself here. I wanted the stamp of approval in my own country. I told my dad I wanted to play for the best club in England, if not the world, and that was United.

I enjoyed my time at Leeds. I made good friends and the lads were brilliant. I knew I would miss them and the fans, who had treated me well. Putting in a transfer request was my very last option. I didn't want to do it. I wanted them to admit they had to sell me, but they didn't. God knows what they'd have done if I'd turned round and said, 'I'll stay.' They'd have topped themselves.

By putting in a transfer request I saved Ridsdale's skin. They might have gone bust if they hadn't sold me and a few others. I knew it and he knew it. Either Ridsdale or I had to take the bull by the horns and in the end it was me that did it. The club made out that I'd asked to go and they'd done everything to keep me, which was rubbish. I wanted to leave on good terms with the Leeds fans and accept I wanted to have my cake and eat it but then so did Ridsdale. We couldn't both come out smelling of roses.

What was I to do? Sit there and waste a year or two of my career at such a vital stage, watching the club sell other players and diminish the squad. After doing well at the World Cup, my game had to move on. I was impatient and if it wasn't going to happen at Leeds it had to be somewhere else.

I thought about the conversation I had with Butty the night we lost to Brazil and remembered him saying that if I went to United I'd never regret it. I'd also spoken to Andy Cole and Ian Wright who told me, 'Just go, man. You've got to go. They're a massive club.'

I rang Paul Ince as well. He had annoyed the West Ham fans when he left there to go to Old Trafford and had also played for United's arch rivals Liverpool. Incey was a man who didn't worry too much about the consequences of a move. He and my old mentor Iain Dowie also said a move was the right thing for me.

Terms were quickly agreed and on 22 July 2002 I became

a Manchester United player.

The medical went smoothly, no mention of any heart troubles, and I walked out into the middle of the Old Trafford pitch with Sir Alex Ferguson for the official photographs. The only time I'd ever met him before was in the car park after West Ham played at home to United.

I had been going to my car and out of nervousness said, 'All right, boss?' He went, 'All right, son. Good luck,' and then got on the coach. Apparently, he'd tried to sign me before when I was on loan at Bournemouth and Mel Machin had to tell him I wasn't actually his to sell. Then another time he called West Ham and Harry said he would sell me in exchange for David Beckham plus cash! He always drove a hard bargain did Harry.

Sir Alex has an incredible presence about him and when I signed for United I was still in awe of him, thinking, 'Shit, man, Alex Ferguson's your new manager.' He lightened the mood at the press conference when he looked at my suit and said, 'Bloody hell, are you going out after?' It was a magnificent suit – white linen with a thin black pinstripe, but the manager just wasn't ready for it, I guess!

I later found out that if anyone wears any dodgy gear, the gaffer rips it out of them. He reckons he's a stylish dresser, which I'd better not comment on in case it gets me into trouble.

I didn't know whether to laugh or not because he had a reputation for blowing a fuse. But he was charm itself and gave my parents and Rebecca the red-carpet treatment. After the press conference was over, he said, 'Well done, son,' and even that gave me a buzz. I hadn't kicked a ball for United yet and he was praising me. I felt ten feet tall.

He told me I'd love it at United, that the fans were fantastic and to make sure I enjoyed it.

When I went from West Ham to Leeds for £18 million it was the British record transfer fee and the world record for a defender. Now the £30 million move to United had broken both records again. It was big news, but there were some commentators who felt I was overpriced. I was going to have to prove myself all over again.

I liked the Leeds area and the people. But as soon as I made my mind up to go I never looked back.

I got stacks of mail, much of it abusive, but not all. I got one letter which said, 'Thanks for all you did for the club. I don't agree with what you've done and why you've left, but I appreciate what you did when you were here.' But there were plenty which said, 'You've only done it for money.' And I'm not going to dignify the disgusting ones by giving them a mention.

I got death threats over the phone as well, with fans telling me they were going to bomb my house and kill me. I didn't take them too seriously, although I had to change my mobile number.

The nastiness didn't worry me, just like chants from opposition fans have never got to me. The more they shout and scream the more I love it, especially when we win.

Other than as a player, I've only ever been back to Leeds twice, once to a restaurant, the other time to a club. I moved to Manchester and that was that. No turning back.

I was disappointed with how it all ended and how the Leeds fans felt about me. But I knew that one day the truth would come out and hoped they would understand.

I would like to make my peace with them because they were good to me, but if they are not interested then that's the way it goes.

We Are the Champions

But from then on I realised what United were all about. Guts and character. The difference at United was that they could draw on the recent experiences of having won other titles from all sorts of positions. United never knew when they were beaten.

On my first day at United I got a bollocking from Roy Keane.

I knew that going on a training pitch with players of the stature of Keane, Becks, Ryan Giggs, the Nevilles, Ruud van Nistelrooy and Scholesy was going to be a daunting prospect. In fact I wondered how I'd get in the team.

And, if you've just cost £30m they are going to want to see what that buys. They want to know what you've got and will test you out.

Keaney – that's what the players called Roy, rather than Keano – was never going to let me break in gently and after I'd played a square ball he went mental and barked, 'Pass the fucking ball forward.' I looked at him, his face all contorted, and he goes, 'It's fucking easy going sideways, pass it forward.'

Keaney was the manager's voice on the field. He could read a game better than anyone and I realised United was going to be very different to anywhere else I'd been.

Perfection is expected on the training field as well as in games and I learned from Roy that you cannot develop from being a good player to a top player if you play safe all the time.

You've got to take chances. I don't mean chances as in when I was at West Ham trying to dribble round the strikers, but you have to try to affect the game rather than wait for others to do it. At United everyone takes responsibility.

The attention on the players is like nowhere else either. Everywhere I went I was followed by photographers. It was a different league to anything I'd experienced before.

Putting the Man United strip on for the first time, it felt the same as when you got a new kit as a kid. It was exciting. I was tugging at it all over, thinking to myself, 'This is how Man United socks are, this is how they feel. This is how their shirts feel. These are their shorts.' Even the texture of it gave me goosebumps.

Just because you are a professional footballer doesn't mean

you should be dispassionate. It was my new job and I was very proud of it.

My first United game was as a second-half sub at Bournemouth in a testimonial game for Mel Machin. The wheel had come full circle. It was great to see Mel again and to thank him for the part he'd played in getting me to where I was in my career.

My first game at Old Trafford was a friendly against Boca Juniors, Maradona's old team. I came in after the warm-up, with the crowd chanting, 'Rio, Rio.' At least I think they were.

Roy goes, 'Are they chanting for me or you?' We had a giggle because Rio and Keano sound pretty much the same when 60,000 fans are singing at the same time. The day turned sour when I jumped over my own goalkeeper, Roy Carroll, and twisted my ankle in the turf. I'd done my ankle a couple of times before at West Ham and Leeds, so I knew I'd be out for a couple of weeks.

I was gutted that I was going to miss the start of the season at an important time of the year, when players are getting properly fit for the long campaign ahead.

When I returned, my fitness was behind everyone else's. It was like having a fortnight off school and when you come back everyone's moved on to new stuff and for the rest of term they keep referring to the bits you missed.

I made my debut in the second leg of the Champions League qualifier against Zalaegerszeg of Hungary.

United had failed to get into the competition automatically, having started the previous season badly, then gone on a brilliant run to top the league before tailing off again by losing at home to Middlesbrough in March and seeing Arsenal win the title with a victory at Old Trafford. The fans did not enjoy that.

When I'd been to Old Trafford before I was always delighted with a draw. Now the boot was on the other foot. You were always expected to win, no excuses.

We were 1–0 down from the first leg out there, which was a shock, but we won the return 5–0 and it was a nice easy start for me.

In September I went back to Leeds, expecting the worst from the fans. I felt a little nervous, but it was nothing like as bad as I had expected. It had been hyped up in the media, but, compared to what Sol Campbell suffered from Spurs fans when he moved to Arsenal, it was a breeze. The worst aspect of the day was that we lost the game 1–0 when I had so wanted to win at my old stamping ground. I was gutted.

We were ninth in the table and the obituaries were already being written. We stumbled along to Christmas, winning a few, drawing a few and losing games like Manchester City away, which did not go down too well, as you can imagine. Then we lost at Blackburn on 22 December and suffered a traditional nightmare against Middlesbrough at the Riverside on Boxing Day.

This was not quite how I'd imagined it going when I'd signed.

But from then on I realised what United were all about. Guts and character. The difference at United, compared to West Ham and Leeds, was that they could draw on the recent experiences of having won other titles from all sorts of positions. United never knew when they were beaten.

From Boxing Day, through to the end of the season we didn't lose a single Premiership game. We won 15 and drew three to take 48 points out of 54 and won the title by five points from Arsenal. The defining moment came when we won 6–2 at Newcastle in April, which took us top of the table for the first time that season.

My mate Kieron Dyer had said that week in the papers that his aim was to get Scholesy's England place. I don't know if Paul saw it, but his answer was to score a hat-trick at St James' Park.

Kieron came off the pitch and said to me, 'Bloody hell!' I

laughed and told Kieron he should not say things like that about Scholesy, who is one of the best players I've ever played with. He can put a ball on a sixpence. Kieron is always honest in interviews and, having been asked the question, he was not going to say that he didn't have a chance of replacing Scholesy.

Scholesy was second top scorer behind Ruud van Nistelrooy that year and was almost unplayable.

Every time we needed to pull something special out of the bag we just seemed to be able to do it – a piece of Scholesy brilliance, a Ruud special, some Giggsy magic or a Becks cross or free kick.

For instance, there was a dour game at Southampton at the beginning of February which was changed by Becks brilliantly setting up two goals for Ruud and Ryan.

That summed Becks up. Sometimes he would not get the headlines, but he'd be the one who made the goals. We have missed the sort of deliveries he can produce since he left for Real Madrid. Any team would.

Ruud carried on scoring goals, but he felt Becks's absence more than anyone else. He had thrived on those pinpoint crosses.

We actually clinched the title without kicking a ball because Leeds won 3–2 at Arsenal. It was a double celebration for me because it meant my old team-mates stayed up and we were champions.

Their game was played on a Sunday, the day after we'd beaten Charlton, and I was still speaking to loads of the lads from Leeds at the time, telling them they had to do it. I was pacing round my rented house in Wilmslow, but I couldn't watch the game. I was too nervous. I told my mates to text me as soon as they knew the score and I can still see the message coming through saying Leeds had scored and won.

Oh my God, that feeling. I went absolutely ballistic. There are holes in the walls of that house from where I punched them and then I ran outside and jumped around in the road in my bare feet, screaming like an idiot.

We'd been on the piss for a week, celebrating, by the time we played at Everton on 11 May, the last game of the season. I was marking Wayne Rooney and he said he could smell the booze on me. Somehow we managed to win 2–1!

I'd rather have won the trophy by beating someone at Old Trafford, but it was great to get presented with it on the final day of the season in front of all our travelling supporters. It was my first winners' medal in senior football and I was delighted that I'd broken a hoodoo at last. But, deep down, I didn't feel I'd played consistently well since my arrival. My contribution wasn't all that it should have been.

Maybe I'm being unduly hard on myself, but I know I didn't play to my true abilities. I was solid, but no more than that. I was just part of the team. I was just there. I'd been getting through games without putting a marker down and saying, 'This is me, I'm the main defender now.'

Perhaps the achievement was tainted by the fact that we lost the Worthington Cup final, were knocked out of the Champions League by Real Madrid and were beaten in the FA Cup fifth round by Arsenal.

The Worthington was my first major final, but we were comfortably beaten 2–0 by Liverpool. I had a stinker and the team likewise. I didn't want the losers' medal, I gave it to my sister Sian.

Then, against Real in the quarter-finals, we scored five times over the two legs and still got beaten 6–5 on aggregate. Neither defence could cope.

Raul was unstoppable in the first leg in Madrid, which Real won 3–1. He played in positions where you couldn't pick him up. Yet we had enough chances out there to have got at least a draw or even win it.

Both ties were so open, brilliant football for the spectators. But not so much fun if you're a defender. We beat them 4–3 in Manchester, with Ronaldo scoring a hat-trick for Real and getting a standing ovation. We got two late goals from Becks, who had come on as a second-half sub. Becks being on the bench had caused something of a stir because, although he had been out injured, he was fit again by then and yet couldn't get back in the team.

There was a lot of talk that Becks could be on his way out to either Barcelona or Real and I'm sure he did his chances of going to Real no harm with his performance. It was difficult to tell whether he'd be leaving or not. Becks didn't say much about it, although there were signs all was not going smoothly.

Relations between him and the manager had become strained after that FA Cup defeat against Arsenal in February. You might remember it. That was the day the gaffer kicked a boot and it struck Becks above the eyebrow. It would be fair to say the gaffer was steaming in the dressing room that day. He said something to Becks about how he'd let someone run through for one of their goals. Becks didn't agree and a few words were exchanged, but a dressing-room argument after a defeat is not unusual.

The manager says his piece and if someone doesn't agree they might challenge him. It happens all the time. But the boss always has the final word.

There was a pile of our boots lying in the middle of the floor and the boss just kicked out at them in anger. It was like slow motion as this boot flew through the air and smacked Becks on the forehead.

If the gaffer tried a hundred times to do it again he couldn't. The best player in the world could not have pulled it off deliberately. He hadn't lined it up or anything, he'd just swung his foot and – bang! – it whacks Becks.

You could tell the manager was upset about what happened and he apologised to Becks as David went off to see the doctor. The dressing room was silent for a few minutes, but feelings had been running high and we all knew it was just one of those things. Becks wasn't going to talk about it to anyone and the gaffer certainly wasn't. But the story came out in the *Sun* on the Monday with the headline 'Fergie Decks Becks'. That day Becks was pictured going to training with his hair pulled back under a hairband so it was hard not to see the plasters. Some people say he did it deliberately but only he knows the truth about that.

The world went mad. I'd never known so much commotion about a player with two butterfly stitches in his eyebrow. For the first time, I began to wonder if Becks would still be at United the following season, even though he loved Manchester. He knew loads of people there and was comfortable in the surroundings.

When the manager finally decided to let him go, it was still a shock. There was a lot of talk about Ronaldinho coming in as a replacement. I remember walking on to the training pitch one day, having seen mention of it in the papers, and asking the manager about it. He seemed quite confident that Ronaldinho would be coming and I was buzzing.

But he went to Barcelona instead who, ironically, had lost out in a bid for Becks. There were also suggestions that Kieron Dyer might be coming from Newcastle. But later that summer, the Portuguese winger Cristiano Ronaldo played against us for Sporting Lisbon in a pre-season friendly and he was unbelievable.

John O'Shea, who was marking him, needed an oxygen mask at the end of the first half! To be fair to John, the game came after a long and tiring pre-season trip to the USA and this was our last stop before home.

At half time me, Scholesy and Butty were going, 'Forget anyone else, we've got to get this kid.' After the game we said to the gaffer, 'You going to get him or what?' We were left sitting on the coach for ages and everyone was messing about having a laugh, saying the gaffer was upstairs doing the deal for Ronaldo. As it happens he was. A week later Ronaldo joined Manchester United for £12 million.

Ronaldo arrived after we had sold Juan Sebastian Veron to Chelsea. Seba had travelled to Portugal for that friendly, but left on the morning of the game. I thought he was a fantastic player. His passing was up there with anyone I'd ever played with.

But I don't think he and Keaney could play in the same team as they had similar styles. They were both the sort of players that every move goes through – 'go to' players I call them. I reckon that's why Veron was not a major success at United.

We had a shocker of an England performance in February 2003 when we lost 3–1 at home to Australia at Upton Park. The only notable thing about the night from an England point of view was that 17-year-old Wayne Rooney made his debut and it was obvious that he was destined to be something special.

Sven played two different England teams, one in each half. The so-called first team, in which I was playing, lost 2–0 and were dreadful, while Rooney's side drew 1–1 in the second half. It was an embarrassing night and did not bode well for success in the remainder of our Euro 2004 qualifying campaign.

We had started with an unconvincing win in Slovakia and an awful performance against Macedonia at Southampton, where we drew 2–2 and could have lost. But we went on to win in Liechtenstein before the big one against Turkey at Sunderland in April. The Turks were our main rivals for automatic qualification and it was going to be a tense battle.

There had been growing calls for Rooney to start against the Turks, but there weren't many who actually thought Sven would do it in such a vital game, which we had to win. But Wazza – which is Wayne's nickname – blew everyone away in training. His confidence and sheer ability shone through.

During one session he went from halfway past a number of defenders and chipped this shot over Paul Robinson from the corner of the box. I was at the back laughing, it was so good. The kid was amazing, an absolute joke. He was barging seasoned internationals off the ball like they weren't there, then releasing defence-splitting passes. He wasn't fazed by anything. He wasn't taking the piss either. He was a humble lad and was just playing like he would have done in the schoolyard.

So Rooney got the thumbs up to make his first ever England start. Me and Frank Lampard sat there looking at him in the changing rooms and he was cool as you like. The match was a massive occasion and critical for England, but he acted like he'd seen it all before. No nerves, nothing. He could have been going out for a kickabout with his mates.

Turkey were a technically gifted side who had reached the semi-finals of the World Cup only nine months earlier. But Wazza took them on like a pro in his prime. He was getting the ball, turning, holding off defenders and bringing others into the game.

Youngsters usually have fits and spurts in games. They flit in and out of the action and can do the easy things wrong and the hard things well. Rooney was doing the easy things really well and the hard things incredibly well. We knew we had a great player on our hands.

The match was one of my favourite games for England. The atmosphere at Sunderland was electric and the 2–0 win made it a cracking night.

That summer of 2003 we went on an England training trip

to La Manga and it was there that I supposedly threatened a security guard. It was a load of nonsense.

Me and John Terry were playing pool after dinner and a few drinks and the guy told us it was time to go to bed. We thought, 'What are you talking about?' He tried to take the snooker cue off me but I wouldn't let him have it. Then he stomped off.

That's all that happened, but next day when I woke up I was being accused by the hotel staff of throttling the geezer. Predictably it made the papers anyway and it was another black mark against me on England duty.

We went on to South Africa for a friendly and the chance of a lifetime to meet the great Nelson Mandela. Forget the football for a moment, meeting Mandela was the main event.

We had to be up at four in the morning for an hour's journey to get a plane to his home. Some players were umming and ahing about getting up early and having to go and some didn't even bother.

What was the matter with them? They were never going to get another opportunity to meet a man who had done so much for people, someone who had sacrificed the best years of his life and spent over a quarter of a century in prison just so others could be free. How dare they moan about having to get up early. No wonder footballers get a bad name at times.

Becks, as the captain, was to sit next to Mandela, with the rest of us gathered round. But there was no way on earth I was going to stay in the background. I asked a PR woman when I could meet Mandela and she gave me some rubbish about there not being enough time. When Mandela walked in he was going, 'Where's David? Where's David?'

He was dressed in this silky paisley shirt and was more frail than I had imagined, but the whole room went quiet in his presence and when he started speaking he was bang on the button.

He knew what he was talking about and there was an incredible aura about him. He had people running around after him left, right and centre and there were about 50 kids there who were all part of his extended family.

After he'd finished speaking a group photo was taken with him and Becks sat on chairs and the rest of us at the back. That wasn't enough for me. I said to the woman, 'I need to meet him. Just a couple of words and a photo. It might be the only opportunity I get to meet the great man and you are rushing me out. I've come all this way. Please!'

She threw her hands in the air and said I would have to ask him myself, so I told the lads I wasn't leaving till I'd talked to him. I went up on the stage and said, 'Mr Mandela, please can I have a picture taken with you?' and he went, 'Okay, no problem,' while the woman was flapping that I'd had the cheek to do what she'd suggested.

Trevor Sinclair jumped in on the act and we sat on two chairs either side of Mandela, with a few of the other lads behind. That's a picture which I am proud to display in my house, I can tell you.

That same summer I had the most fantastic time in the South of France with my mates – I always try to fit in a break with the lads before having a holiday with Rebecca – which came about after I'd met a bloke in Monaco who was a Manchester United fan.

I've been to Monaco for the Grand Prix a few times and it's a brilliant experience. I've been in the pits, met the mechanics and seen all the drivers. I've touched the cars and walked on the grid. It's one of the perks of being a sportsman.

After one race, we were walking by the marina, having a good close-up look at all the millionaires' boats. David

Coulthard was on this boat and one of his people asked if I'd come on board and have a picture taken with Coulthard and a couple of models.

When I got off, the boat next door was hosting a party and there were loads of people packed on board. The owner, a guy called Ian, ran down the gangplank and invited me and my mates aboard.

The drink was flowing and Ian said he'd do me a deal. He said that if I could get him four tickets for every Man United game in the Champions League the following season, I could have his boat fully staffed for ten days and sail wherever I wanted with my mates.

I was in heaven. You might think footballers are rich, but this really was how the other half lived. It was a different league.

I already had the tickets anyway but I made out that I'd have a word with the girl at the club and see what I could do and pretended to ring her there and then. I put the phone down and said, 'Listen, no probs. It's sorted.' He was made up.

I got the boat as he'd promised and I invited my cousin Bernard and all my mates, like Gavin Rose, Justin, Courtney, and Weasel. There are times in your life when you just can't believe what's happening and that boat trip was one of them. We could go anywhere we wanted. We boarded the boat in Cannes and told the captain to take us to St Tropez.

There were two waitresses serving us drinks non-stop all day. Before your glass was empty they had filled it up again. We lived like kings. You'd be sat at breakfast and the chef would ask what you wanted for lunch. We would say, 'Whatever you're cooking. Just do anything,' but that wasn't good enough for him. He would bring out a menu which was better than any you'd get in a top London restaurant. After lunch he'd be asking what you wanted for dinner.

The captain got permission to dock in St Tropez, which is notoriously difficult, and we tied up on the marina, where all the bars are. We were hanging out on the deck with music playing and everyone was looking at us and taking pictures. They must have thought we were rap stars. We were these kids from a council estate in Peckham and here we were in paradise. We couldn't stop smiling at each other.

I got a buzz out of being able to take my mates away like that. It was wicked.

There's rich, like a Premiership footballer, and then there's super-rich. But many of those I've met in Monaco had to work hard for their money. I'm always intrigued by businessmen like Ian. I like finding out how they made their money, which in his case was through stocks and shares. It's amazing what it's possible to achieve if you put your mind to it.

I was raring to go when I came back for the 2003–04 campaign. It was one of the best pre-seasons I've ever been involved in.

We played really well against Barcelona and Juventus, then we had that game with Sporting Lisbon after which Cristiano Ronaldo signed. We beat Arsenal on penalties in the Community Shield following a 1–1 draw and I got my first United goal of sorts in the shoot-out.

What a nerve-wracking moment. It was only the Shield, but walking up to take a penalty with 60,000 watching, knowing you have to score, scrambles your mind. I could only imagine what it must be like if you had to do it in the World Cup. I couldn't afford to miss because by the time it came to mine it was sudden death and, thankfully, I tucked it away. The relief was enormous.

We won our first three league games, somehow lost at Southampton, beat Charlton and then came up against Arsenal again at Old Trafford and it was mayhem.

Looking forward to being a better player - in big games...

...and they don't come very much bigger. Champions League semi.

Three in five games.
No. 1. Deportivo.

No. 3. The Hammers.
It would be, wouldn't it?

Nice threads!

First game.

Spot on. 100% record.

First match
after the ban.
Magical.

A new contract.
Chelsea done over.
A turning point.

Sweet!

You could say it was a physical game – Patrick Vieira got sent off for having a swing at Ruud. But then we got a late penalty, which Ruud smashed against the bar, sparking mad celebrations by the Arsenal players, especially Martin Keown who jumped up and down around Ruud like a nutter.

We went down the tunnel and there was a lot of shouting and swearing, pushing and shoving and various people accusing each other of this and that. But I wasn't aware of how badly Arsenal had behaved till I saw the pictures in the papers the next day. In the end a lot of their players got done by the FA, but so did Giggsy and Ronaldo for some reason, which they weren't too happy about.

Some Arsenal players had been whingeing throughout the match, but I couldn't see why; there were just a few mistimed tackles.

The best way to play Arsenal at that time was to get in their faces because they seemed to find that difficult to handle. There's a few of them who don't like the physical side and, as long as you stay within the rules, challenging strongly is a good way to rile them.

I'm not saying we single out individuals, but Robert Pires and Jose Antonio Reyes don't seem to like it when every ball gets so keenly contested and they can go down rather easily in my view. They did that day and were lucky to draw.

I wasn't so lucky a few days later.

Branded a Drugs Cheat

It was clear I was in trouble. Gill told me
that the FA were saying I might not be able
to play against Turkey. I couldn't believe it.
It was such a massive game for the country
and that was more important to me than
anything else about the situation. What
were they on about? Everyone knew
it was a mistake, didn't they?

When I got up to go to training on Tuesday, 23 September 2003, I had no inkling of the monumental events which were about to engulf me.

It was the day I missed a drugs test, an incident which landed me with an eight-month ban and gave anyone who fancied it the opportunity to give me a right good kicking.

But you know what? People said to me at the time that they wondered whether if David Beckham – and this was in no way ever meant as a slant at Becks – had done the same thing, there was any chance on earth he would have received a ban. He was the England captain, the biggest name in football and the FA's commercial linchpin. The suits would have found a way to let him off, surely? That was their thinking. At worse he would have got a slap on the wrists. They wouldn't have banned the England captain, not the man who was the face of the England team around the world.

I listened. Maybe they were right, but for me, it felt like I was an easier target.

There has been a lot of speculation, rumour and innuendo about what actually happened. Here's the truth.

I was still thinking about the fallout from the Arsenal game, mainly about how we should have won rather than the aggro, as I arrived at our Carrington training ground. It was just an ordinary day and I felt fine.

We jogged out for a fairly light 45-minute session and the club doctor Mike Stone told me, Nicky Butt, Ryan Giggs and John O'Shea that we had to attend a drugs test at the end of it.

Fine, no problem there. I'd had many a drugs test after games, and one at West Ham after training. There was no specific time we had to do the test, just sometime after training. You didn't get a fixed appointment or anything like that, you popped along when you were ready.

In the changing room I was having a massage and a bit of

banter with the lads, like I would on most days. Then I went in the shower, which was when Dr Stone shouted to me, 'Rio, the drugs test. Do it before you go.' So I said, 'Yeah, no probs.'

Twenty minutes later I'd finished getting ready and walked straight out the door to my car. There were no testers waiting for me. They were in a room upstairs in the doctor's office.

When I walked out I didn't go past anybody, so there was nothing to remind me again that I had to have a test. The other players being tested had either already gone upstairs or were in the gym. It's not like we waited for each other so we could go and pee in a bottle together.

I know I should have remembered. I'd already been told twice, the last time only twenty minutes earlier, but I forgot. Not much of an excuse, but that's what happened. At the time, I was in the process of moving house and all I was thinking about was that I had to go into town to get some bed-linen that Rebecca had asked me to pick up.

So as soon as I was ready I just jumped in the car – which was being driven by my friend Jason Worthington because I'd been banned for speeding under the totting-up procedure – and headed off to Harvey Nichols in Manchester city centre.

While walking around I bumped into Eyal Berkovic, my old team-mate from West Ham who was then at Manchester City. We decided to head off for some lunch and a chat.

As usual, I had my phone on silent because it rings all the time and I get loads of text messages. If I'm busy I leave them until I'm free, then I check all my messages and missed calls. I didn't bother with the phone until I'd ordered my food. Doctor Stone had sent a text and a voice message saying, 'Rio, come back to the training ground, you've got your drugs test.'

When I saw this, I thought, 'Oh fuck,' not because I was worried about the consequences but because it meant I'd have to go back to the training ground. I really didn't think it was that big a deal, although I thought I'd have to take it that day.

I phoned the doctor straight away and said, 'Doc, I'm in town. It will take me 20 minutes to get to you.' He told me they'd just left, so I said, 'Can you give them a ring and tell them to come back. I'll be there in 20 minutes.'

He didn't have their number and went, 'This could be serious. You can get in trouble for this, really bad trouble.' I told him I would ring the FA and they would be able to sort it out.

As my luck would have it, Michelle Farrar, the England players' liaison officer, was away and those filling in for her could not advise me on what to do. Also, the man who ran the FA's drugs-testing department was on holiday and no one had the number of the people who actually came out to do the test.

The testers are independent. They do tests on behalf of the FA, but are not their employees. Having said that, I was astonished that no one at the FA was able to give me even a general number I could contact. There was absolutely nothing they could do for me.

After a few inquiries, a lady at the FA rang me back and said I would be able to take a test a couple of days later, but she didn't know whether that would be the end of the matter.

Despite what Dr Stone had said, I wasn't worried as I knew I had nothing to hide. When I got home to Rebecca I casually remarked I'd missed the test then went on talking about the house move.

On the Thursday, I did a test and, of course, passed with flying colours. I don't know why I bothered, given what was to happen.

Doctor Stone was still worried, no doubt about it. He repeated his fear that I could be in trouble. But when he told me I could get a two-year ban I thought he was having a laugh.

Even he admitted he didn't think it likely, he was just painting the worst case scenario. I'd done another test and I'd passed and, at worst, I thought I'd get a telling off for forgetting.

If I'd known what the consequences were going to be I'd have asked about getting a test done privately myself that same Tuesday, although later I found out that for some reason that would have been against FA regulations.

I knew I hadn't been under the influence of any drugs. Despite the rumours to the contrary, I've never taken any illegal substances in my life, not even cannabis. I challenge anyone to prove otherwise. I know no one can.

I didn't think for a second that I would get banned, despite the doctor's warning. I carried on playing and looking forward to England's crucial European Championship qualifier against Turkey in Istanbul, where a draw would get us through to the finals.

United beat Birmingham 3–0 on the Saturday at Old Trafford, after which I travelled down to London to see my family ahead of meeting up with the England squad. On the Sunday morning I got a phone call from FA executive director David Davies and the seriousness of my situation began to register. I remember him saying something like, 'Rio, I've been speaking with Sven and people from the FA about your situation with the drugs test. We need to sit down and talk to you and United because we're having loads of problems with this.'

I rang the Manchester United chief executive David Gill who had spoken to Maurice Watkins, the club solicitor who was also a United director. Gill told me we had to go immediately to Davies's house in Birmingham for a meeting and that the FA would be bringing a legal advisor.

I'm thinking, 'Bloody hell, all this fuss over me missing a drugs test. I took one within 48 hours and it was negative. What's the problem?'

As I sat in David Gill's car outside Davies's house it was clear I was in trouble. Gill told me that the FA were saying I might not be able to play against Turkey. I couldn't believe it. It was such a massive game for the country and that was more important to me than anything else about the situation. What were they on about? Everyone knew it was a mistake, didn't they?

Gill and Watkins explained that the FA felt they couldn't let anyone play for the national team who was under suspicion of having drugs in their system. Yet the sample I'd given later was negative, so why was I under suspicion? I'd explained the circumstances. It stank.

They feared England might be chucked out of the European Championships, but, as I'd been allowed to carry on playing for United in the Premiership and the Champions League since the missed test, I thought that was a load of cobblers.

I sat there, dumbstruck, thinking, 'This is a joke. Are they taking the piss?'

We went into the house and I don't even know why I was there. I think the decision about me not playing for England had already been made.

I can see it all so clearly in my mind. I said hello to Davies and the legal advisor. As I was about to sit down with them at the table they told me to go into the kitchen while they sorted it out. I'd been asked to come along but they weren't going to involve me in the meeting. I didn't get that.

I slumped off to the kitchen and had tea and biscuits with David's wife Susan.

When I was called back into the sitting room after about an hour and a half, Davies told me I wasn't going to be able to play against Turkey. I was nearly sick on the spot. I said, 'Why? What are you talking about?' and he said, 'You've missed a drug tests and FIFA could ban you for up to two years.'

I argued that I hadn't taken anything and had passed the

test two days later. I sat there and thought they had found me guilty before I'd even been able to mount a defence. But Davies insisted that the FA couldn't afford to let me play.

The emotions were boiling up inside me and I told them, 'I've not been found guilty of anything. I've not taken drugs and now you're going to make it seem like I have. I've been forgetful and that's it.' Davies accepted my point but said it didn't alter the FA's position.

I was raging by now and said, 'So you want to risk not qualifying for the European Championships then? You would rather go into this game without someone who usually plays in the team. I took another drugs test as soon as I could. I even offered to go back that same day. I did everything to put the situation right, what more do you want?'

They all just stared at me and waited for me to calm down. I could see I wasn't going to win the argument, so now the question was: what to do next? The public had no idea I'd missed a test so I asked the FA to say I was injured, rather than portray me as guilty before I'd had a chance to prove my innocence.

But the FA claimed they had already taken phone calls from the press asking about me missing a test. That seemed strange because there had been nothing in the papers that day and my agent hadn't had any calls. I said, 'You are taking the piss now. It's a fucking liberty. Who told them?' As far as I could see, it didn't benefit any of us for this to come out.

Had someone inside the FA tipped the press off? God knows. Whatever had happened, it wasn't good news for me.

I'd always respected Davies, but I was completely gone by now and told him I thought the FA was trying to stitch me up. I was shouting at him because he was the one telling me all this. But, in my mind, Davies was only the middle man doing, as I realised he had to, what the FA's new chief executive, Mark Palios, had asked him to do.

I pleaded with Davies and said, 'How can you do this? Everyone's just going to think I'm guilty. Everyone's going to think I've taken drugs. All you have to do is say I'm injured while we get this sorted out or it's just going to cause a big commotion.'

Saying I was injured would have given everyone a chance to get their heads together. It was not just me who was facing a lot of hard questions; the FA were going to have to do the same. But Davies and the legal bloke weren't having it. They insisted they had to say I'd missed a drugs test.

There was something odd about how it was panning out. Wasn't there another approach? To keep things under wraps for a bit longer as we tried to sort it out? But no. Somehow events were already picking up speed and couldn't be stopped.

And where was Palios when I could have done with him to sit down and explain it all to me? Would that have been too awkward for him?

Palios wanted his FA to be an organisation admired around the world as a tough no-nonsense outfit who were not afraid to crack down hard on their own and I felt like he was going to try and use my situation as the perfect example of that approach.

As I saw it, he must have thought, 'Fuck Rio Ferdinand, I'm going to do him,' and Davies was his messenger, bringing the bad tidings.

One of my first questions when I walked into Davies's house had been, 'Why ain't Mark Palios here?' After all, he was the man making the decisions. Why leave it to Davies, a man I had, and still have, a good relationship with?

I tried to contact Palios at least ten times, as did Pini and Alex Ferguson. But he wouldn't talk to any of us.

I told his PA I'd travel anywhere to speak to him face to face so he could tell me exactly what was going on. I tried for weeks and weeks but got absolutely nowhere. Whenever I got through to his office I was told, 'He's in a meeting,' or 'He's out at the moment,' or 'He's gone to the toilet,' any excuse they could find.

Looking back on it all now, I still think about how it could have been handled differently by the FA. There must surely have been a way I could have continued playing for England while things were being sorted. And did they have to be quite so full-steam ahead when it came to instigating proceedings against me? Couldn't they have accepted the fact I'd later tested negative and merely dealt with the fact I'd been careless in the first place? And at the same time accepted that the drugs-testing procedures were too lax and had to be tightened up in light of the case.

And surely it isn't too much to ask to be able to speak to the top people at the FA. But I couldn't seem to get hold of them.

I returned to London from Birmingham, absolutely shell-shocked, and told my mum and dad that they were not going to let me play for England. Mum would have gone to the FA the next day and smashed Palios's door down if I'd let her.

I spoke to Sven-Göran Eriksson on the phone and he was very apologetic and said, 'I'm very sorry. I've tried. I've spoken to the people at the FA, everyone you can imagine I've spoken to, but they don't want you to play.

'I need you in my team. I want you to be in the team. But they won't let me play you.'

I spoke to Sven many times after that and I know he did his best for me. He said that he couldn't imagine it happening anywhere else in the world. He felt that it would not have been made public and that it would have been sorted out. He

told me they all knew I hadn't taken any drugs.

Alex Ferguson said it was out of order that I wasn't allowed to play for England, but told me that I should have been at the test and forgetting was no excuse. He said I was responsible for making sure I attended, nobody else, which I totally agreed with. But he also said he would stand by me all the way.

I explained to him that I'd completely forgotten and, although I had walked out of the training ground, I had tried to go back and do it when I picked up the doctor's message, only to be told the testers had gone.

I knew that forgetting was a pretty lame defence for my actions, but it was the truth. I never remember anything. I get phone calls from people saying, 'Where are you?' when we've arranged a meeting and it's completely gone out of my head. There are just too many things going on at the same time.

I've started writing appointments down now and checking the calendar because it was happening too often.

Sir Alex explained that when you play for a big club like Manchester United these are some of the trials you have to face. I felt that the manager was not only angry with me, but also with the FA and the fact that Palios wouldn't ring him back made him even more annoyed.

News of my missed-test nightmare broke in the papers as the squad met up at the Sopwell House Hotel in St Albans. It had become a very big story. You would have thought there was nothing else going on in the world. It was not just making headlines on Sky Sports, but on the main terrestrial channels as well. Unbeknown to me, the players, led by my United team-mate Gary Neville, immediately called a meeting to discuss my case and voted to go on strike unless I was named in the squad.

Kieron Dyer rang me up to let me know exactly what was

going on and I'll never forget what he said: 'We ain't going to play, Rio. Gary Neville ain't fucking about. He's a fucking soldier! He is fighting your corner and saying that if you're not picked then the lads ain't going to Turkey.'

Gary, whose nickname in the media is Red Nev, was in no mood to back down. I gather there was some apprehension from Becks, Michael Owen and David James who, though they supported the principle, felt a strike was going too far.

I understand how difficult it would have been for Becks to go all the way with a strike because he was the England captain. He'd made it clear that he was on my side and I could not ask for more than that. He went as far as he could go.

To be truthful, I didn't feel comfortable about the strike call anyway. The PFA were supporting the players, but I had a couple of conversations with the chief executive, Gordon Taylor, and told him I was worried about how far it was going. The FA were threatening to select a whole new squad to go to Turkey instead of us. They said that if England didn't play the match not only could we be booted out of Euro 2004 but the next World Cup as well. I couldn't have that on my conscience, however wronged I felt.

I spoke to Jamo, Kieron, Butty and then Gary and said, 'You can't do it. Just go and win the game.' I appreciated what my team-mates had done for me. The point had been made. The fact that they had the balls to stand up to the FA and tell them they were wrong was more than enough for me. They got a hard time from the press for the position they adopted. I can't thank them enough.

I'd always got on fine with Gary Neville, but we weren't best pals or anything. Yet he had put his neck on the line for me. He was quite prepared to take it all the way and potentially harm his own England career in the process. He really wouldn't have played, he felt that strongly, and I know the same went for Butty, Scholesy, Kieron and Ashley Cole.

Gary is so different from how he is portrayed in the papers. He's a good lad who likes a laugh at the right times, but he is very serious when it comes to football. He's a top professional who goes to bed earlier than most schoolkids and wakes up before they do as well. His England career meant everything to him, but it seemed his principles were just as important. What he did wasn't just for me or because I was from Manchester United; he would have defended anyone's right, even a Liverpool player's, not to be hanged before their trial.

I had always respected Gary as a professional footballer. As a man, there is no praise high enough for him. If you've got a problem and you want someone in your corner, there is no one better. If he's got an opinion he delivers it without hesitation. I prefer someone like that. You know where you stand with Gary – the FA certainly did.

The lads went to Turkey and got the point required to qualify for Euro 2004 and I was delighted. I couldn't watch the game, I was too nervous. I couldn't imagine what life for me and the team would have been like if they'd lost. We'd all have been slaughtered. I flicked on to Sky at the end of the game to get the result and there was a feeling of huge relief.

There's no doubt that there were plenty of people who believed I was a druggie. I'd told the FA that if the reason for my absence was made public this is what would happen and it did. Yet this was the perfect opportunity for anybody who had ever seen me taking drugs or sold me drugs to come out and sell a massive story, but nobody did. Because such a story didn't exist.

My mum's friends were being offered £5,000 for proof I was at it and one bloke tried to sell a story that I'd been in a

Liverpool club asking where I could get some cocaine. He didn't do his homework very well. The night he claimed I'd been in the club I was miles away, staying in a hotel the night before a United game. What a mug!

I've always likened what I did to forgetting your car keys, leaving them on the table and walking out the front door, then having to turn round and go back in and get them when you realise you can't get in the car. It happens all the time. Some people forget important birthdays or their wedding anniversaries. There isn't a human being alive who hasn't forgotten something important. Yet for reasons I don't understand I wasn't allowed to forget a drugs test.

Anyone who knows me – my family, my mates, other players – will tell you I'm forgetful. I'm always thinking about 110 different things at once, so when I had my mind on moving into my new house it was understandable that I forgot the drugs test. Don't they say moving house is one of the three most stressful things you can do in your life?

I admit that if I was looking at the case as an outsider I would maybe think, 'Rio's got something to hide.' But the fact was I didn't. There were idiots who would shout out in the street things like, 'Fancy doing a line?' I tried not to rise to the bait but it wasn't easy.

While I wasn't happy when my phone records came out in the papers, they did show I rang the club doctor within a minute of picking up his message. They also showed how often I rang the FA that day. If I'd been trying to hide I would have switched my phone off altogether.

A newspaper claimed a call to my own doctor not long after I'd left training proved I was up to something, but I'd only rung him because I'd been suffering from a kidney complaint and wanted to know the results of some tests he'd done. I even checked a few weeks later to see if the medication he'd given me would have produced a positive test, but the doctor said it wouldn't have.

We began to look into precedents – players who had missed a test in England and didn't get banned.

We discovered that Manchester City midfielder Christian Negouai had missed a drugs test and had got away with a £2,000 fine and no ban. His explanation was that he'd been picking his parents up at the airport and the FA accepted it. I thought that meant I was bound to be given the benefit of the doubt, especially as I'd tried to get back to do the test.

There was also an unnamed player from a lower league club who took cocaine and got off on the grounds that he was under stress because his wife had depression. There were players in Europe who were found to have actually taken performance-enhancing drugs and got bans of between two and five months. Jaap Stam, the former Manchester United defender, only got a five-month ban, despite testing positive for the steroid nandrolone, as did his Dutch team-mate Edgar Davids.

Yet, in the end, those cases were to make no difference at all.

Mum was panicking. She rang up the gaffer, David Gill and Maurice Watkins, wanting to know what was going on. She was going mad and hammering on the table at one particular meeting in the PFA offices in Manchester. I'm always glad to have her support, but once she starts talking she can't stop. I like to speak up for myself now that I'm older.

My mum and dad felt that it wasn't a good idea to have Maurice acting on my behalf, as he was also Man United's solicitor. They felt that I should have my own legal team who were not connected to the club.

Maurice and his assistant, Edward Canty, were superb. They were very professional and did everything they could for me, but my parents felt that their first responsibility would have to be to protect United and I would come second to that. But I was never under pressure to use Maurice. The club said they could get him to represent me if I wanted and I said yes. It was my choice.

The papers usually get a steer from their sources and they were saying I'd get a three-month ban maximum. I still felt that was three months too long, but it would mean I'd only miss part of the season with United and be back for the big games at the end, as well as the European Championships.

We were top of the league and I was playing some of the best football of my career. I was getting plenty of abuse at opposition grounds, but the Man United fans were brilliant to me.

I so wanted to tell my side of the story in the papers, but I was advised against it by my lawyers. Given the time over again, I'd have ignored that advice because going public might have helped me – especially after the verdict because people would have seen how disproportionate the ban was.

On 28 October the FA charged me.

Their statement read: 'The FA has today charged Rio Ferdinand with misconduct for a breach of FA Rule E26, with reference to Regulation 1(c) of the FA Doping Control Regulations. Regulation 1(c) refers to "the failure or refusal by a player to submit to drug testing as required by a competent official". The charge relates to the selection of Rio Ferdinand to submit to out-of-competition testing on 23rd September 2003 as part of The FA's Doping Control Programme.'

I felt that I'd neither failed nor refused the test. I'd forgotten. I'd offered to return to take the test on the same day and there had been no specific time given for when I had to take it.

But the FA weren't seeing it like that. And nor were the press who seemed to relish 'anti-Rio' articles.

It felt like my head was about to be served up on a plate.

Trial of Strength

I lost it completely and shouted, 'Fucking hell, why don't you just fuck me all of you! You might as well. It's a fucking joke. You are treating me like a druggie and I'm not. Why don't you just go out there and tell the press I'm a druggie, even though I've proved to you lot that I'm not.'

My hearing – if that's the right word, since I didn't feel anyone was much listening to me – was set to take place at Bolton's Reebok Stadium just before Christmas.

You couldn't move for the press and TV cameras. Unfortunately, they weren't allowed into the hearing itself. Frankly, I'd have happily invited the media in because I really believe that if they had heard the evidence I'd have been treated far more sympathetically by the public.

I'd become really involved with the preparation of my case with my legal team. I was in and out of their office all the time after training, calling and texting, wanting to discuss ideas, ask questions. Some people might think that I just sat back and left it to the lawyers, saying and doing whatever they said. No chance. I couldn't leave it – it was my career we're talking about here.

There was a formal courtroom-like atmosphere. Mark Palios had stressed on television a few days previously that, 'The commission hearing the Rio Ferdinand case is totally independent.' The panel comprised three FA councillors – the head of the disciplinary committee Barry Bright and FA men Frank Pattison and Peter Heard.

I thought it odd at the time – as did a number of people within football who spoke about it in the press – that all three came from within the Association. But that's apparently what the rules are for such hearings. All quite internal. I also learned from the press that one of the panel members, Peter Heard, had co-founded a property company called Churston Heard which did over £1 million worth of business for the FA.

My memories of that day are clear. Sir Alex, Nicky Butt, Doctor Stone, Eyal Berkovic and Jason Worthington, my driver on the day in question, all gave evidence, while Sven sent a fantastic letter supporting me.

Butty and Sir Alex were asked about what sort of person I was and whether I would have tried to hide anything. Butty also spoke about the testing procedure that day and how lax it all was. That was not an excuse, it was just a fact.

The chief drugs-tester and one of the testers who had been there on the day talked about the procedures and, in my view, simply underlined the argument that there were not sufficient guidelines in place. They admitted that various aspects could be tightened up and that there were many grey areas.

Doctor Stone told it exactly as it was and I accept that it must have been hard for him. He was caught between a rock and a hard place. He said that, with hindsight, he should have stayed downstairs and made sure I went to the test, but that was not really how it worked. I don't blame him at all. As the testers had admitted, there were no strict rules about how a test should be conducted.

Since my case the drug-testing procedure has changed completely. They've almost got handcuffs on you from the moment your name is picked out at training. You can't go anywhere without a tester following you.

I gave evidence for about an hour and the FA's lawyer, Mark Gay, kept hammering me as I tried to drive home the fact that I'd forgotten the test and never had any intention of dodging it.

I felt we'd put forward a good defence, led by my barrister, Ronald Thwaites QC. As I paced around the room waiting for the verdict, I was confident it was all going to be okay, that I would be able to get back playing for Man United at some point in the season and go to the European Championships. I was already thinking about the future. I couldn't wait to play again.

No way was I prepared for what came next. Bright read out the verdict: 'You will be banned for eight months.'

I thought I'd heard it wrong. Maybe he'd said eight weeks. That would have been more likely. But no, eight fucking months. I could not believe it. They were taking away from me the game I loved. I was in tears. My body went all hot, my head was spinning, the sweat was pouring off me. I just couldn't understand how on earth they had come to that decision. What were they hoping to achieve?

The FA immediately issued a statement which said: 'The commission unanimously found that the charge was proved against Rio Ferdinand.

'It was further decided that he be suspended for eight months from 12 January 2004 and fined a sum of £50,000.

'Having requested a personal hearing, he is subject to pay the costs of the hearing. Such decisions are subject to the right of appeal.'

I then had to stand in front of the media as Maurice Watkins read a statement which said: 'We are extremely disappointed by the result in this case. It is a particularly savage and unprecedented sentence which makes an appeal inevitable.

'We can confirm that Rio has the full support of Manchester United and the PFA.'

The room was a blur. I thought I was going to keel over. I wanted to get out of there as quickly as possible.

I hadn't taken any drugs yet I was going to miss the rest of the season and Euro 2004. It just couldn't be right.

The gaffer was superb. He was gutted for me and thought I'd been hard done by. He's a people person and knows exactly how to deal with all sorts of situations. I knew he was angry with me for what I might have cost United in terms of challenging for trophies. But he knew that I recognised I'd made a mistake by missing the test in the first place and probably felt that coming down on me like a ton of bricks would have made it far worse. I needed his support and he gave it without any hesitation.

He told me that whatever decision I made regarding an appeal he would support me. I was determined to take it further. There's no way I could have accepted that decision. I knew there was a danger that the sentence could be increased, but I didn't care. As far as I was concerned I had been the victim of a gross injustice. That's what it felt like to me.

I had 12 days to appeal, but the FA seemed to be mucking about and didn't give us some of the documents as quickly as we would have liked. There were all these mad things going on behind the scenes and we only just made the deadline.

It was clear the appeal was not going to be held for some time, but in the meantime I could keep playing. The problem with that was that the longer I played the more chance there was that I could still miss the end of the season and Euro 2004, even if the ban was reduced.

I reasoned that if I started the ban in January and it was cut to, say, three months, as I expected it to be, I could still be involved at the business end of the season for Manchester United and go to the Euros. Sven had told me that as long as I could prove my fitness I'd make the plane.

I began the ban on 20 January, just after we lost at Wolves, and, just as with the first hearing, I worked hard with the lawyers on my appeal. By the time I went to the hearing at the Radisson Hotel near Heathrow airport on Thursday, 18 March, I was confident of a good result. I even thought the ban might be scrapped altogether.

I'd had to grow my hair into a big afro so that I could have a hair-follicle test. The test checks for any drugs in your system over the previous six months and is used by the army and top companies in the city to prove recruits are drug-free. I knew I was clean and the test confirmed it once and for all. There was nothing in my system.

I remember the day of the appeal clearly. Gay was again the FA prosecutor, but it was a different panel hearing the evidence this time and the chairman, Ian Mill QC, wasn't from the FA.

There were two other FA blokes trying the case with him, the chairman of the FA, Geoff Thompson, who hadn't spoken a word to me since I'd first missed the test, and Roger Burden, an FA councillor.

I thought I might have more chance this time round but it wasn't to be. The FA seemed determined to make it stick. My defence argued that the ban should be reduced, citing the cases in Europe involving the taking of performance-enhancing drugs for which players had been banned for comparatively short periods. I hated being compared to drug-takers, but it was necessary for my case.

I didn't have to give evidence this time but my lawyer highlighted the Negouai case and the fact that the City player had not been banned, even though he hadn't contacted the club or the FA like I had. It all sounded very good to me.

I was kidding myself. They decided to uphold the eight-month ban. I was devastated. I just slumped in my chair as if all the life had been sucked out of me. I stared at the ceiling like a zombie for a couple of minutes.

Then Gay told the panel that he didn't think it was enough, implying that I should have been given a two-year ban and that they'd been very lenient on me.

I lost it completely and shouted, 'Fucking hell, why don't you just fuck me all of you! You might as well. It's a fucking joke. You are treating me like a druggie and I'm not. Why don't you just go out there and tell the press I'm a druggie, even though I've proved to you lot that I'm not.'

Ronald Thwaites argued that the statement which would be read out to the press should include a line saying that it had been proved that I hadn't taken drugs. It was a small consolation, but it was important. Gay, on behalf of the FA, was totally against it.

I looked at him and said: 'What more do you want, do you think I'm a drug taker? Do you want people to think I'm a drug taker? Go on, do it then, fucking do it.'

I was ready to tear the place down until the panel agreed

that the line should go in. It was a victory of sorts and removed any stain on my character.

The FA statement said: 'In reaching its conclusion, the appeal board has discounted the possibility that Mr Ferdinand's reasons for not taking the test were drugs related. But, having considered the matter very fully, the appeal board have today dismissed Mr Ferdinand's appeals, both against conviction and sanction. They have also rejected the FA's contention that the period of suspension should be increased.'

It was ironic that Gay had spent the previous two months fighting like mad to get the tennis player Greg Rusedski cleared after he tested for nandrolone.

Up until the verdict I'd thought I might make it to the back-end of the season with United, hopefully win the league, then head off triumphantly to the European Championships.

All that had been taken away and, to rub salt in the wounds, I was going to miss the beginning of the next season as well.

I always accepted that I'd made a mistake by not taking the drug test and never put the blame on anyone else. I argued mitigating circumstances, but I took responsibility for the situation I was in. The fact was that there was no one else to blame but me and I knew there had to be a punishment. I wouldn't have agreed with getting a three-month ban, but I would have accepted it. I'd let myself, the club, the country and the boys in the United and England teams down.

But I felt victimised. If other people before me had been banned for eight months for missing a test, then the precedent would have been set and I wouldn't have had an argument. I would have known from day one what to expect.

The Negouai case was so similar to mine that I thought I couldn't fail with my appeal and I still don't understand why I was treated differently.

Whenever I have to talk about it and analyse it, I cannot

help but feel bitter. It does my head in. It's a major chunk of my football career gone and I cannot get it back. Had I been injured for eight months I would just have had to get on with it, but in my eyes this was an injustice which could have been rectified.

What killed me was that no one at the top of the FA was big enough to come and speak to me and explain what they were doing and why. There were so many questions I wanted to ask. I played for England and, if you like, for the FA. I was part of their team, I wasn't the enemy.

At one point I almost felt like going down to Soho Square and standing outside FA headquarters with a placard saying 'Rio is innocent'. That would have made Palios and the rest of them jump. Knowing them, though, they would probably have tried to disappear out the back entrance to avoid me.

Is it any wonder I still feel bitter when only last summer two players tested positive for cocaine and got shorter bans than me?

Wolves striker Chris Cornes got a six-month ban and West Ham's Shaun Newton a seven-month suspension. Where's the logic? How do they justify my ban now? It seems you get a bit of sympathy if you've taken something, but none if you haven't.

In my view, there's no one who can relate to the players in the FA at the moment. The best man in charge in my time was Adam Crozier, who left to become boss of the Royal Mail. It wasn't so much that he was close to the players in age, it was his outlook.

He was a democrat, he liked to converse with people. If he had been in charge when I missed the test, there is no way he wouldn't have discussed it directly with me. And I'm sure he would have spoken to Sir Alex as well.

I'm not licking his arse. I didn't have much to do with Crozier, but that was how he worked. Some people liked him, some people didn't. But he would let people air their views.

Before my first hearing he would have spoken to me, as he

would have done to any player in the same situation. It's just common decency. It's the right thing to do. Crozier recognised that and I think the new chief executive Brian Barwick will too, but Palios didn't see it that way.

I had wanted to sit down with Palios so he could look into my eyes and see the truth. I had wanted to read his face, to see if he was lying or being straight and whether he was an honest and genuine person. You can learn a lot by looking at someone rather than speaking to them over the phone or having someone else relay what they've said.

But, for whatever reason, Palios didn't seem to think a get-together was required. He wouldn't even return the calls of one of Britain's most respected and successful managers ever, Sir Alex Ferguson.

Imagine it. The gaffer is asking to speak to him concerning the situation of one of his players, who is also an England player, and Palios blanks him. Why didn't he meet me and just say, 'Listen, Rio, this is what's happening. I'm the Chief Executive of the FA, the buck stops with me and this is the procedure that has to happen'?

Maybe he didn't think football meant as much to me as it did. He probably thought I didn't care and that, as I would still get paid, I would enjoy the time off.

But I was an England player who performed on behalf of the FA. You'd think there would have been some opportunity for dialogue, some form of conversation or communication between myself and them, but there wasn't. I reckon Palios would have got a lot more respect from my manager, myself, the players and many other people if he'd talked to us.

By the time I returned from my ban he had resigned following his relationship with the FA secretary Faria Alam. I don't know what he's doing now and I don't care. I wouldn't want to speak to him anyway.

During my ban, I kept going to all our home games and many of the away matches. I trained harder than ever and stayed involved as much as possible.

I wasn't feeling guilty as we dropped down the league, but I was annoyed that I couldn't help out. If I'd kept playing, maybe the outcome would have been the same, but I couldn't help feeling it was the FA's decision, not me, which was buggering up United's season.

And it bothered me that young kids might still think I was a druggie.

A lot of what I do off the pitch for charity and good causes involves kids. I like helping children and I love doing anything that I feel might inspire them. I've always enjoyed doing question and answer sessions where you can give youngsters a real insight into what your life is like. If my case has made children think less of me then I would be gutted about that. Hopefully it hasn't.

The manager, the chairman, the fans and the players at United stood by me and I couldn't be more thankful to them for that.

A lot was made of the fact that the club kept paying my wages while I was suspended, but they did the same with Eric Cantona when he was banned for jumping into the crowd. The club is contractually obliged to pay you.

If it's any consolation to those who wanted to grind me down still further, I did have to pay the costs of the case, apart from the cost of the hearing. I had to pay for the hire of the venues for my first case and the appeal hearing. They also tried to bill me for meals and wine for all the FA people who were banning me, as well as their drinks at the bar. One of them even had his wife there and I was supposed to be paying for her as well. I told them where they could stick things like that.

THIRTEEN

A Test of Character

I walked into the restaurant and saw Kenyon sitting there with Pini. I vaguely thought about turning back round, but as I wasn't there to talk about anything that concerned him, I figured it didn't matter. How I wish I'd stuck with my first instinct.

When I was banned I probably trained harder than ever before. I've never been so focused because I knew that when I came back I had to be dead right.

There would be no room for any slackness and all eyes would be on me. I would be under even more pressure if I looked off the pace. I only missed ten days of training during the entire length of the ban.

I had to serve every day of my sentence. Even in prison they let you out early for good behaviour. Not the FA. They would not even let me play friendlies against other clubs behind closed doors.

I had one week off when I went to Mauritius and, unbelievably, saw Ian Mill, the QC who had headed the appeal panel, at the airport. He was on the same bloody flight! He was about 20 yards away and I pointed him out to Rebecca. I was not about to go over and have a cosy chat, I can tell you. That wouldn't have been wise. My emotions were still raw.

The ban meant that I missed my first chance of playing in an FA Cup final when we beat Millwall. I went to the Millennium Stadium, but just stood around like a spare part really. It was some consolation for the fact that we'd fallen away in the league to finish third behind Arsenal and Chelsea.

I was delighted for the lads and was cheering them on, but I so would have loved to have been involved. I walked out on the pitch before kick-off and it hurt knowing I wouldn't be able to play. I had watched loads of Cup finals as a kid and always dreamed of playing in one.

I thought the day might be an opportunity to get hold of a few FA people and give them a piece of my mind. In the end, I didn't bother. It wasn't the time or the place. I went on the pitch at the end, but didn't touch the cup. God knows what the FA would have done to me if I had. They might have banned me for life!

But they had nothing to worry about, I didn't feel part of it. I left early and gave the celebration parties the big swerve.

I went off to Monaco again for the Grand Prix and then to Miami with Wes Brown and a few others during Euro 2004 and we were like fans on holiday. We took over this pizza restaurant and never stopped singing Rooney songs. I was dancing on the chairs when he scored his two goals against Croatia.

There was no jealousy on my part about the boys being there without me. Bitterness yes, but jealousy no.

When I'd missed Euro 2000, all my fury had been directed at Keegan, but I had also been young and immature. This was different. This time the FA had taken it away from me, not the manager.

The lads had stood up for me over my missed drugs test and had put their England careers on the line and I was willing them to go all the way and win it, even though I wasn't there. We came close, but Wazza's injury in the quarter-final against Portugal probably cost us.

I was gutted when we went out. Sol Campbell had a perfectly good goal disallowed, as far as I could see, and it was history repeating itself. I had been on the bench when he had had one ruled out against Argentina at France 98. It was uncanny that it should happen again.

I had a good time in Miami. It was nice and easy-going and relaxing. There were no paparazzi chasing me and nobody recognised me unless I was in the bar watching the football.

I started looking forward to reclaiming my place in the Manchester United team.

I went back to America a month later for a pre-season tour with United, but I still wasn't allowed to take part in any games. I couldn't even play against a non-league team at the training ground wearing bibs. I thought the FA might give me a break, but no.

I kept working with Michael Clegg and Valter di Salvo, the

United weight-training and fitness coaches, and was raring to get back into action. My return date, 20 September, was imprinted on my brain.

One positive thing I did during the ban, which has stood me in good stead ever since, was to consult a sports psychologist called Keith Power. I decided that when I returned I had to be right, not only physically but mentally too, so I thought I would give the psychology a go.

David James had told me about Keith and though I had been sceptical about such people in the past – in fact I thought it was a load of bollocks – I was looking for a new start and went into it with an open mind. I've never regretted it.

Keith gave me some great ideas about preparing for games and how to implant images in your mind of winning tackles or making interceptions or headers, anything that is in your favour. It's something I now do every night before a game and in the mornings. It has helped me enormously.

It hadn't occurred to me that Wazza would be a United player by the time I pulled the shirt on again.

When the rumours started that he might be joining us I was on the phone to anyone I could think of to find out the latest news.

I spoke to Frank and Gary Neville to ask how good he'd been during England games and training and they were almost lost for the words to describe him. I kept my fingers crossed that we'd get him, especially as we'd missed out on Ronaldinho the year before.

Newcastle were in for Wazza as well, but I didn't think for a moment he would go there, even though they put a big bid in. I don't mean to be disrespectful to Newcastle, but I couldn't see him moving there if Man United were interested.

The whispers were that he would come to United if Everton decided to let him go.

I thought he would be great for United. He was young, he had the talent to do anything with a football and could go as far as he wanted. Old Trafford was going to be the best stage for him to perform on. Whenever there is speculation in the papers, I quiz the gaffer about it. He said Rooney was a fantastic footballer and he'd love to get him.

The gaffer was good as his word and Wazza signed for United in the worst jumper you have ever seen. Why he didn't wear a suit or something more presentable to sign for the biggest move of his life, I don't know. As I was to find out, Wazza's not bothered about his gear, or that's what he tries to tell me anyway.

To get Rooney after the European Championships he'd had was a brilliant boost for us.

He integrated straight away. There were some high-profile players who were big personalities in the changing room, but he just walked in and it was like water off a duck's back to him. He was just the same as he was when he'd made his full England debut in that massive Euro 2004 qualifier against Turkey. As soon as he arrived, it was as if he'd been there ten years.

Wazza's an easy lad to talk to. If he doesn't know you, he comes across as quite a shy fella. But in surroundings he's comfortable in, in the dressing room or on a training field, he's just one of the lads.

It helped that he already knew the England lads. It was the same for me when I signed for United because I knew Gaz and Phil Neville, Becks, Scholesy, Butty and Wes Brown.

When the fixtures came out I noticed we would be playing Liverpool on the day my ban ended and I wondered if the manager would put me in. But that didn't seem realistic and, if I'm honest, the thought of it scared me.

It was going to be like the first day of pre-season, when you shit yourself because you know you're going to be in all sorts of pain from the hill-running, the circuits and the ball work. Then for the next few days you can't walk properly because you're so stiff. After an hour of your first game you always feel knackered.

I thought that if I was going to play against Liverpool I'd be done in long before the end and, with it being on TV, the whole country would be watching and I'd look a right mug. I wasn't convinced I could do it and thought I should have some reserve games first to get myself in proper shape.

I kept those views to myself, though, and as match day drew closer I changed my mind. I'd been out long enough. I just wanted to play and get stuck into it.

Two days before the game the gaffer came up to me and said, 'Listen, I'm going to play you against Liverpool. I feel you're fit enough, and I think your head's in the right place.' Then he goes, 'Do you feel ready?'

What else was I to say except 'yes'?

Physically I felt in perfect condition, but it doesn't matter if you practise against some of the best players in the world in training every day – people like van Nistelrooy, Scholes or Giggs – a proper game with a hyped-up opposition in front of 67,000 screaming fans is another world.

You could invite the fittest man on the planet, a Linford Christie or a Colin Jackson, to come and train with United and then ask him to play a game and he would be out on his feet. He wouldn't be able to do it, because it requires a different type of fitness.

But if the gaffer had had any inkling that I wasn't properly ready he wouldn't have played me. He had more faith in my capacity to get through it than I did myself.

While I was nervous about my match fitness, I wasn't nervous about the actual match, if that doesn't sound like double-Dutch.

The attention on me turned out to be not so intense as it might have been because that was the day the legendary former Nottingham Forest manager Brian Clough died, which rather put the importance of my comeback into perspective.

Running out on to the pitch into the Old Trafford cauldron was absolutely magical. I'd missed it so much. The fans were cheering and singing my name. I got a good early tackle in on Djibril Cisse as the ball went down the line. That gave me a lot of confidence and with the fans giving it 'Ree-oh, Ree-oh' I got carried along.

I didn't have any problems with my fitness. I felt sharp and on top of my game. But I got hungry in the second half and desperately needed a sugar boost. So I grabbed a Frosties bar, which is something I have in the morning before training.

I got Man of the Match, but it should have been Mikael Silvestre for the two goals he scored in our 2–1 win. My first game back, to win, and to be so embraced by the fans – I couldn't have wished for more.

About four games later, I suffered a dip in fitness. It was like I'd hit a wall. But the coach had warned me that could happen and I got through it.

Eight days after my return, Wazza made a sensational debut in the Champions League match against Fenerbahce at Old Trafford. Because of his injury at Euro 2004 he hadn't been able to play straight after signing and his first game was highly anticipated. There were questions as to whether he would be the same player, how long it would take him to get back into the groove and even whether he would fit in at United. Wazza blew all those worries out of the water with a hat-trick. I thought, 'Oh my God, we've just signed Superman.'

He crashed one into the roof of the net, drilled in another and finished by curling in a free kick as we won 6–2. Lifelong United followers say it's the greatest debut ever in a red shirt and it's hard to argue with that.

In training we always muck about for a couple of minutes before we start properly and Wazza, like Scholesy, is always

trying different things saying, 'I'm going to hit the crossbar from here' or 'I'm going to hit the corner flag' or 'I'm going to try to drill it off the floor. Where do you want it?' You've got to be on your guard because Wazza and Scholesy will aim to knock your head off if you haven't got your wits about you. If I tried to hit a ball as hard as they do before training I'd pull a hamstring. I need to do my stretches first!

Wazza has such enthusiasm for the game, he's like a kid. But when you put him on a pitch he's got the mind of a seasoned professional.

Like him, I came through very young, but as a defender the game comes to you and you have to stop players from scoring. Wazza has to do the hardest and most important job of all – stick the ball in the net. He's a forward, a match-winner. It's a totally different pressure to what I was under at his age. He's already at the Beckham level, with the paparazzi all over him wherever he goes.

Wazza believes he will be better than Cantona and Best. He actually said so once, half-jokingly, when we were in the dressing room. We were talking about Best, Bryan Robson and Cantona and how they are legends at United and he went, 'I'll be the best player to play for United,' and smiled.

Deep down he does really believe it, but he's not being cocky. People can see he's so good that it's possible he will be the best United player of all time, provided he can steer clear of the unfortunate injuries which are getting in his way. He's not just about silky skills. He's got the end product, he's clinical and he puts others in on goal.

Having gone straight back into the United team, I also returned to the England side for our World Cup qualifier against Wales in October. It was my first international for 14 months, but the fact that it was at Old Trafford made it easier.

I had a few butterflies, but that was because I feared that I might feel like thumping certain members of the FA if I bumped into them. There were some that I thought I got on okay with but they hadn't spoken to me at all during the ban. But the sting had been taken out of it somewhat because by then Palios was gone.

While I was delighted to be back with England, I wasn't happy at having to speak to the media. It's fair to say that I did it through gritted teeth. I wasn't entirely sure how I would react, but when I got out in front of them I was absolutely boiling. I knew I had to restrain myself. If I'd lost it with them I'd have got an absolute coating.

Many of these guys had put a gun to my head in the papers, on the radio and on the TV. I recognised them all, those who said I should have been banned for life or that I was lucky or implied that I must have taken something, without knowing the full details of the case, and yet here they were, wanting to have a nice little chat with me. I suppose it's part of the job.

As they were asking their questions – 'How's it been?' 'What's it like to be back?' – I was seething inside. If only they could have read my mind.

I've always believed the press has a right to their opinions, but they should base them on facts not fiction. They had no proof that anything had happened other than a missed drugs test. They didn't know the reasons behind it. But I got through their questions, and somehow kept my cool.

As I've said, I'd wanted to hold a press conference when the whole thing started, but the legal advice was that it would affect my case. And I was concerned that if I had done so the FA might have really gone for the jugular. I reckon now that it was probably a mistake not to have said anything, not to have laid all the facts on the table there and then, but I was fearful the FA would come down hard on me for trying to influence the public. It was difficult to think straight at the time, with so much going on.

We had a comfortable win over Wales and flew on to our next game in Azerbaijan, where David Davies asked if he could have a chat with me in the hotel after dinner. He said, 'I never had any intention of trying to hurt you. It was never my idea to get you in any kind of trouble. It was nothing personal, it was just the way it went. I didn't have much to do with it.' He added that he hoped it wouldn't affect our relationship and I just replied, 'Yeah, okay. No problem.'

We weren't great buddies, but he and Sven were the two people who spoke to me during the ban. I didn't see Davies as part of what I regarded as the FA 'mafia'. He was caught in the middle of the situation and was not comfortable with it. I had nothing against him.

Having returned to action, I then dropped myself back in the mire. My grandmother on my dad's side died and I was given compassionate leave to attend the funeral rather than travel to Sparta Prague to play in our Champions League game. But I was photographed coming out of a London nightclub, the Embassy, the day before the funeral, when the team was heading off to the Czech Republic.

I had only popped in to see a friend of mine, Estelle, who was launching her new album and I actually left at 12.30a.m., sober as a judge. But the papers claimed I left at 4a.m. and was pissed. Either way, I probably shouldn't have been there. It was a bit daft on my part and the manager wasn't happy. Let's just say he let me know about it!

Our old pals Arsenal came to Old Trafford the following weekend for another battle, which became known as Pizzagate. They were trying to establish a run of 50 games unbeaten, which would have been a big, big achievement for them, obviously.

The gaffer made it abundantly clear beforehand that he didn't want them celebrating at our ground again, like they had when they won the Premiership at Old Trafford in 2002. That had hurt United deeply, especially the boss, and those words, 'Don't let them do it again,' were ringing in our ears.

We went out there and got right in their faces. Wazza won a penalty early on, but they claimed Sol Campbell didn't touch him. It was one of those which could have gone either way. Sol said a few things to the referee, but nothing to Wazza. I could sympathise with Sol. As a defender, I wouldn't have been happy if that penalty had been given against me. But we weren't going to argue as Ruud van Nistelrooy put the kick away.

Wazza got the second at the death on his nineteenth birthday and the whole place was buzzing.

I clapped the fans, happy that we'd done a good job, and headed down the tunnel. Just as I was about to turn the corner to the dressing room I heard shouting in front of us, so me and Patrick Vieira went running towards it, getting faster and faster when we saw a load of Arsenal players rucking with our security staff.

I battled my way through the crowd and found myself right in the middle. The security guards had split the two teams and everyone was trying to get at each other. I was baffled as to what it was all about and tried to push everyone away.

I don't remember either of the managers being there. Their full-back, Lauren, was at the front, giving it plenty.

Apparently that's when some pizza and soup were thrown, but I swear I never saw it.

We always have pizza and soup in our dressing room, but our dressing room was right down the other end, so it must have come out of Arsenal's. I've no idea who started chucking it and the gaffer never said anything to us about it. There was no soup dripping off his face, although apparently he did get hit with a slice of pizza.

I've got mates in the Arsenal team, like Sol and Ashley Cole, but when you are battling for your club, friendships are forgotten. Whenever I line up against Arsenal I don't think, 'There are my mates Ashley and Sol. That's nice.' It's the same whenever you have friends in the opposition.

There's a real rivalry between United and Arsenal and you can feel the tension before kick-off. All sorts of things have contributed to that. Ruud and Vieira. Keane and Vieira. To name a couple. Gaz Neville and Reyes always had good tussles. Pires is a bit of a diver and if someone gives him a proper hard tackle he starts crying. Well, not literally, but you know what I mean. Things like that have all been added to the mix to make the games what they are now.

But one Arsenal player I admire is Thierry Henry. He is a nice guy, really easy going. I've got nothing against Arsène Wenger either, in fact I quite admire him. He changed Arsenal from being a boring team into an entertaining one. He brought in loads of unknown players who are now recognised all around the world.

I don't have problems with too many players, but Robbie Savage is one I did get upset with. I'll explain that later on.

Craig Bellamy's another who gets on opponents' nerves, but he makes me laugh. He hammers his own players as well as the other team. He'll go, 'He's rubbish' and 'That was crap' and 'Give me the ball and I'll skin Ferdinand alive.' It's like being in the school playground. It's funny.

We had high hopes of silverware that season, but it didn't happen for us. We lost to Chelsea in the Carling Cup semi-finals. That was when Mourinho went on about our gaffer influencing the ref at half-time. Mourinho did the same thing in the Champions League against Barcelona and both times Chelsea went through.

We went out of the Champions League in the first knockout

stage against AC Milan, losing both legs 1–0. We had the better chances in both games, but when they got theirs they took them. They were probably the best club team I've ever played against. Paolo Maldini was brilliant at the back. He's got to be one of the finest defenders the game has ever seen.

He was 36, playing against 20-year-old Ronaldo, who was in exceptional form, and experience won out. Also, the Brazilian Kaka was outstanding in midfield. He was quicker with the ball than he was without it.

There was a stage in the season when we thought we would catch Chelsea in the title race, but they were just too consistent and we lost some silly games.

One of those was in April at Norwich, who were relegated a month later. I was so pissed off about it as I headed into London afterwards. I hadn't played great and neither had the team.

I rang Pini and said I'd like to meet him to talk about sorting out a new contract at United. It was about the right time. There were just over two years to run on my agreement and United don't like contracts running down if they've paid a lot of money for you.

Pini told me he was having a meeting with the Chelsea chief executive Peter Kenyon that night, but what he didn't tell me was that he would be with Kenyon when I turned up. Kenyon had been the chief executive at Old Trafford when I signed and obviously things were extremely sensitive between United and Chelsea.

I walked into the restaurant and saw Kenyon sitting there with Pini. I vaguely thought about turning back round, but as I wasn't there to talk about anything that concerned him, I figured it didn't matter. How I wish I'd stuck with my first instinct.

I had a few nibbles and then we got into a couple of taxis, me and Pini in one and Peter Kenyon and his girlfriend in another. I was going on into town and the rest of them were going to a Greek bar.

When we got to the bar, the guy who owned it wanted to have a picture taken with me. Then some girls on a hen night wanted a photo, then some belly-dancer wanted one, and so on.

What happened? One of those photos ended up on the front page of the paper with Kenyon's face in the background. What made it worse was that it was not long after the news about Chelsea supposedly having an illegal meeting with Ashley Cole. The rumours that Chelsea were interested in me had already turned up in the papers. But I couldn't believe anyone would think I would be organising a move to Chelsea over dinner and drinks in a packed restaurant and bar.

Me and Pini talked about it afterwards and he could see I wasn't happy and admitted that he should have told me not to come to the restaurant. But I should have left when I saw Kenyon there, so it wasn't all Pini's fault.

Sometimes you allow yourself to trust in the system and hope that people won't interpret incidents in a certain way. But often they do. I know I was naïve. I understand why the public thought there might be something in it and it was definitely a mistake on my part. A red light should have come on in my head, but it didn't.

The gaffer went mad when I went into training the day it was in the papers. I was going to go and see him to explain anyway, but he called me in first thing and went absolutely bananas.

He said, 'What the hell's going on?' I told him, 'Boss, I don't want to go anywhere else. I was there but nothing was spoken about.' I don't think it even mattered what had been said in the meeting. I shouldn't have been there, full stop. I can see that I screwed up.

The manager hammered me and quite rightly. I got the treatment. I'd never seen him so angry; it was far worse than when I missed the drugs test. Much worse. I couldn't say a lot because I was in the wrong. I just said again, 'Boss, I don't want to sign for nobody. I want to sign for Man United. I told you at the beginning, I want to sign for United.'

For a moment I was worried he was going to say, 'Bollocks, I'm going to sell you.' The meeting went on for 15 minutes and he was going, 'You know how people will interpret it. It doesn't matter what you said. It doesn't matter if you were talking about the price of milk, the time of day or the colour of the table you were sitting at. It's just so stupid of you to go there and do that. Once you walked into the restaurant and saw him there, you don't sit down, you go straight back out again.'

The manager is good friends with Pini and he told him what he thought as well. But Pini is friends with lots of people in the game at the highest levels all over the world. He thinks he should be able to sit down and have a meal with anyone he wants.

I knew the general public were not going to give me the benefit of the doubt over this one because of how I'd explained my missed drugs test. First I said I'd forgotten the test and then that I didn't talk to Kenyon about joining Chelsea at dinner. I can see it's hard to believe, without me explaining it, but it's the truth.

I didn't want to sign for anyone other than United. The trouble was, how could I prove that? It didn't help that the meeting had come straight after such a crap defeat at Norwich either. Beaten by a team that we should have been able to put away and then, there I was straight afterwards with Chelsea's chief executive.

I had only myself to blame, though, and all I could say to the manager was that I hadn't spoken to anyone about going to Chelsea or anywhere else and he had to take my word for that. I don't know if he believed me or not.

Soon after, in a game at Charlton, I was booed by the

travelling United fans and it was an horrendous experience. I'd never had to deal with anything like that before. I'd been booed plenty of times by opposition fans, but never by my own. It wasn't something I'd expected. All I kept hearing was 'Fuck off, Rio'.

I understood that they were doing it because of what was being said in the press about the meeting with Kenyon. Not only were the papers saying that I wanted to go to Chelsea, which was rubbish, but also that I should just sign the new contract with United straight away because the club had backed me over my missed drugs test. But everyone has a right to negotiate.

When I walked off I clapped the fans, but they booed me even more. It was a sign of things to come and an uneasy relationship developed between me and the supporters which went on for quite a while.

We reached the FA Cup final, having struggled past Exeter by 2–0 in a third-round replay, Middlesbrough 3–0 in the fourth round, Everton 2–0 in the fifth, Southampton 4–0 in the quarter-finals and Newcastle 4–1 in the semi-final.

Our Cup form was good. We conceded one goal in the whole competition and scored 15, yet we lost the final in Cardiff to Arsenal on penalties, which was an absolute travesty.

We pummelled Arsenal. I've never seen them play so defensively. They had one shot at goal in 120 minutes. They were poor. We hit the post, the crossbar, had shots cleared off the line, everything. Rooney and Ronaldo were on fire. But it wasn't our day.

It was my first FA Cup final and it left a bitter taste in my mouth when Arsenal lifted that cup. They knew they'd got away with murder. I don't even know where the losers' medal is and I don't want to know.

The only bonus at the end of that trophy-less season was that I was back playing football again.

Brothers in Arms

Everyone had been asking us who was going to win. Anton wanted to beat me so much and I wanted to beat him. I knew if he won he would go on about it for ages.

My brother Anton is a top footballer in his own right. There are people I respect, like Dave Goodwin, who reckon he will be as good as or better than me. Only time will tell, but I hope he's correct.

Yet, it doesn't seem so long ago that I went to the hospital to see Anton on the day he was born.

We nicknamed him Tintin, after the cartoon character, because he had this little bit of hair curled up at the front which stayed like that for years. When me and my brothers and sisters were kids we all had two little teeth sticking out and big, fat, rosy cheeks.

I couldn't wait for Anton to walk so I could start playing football with him. By the time he was four I had him playing in the living room of our little flat, using the radiator as one goal and the sofa the other. It wasn't very fair, really, seeing as I was 11, but a game's a game!

Even as a little 'un he had a powerful shot on him. I'd go in goal for him and you could guarantee he would break something. Mum and Dad were always shouting, 'Stop playing football in there' and we'd go, 'We're not, we're not' and then we'd carry on playing.

Anton always ended up crying, because he'd either got beat and I would torment him (nice, eh?) or I would tackle him and he would claim he'd been hurt. Older brothers will know what I mean: the younger ones are always the same, they try to get you into trouble. And it's never our fault . . .

So my mum would shout out, 'Stop bullying him. Stop hitting him. Rio, what's wrong with you?' and I'd say, 'He's lying, he's lying.'

We shared a room and had bunk beds until we moved to Latona Road, where I was on one of those beds which folded up into a couch and my feet used to stick out of the end against the wall.

Our friends, the Zort family, had a young lad called Osman who was about Anton's age. The two of them would play against each other on the back grass – our 'Wembley' – and I'd be in goal. I would let Osman score to see how Anton would react and whether he had the character to come back. He would scream the place down saying, 'You let him win. I saw you let that ball in.'

Osman had the skills, but Anton had the speed. He was like a little bullet. He would shoot from anywhere as well.

When Anton was seven, he entered a tournament with boys who were three years older than him and he was unbelievable. Paul Elliott, the former Chelsea player, was watching and was so impressed he wanted to take him to his academy.

Anton came on in this game, got the ball, ran through and smashed a shot against the bar. I was sitting on the sideline going mad, shouting, 'That's my brother, that's my bro!'

Everyone was crowding him afterwards, telling him how wicked he was. But he didn't like it. It was all too much and it scared him. He said he had a bellyache and wouldn't play the next game. He'd never had attention like that before and I have to admit it was fairly crazy.

Anton could drop a shoulder, run on and then – bang! – he would shoot. By the time he was 11, Dave Goodwin, who was his district manager as well as mine, told me he was better than I was at the same age and he was right.

There is no history of football in the family, apart from Les Ferdinand. As I've said, Dad was into his kung fu and weights rather than football. Les is my dad's cousin, which makes him my second cousin, but we didn't know him. He's from a different part of the family and, like many Caribbean families, ours is a big one. Dad has loads of cousins. People had asked me if we were related and I always said we were, but I didn't really know. I just boasted that we were.

Then, when Dad went to St Lucia one summer, he asked around and found out that Les was his cousin. When he was playing for QPR while I was there with the schoolboy team, I got my dad to go and talk to him for the first time. Les didn't know we were related either, but he had heard there was a Ferdinand at the club and had always wondered.

We didn't become instant buddies. I was only a schoolboy and he was one of the star players. It was just like, 'Hello, how you doing?' when I saw him. But when I was asked by Terry Venables to train with the Euro 96 squad, Les really looked after me.

A lot of my family was there when I played against Les at Upton Park for the first time in August 1997. I was quite nervous about playing against him because, of course, by then I knew him and looked up to him so much. Once the game started, though, I was all right. We beat Spurs 2–1 and I got Man of the Match, but Les scored for them.

We speak on the phone sometimes and he's helped me out with some good advice. He's a qualified helicopter pilot, which I think is unbelievable. The idea of doing something like that scares the life out of me. I got a lift in Michael Owen's helicopter once and was almost sick. I avoid them if I can.

It's spooky that me and Anton played in the same position for the same district side under the same manager and both went on to West Ham.

Anton was a big Liverpool fan. I liked John Barnes more than the team, but I still followed Liverpool, as did a lot of the boys on our estate, mostly because of Barnes. There was one Arsenal supporter, a Spurs fan and a few were Millwall. We had this video called *Who's the Greatest?* It featured George Best, Barnes, Maradona and Pelé. It was wicked. We played it so much it wore out.

Although we had our own video recorder, we always went

downstairs to watch videos at the Zorts'. We would sit in front of their TV screen for hours, getting on their mum's nerves. They were good lads. Me and Anton are still friends with the four brothers, Ahmet, Sevhan, Osman and Ershan, and when their mum sadly died of cancer recently we all went to the funeral.

Anton loves football as much as I do now, but when he was a kid he wasn't so bothered. Dad said he didn't have the same focus as I did. Anton had other interests and was really into horses. When Mum moved to Mottingham they had stables nearby and Anton went there whenever he had a spare moment, after school and at weekends, whereas any of my spare time revolved around football.

He rode the horses, groomed them and sorted the stables out. He knows everything about horses. He's not into horse-racing and betting, it's the everyday aspect that he likes.

I used to say to him, 'You want to be a horse rider or something? Don't you want to be a footballer?' It used to really get on my nerves. He would say, 'I do, I do' and then get the hump and run upstairs. Dave Goodwin would tell me, 'He's doing all right. He's got the ability. He's better than you were, but he's not producing it for some reason.' That's when I really started telling him he should be concentrating on football, instead of going horse-riding all the time.

I used to talk, eat and sleep football when I was a kid. Anton, on the other hand, had loads of hobbies. Apart from his horses, he enjoyed singing with his mates. One of his friends was even in a proper band. Anton likes to dance as well. He can do a bit of Justin Timberlake, Michael Jackson and Usher. We both used to do the Michael Jackson moonwalk, but he's not as good a dancer as me. I'm one of the best around!

Once Anton became a YTS trainee at West Ham he turned into a different player and football became his priority. He still goes down to the stables, nothing will ever change that, and he's still friends with the people there, but it's not the obsession it once was. I never understood it anyway. I don't like horses, certainly wouldn't dream of riding one. In fact I don't like animals – they're dirty. I hate dogs and cats. I won't have them in the house.

There were a lot of people who doubted Anton and it's been harder for him than it was for me. Just having that tag 'Rio's brother' carries with it an expectation that other lads don't have. It's not that he was in my shadow, it's more that when he got into the first team at West Ham he was having to play right-back, left-back and midfield and was getting a lot of stick because he wasn't playing in his best position. I would say to anyone who would listen that when he got to play centre-back they would see what he was capable of. I guess that was me being the protective older brother.

As a young player you've got to go in and do what's asked of you. That's fine, but Anton wasn't doing himself justice. He was playing well at times, but poorly just as often. I would get more nervous watching him than I did when I was playing myself because I couldn't bear to see him make a mistake. It did my head in.

There was a game where he was full-back and not playing particularly well and the crowd we're giving it, 'You're not as good as your brother, blah, blah, blah.' I wanted to go down to the dugout myself, put him at centre-half and say, 'Now you watch him play.' That would have shut them up.

All the switching around slowed his progress and his confidence dipped. But that's what loads of young players have to go through. Sometimes you don't get into the first team playing your preferred position. You have to work your way into it. I did, and actually scored two goals in five games at West Ham. Anton would call me up and say he felt the manager doubted him. I would tell him just to keep playing and that when he got the chance to play centre-back he'd be all right.

I was right, because as soon as he started playing in that position he got rave reviews. He played centre-back in the 2006 FA Cup final, which West Ham lost to Liverpool.

I'm a lot more relaxed when I go to his games now. Still nervous, but not quite so uptight, thankfully.

Hopefully he will be better than me. He already believes he's quicker than me, but I reckon I'd leave him in my slip-stream!

The resemblance between me and Anton when we play football is amazing. There was a picture in the paper of him jumping on the backs of his West Ham team-mates when they'd scored and I did a double-take. It could easily have been me. When you see film of the two of us running and making little turns it's difficult to tell us apart. He mimics me unintentionally, like when he jumps over the touchline when he goes out on the pitch. That's a superstition I've always had.

We'd never played against each other until United visited West Ham last season. It was a special occasion for our family.

The other United players had been asking what it would be like for me because I'd been booed at Leeds, but I knew the West Ham fans would be brilliant.

Me and Anton spoke a little less that week than we normally would. I was going, 'Watch out for Rooney and Van Nistlerooy. Just watch out for them.' But I didn't give him any of my usual pointers.

Before the game, there was a big build-up about us brothers playing against each other, as you might expect, but there was not as much press attention as there could have been because George Best, the greatest United legend of them all, had died two days beforehand.

That affected everyone connected with United. All the supporters at Upton Park, on both sides, were excellent and paid a fitting tribute to a great player.

I tried to ignore the fact that Anton was in the other team. I've learned to play situations down as much as possible and not get embroiled in emotions after my feelings got the better of me before the World Cup quarter-final against Brazil. There's no doubt that emotions like that can affect your focus.

But it was difficult. Everyone had been asking us who was going to win. Anton wanted to beat me so much and I wanted to beat him. I knew if he won he would go on about it for ages.

There must have been 50 of our family and friends in the main stand. My little brother and sisters were wearing their half-United, half-West Ham shirts which Mum and Dad had made. And, for a second, as both teams lined up to shake hands, I started getting emotional again. I told myself to stop and concentrate on the game.

We went 1–0 down really early on when they broke away and we were left short at the back. I thought about how my family would be feeling – happy for Anton, gutted for me. But I knew Anton would be laughing after the game if the score stayed the same and I vowed that I would go straight back to Manchester without talking to anyone if that happened.

I don't think me and Anton came into contact during the game, apart from one corner. In the end we won 2–1 and I could relax.

As soon as the final whistle went, I looked for Anton. The first thing he did was ask if I'd seen his bit of skill in his own six-yard box when he went round Ruud. That was so me when I was younger. Skills were everything.

All the family gathered in the lounge afterwards. My dad and Lisa were there and Mum and Peter, who's a Man United fan, my cousins, my uncles and auntie and my mates. It was also brilliant that Granddad, who hadn't been in great health, had made it from the Isle of Wight.

My dad said his emotions had been all over the gaff. Mum had been like that too. They had wanted a draw. It was the worst game they'd watched in their lives. Apparently, no one in the family had jumped up when the first goal went in, only when we scored an equaliser. Then they'd stayed in their seats when we got the winner.

I experienced all the emotions they went through and more when Anton played in the FA Cup final against Liverpool at the end of last season.

Sky and the BBC asked me to be a studio expert for the game, but really I just wanted to go and watch with my family. Being me though, I left it far too late to arrange things and when Sky said they would get me to Cardiff by helicopter I accepted the offer, even though I hated flying in them.

I was just hoping Anton played well and that West Ham would win it.

I was watching on the monitor in the Sky studio with Jamie Redknapp before the match and Anton came in to the Millennium Stadium with his headset on, singing. He was very relaxed.

I'd spoken to him a lot the day before and on the morning of the game I sent him a text, giving him a few positive thoughts. I said, 'Make sure you don't let the occasion get to you and think about the game like you would any other. Don't get carried away by the atmosphere.' He didn't really need any advice – it was for my own peace of mind as much as anything else.

The Sky studio was situated in the corner of the stadium where the Liverpool fans were, which was not great news. I wanted to be in the West Ham end. As the game kicked off, I went outside to sit on the balcony and the Liverpool supporters started giving me stick – 'Oi, you fucking Manc twat' and 'I bet you wish you were playing.' All that shit. It got worse and worse – 'You shouldn't be at this end. Fuck off. Get down the other end.'

Then Jamie Carragher put through his own-goal to give West Ham the lead and I couldn't help myself. I was off my seat, celebrating like a mad thing.

I'd forgotten where I was, but my brother's team had just scored and it was brilliant! When Dean Ashton put West Ham two up I was going mental. The Liverpool fans were shouting and pointing at me again and all I could see were rows of angry red faces, then coins started pelting me. A few coins flew past my head at real speed, hit the wall and bounced off the floor.

I turned round to get back into the Sky box, but it was closed. So I had to jump over to another box and get back in that way. Wrighty and Les were in the other box, working for other TV stations. They were more than a bit surprised when I suddenly appeared. Liverpool got one back before half-time and when Stevie G equalised after the break their fans turned round and were laughing and shouting. Unbelievably West Ham made it 3–2 so I ran back out and started celebrating again.

The Liverpool fans were giving Jamie, one of their ex-players, loads of abuse for sitting next to me.

It was a game of such mixed emotions. If it hadn't been for Stevie Gerrard, West Ham would have won the Cup and I would have continued the banter with the Liverpool fans, going bananas. But his amazing goal in the last minute took the match into extra-time and then it went to penalties.

I could barely look. My stomach was in knots.

West Ham were already behind after Paul Konchesky's kick had been saved by Jose Reina and when Anton stepped up he had to score to keep the Hammers in it. I was thinking, 'Anton, just score. Please, please score.'

It was one of those slow-motion moments when the ball seemed to take forever to go from his foot towards the goal. It was not the greatest of kicks and Reina saved. It was all over. Liverpool had won the Cup. Anton was in tears and I was absolutely gutted for him. I wanted to cry myself.

I was so proud that he went up and took one, though. He had the bottle to do it, which says a lot about him. There were a lot of players on that pitch who you thought would have taken one before him because of their experience.

I was in bits. I was on TV, trying to hold it all in when I was ready to break down. I'd never wanted to be there in the first place. I just wanted to go down and see Anton and Jamie could see I was devastated. I was far more upset that he'd missed a penalty than because West Ham had lost. Maybe that's selfish, but as long as Anton plays well I'm happy.

The Liverpool fans loved it, of course, and gave me plenty more stick, but by then I was past caring about them.

I eventually got to see Anton and just said to him, 'Keep your chin up. Don't worry about it. At least you took the penalty. At least you can say that you had the balls to go up there and take one.'

The whole family was upset, but proud because Anton and West Ham did themselves justice and it will go down as one of the best FA Cup finals ever. If they had gone in 2–0 up at half-time they'd have won it, but Steven Gerrard was the difference and I consoled myself with the fact that he looked in great form as we approached the World Cup.

Anton's his own man now, he can swim for himself. We've both been capped by England Under-21s and it would be brilliant to play for England together like the Charltons and the Nevilles.

Anton was actually asked by Sven if he could be on standby for the 2006 World Cup in case there were any injuries, but he couldn't do it because he had just had an operation. So it's come close. You never know, I could lose my place to him.

Hopefully, our little brother Jeremiah is going to be a footballer too. He certainly wants to be. He wants to tackle people and has set his heart on being a centre-back like his brothers. Most young kids want to score goals. Clubs have already asked about Jeremiah joining them, but Mum wouldn't let him go. He's only little, there's plenty of time.

Jeremiah's the entertainer. He's into everything and can talk the pants off anyone. He likes reading poems and singing and dancing. Like me and Anton, he's into Michael Jackson songs. Anton was living in the same house as Jeremiah at one time and used to show him his Michael Jackson moves. He loved it. Whenever he's in my car he sings along to all the rap songs.

When Jeremiah was a baby and I went round to Mum's, I used to wake him up, pinch his big cheeks and kiss him. He was like a new plaything.

Our sister Sian is not really into football. She goes along to watch because we play, but she's more into singing and dancing. She's her own person. Out of all the kids, Chloe's probably the only one who's shy, but she's still individual, like the rest of us. She likes playing the piano, but stopped horse-riding because a horse bit her.

Remy and Anya are twins with very different personalities. Remy's a little hooligan and is always answering back, while Anya tries to be nice, although she can go down Remy's road sometimes. They're little lunatics who run around all over the place like nutters.

Just to recap, in case you're confused, I have one brother, Anton, and five half-brothers and sisters who are Sian and Jeremiah by my mum and Peter, and Chloe, Remy and Anya who are Dad and Lisa's. Society might call them 'half-brothers and half-sisters' but to us, we're all just one big family.

Having so many younger brothers and sisters has been like having my own kids, except I could hand them back when they were acting up! It's disappointing that I'm so far away now and won't get to see the smaller ones grow up the way I did with Anton and Sian. They come to see me as much as they can and stay with me every Christmas and New Year.

I took Chloe, Sian, Jeremiah and Rebecca's niece Liberty to Euro Disney and it was the hardest weekend of my life. I was so tired at the end of it. They were buzzing and we were on the go non-stop. This parenting stuff is going to be harder than I thought!

Our family is music mad. We can't live without it.

I've mentioned I bought a Ferrari once, when I was at Leeds, and when the guy delivered it to my house it didn't have a CD player in it. I went mental and told him to take it back. He looked at me like I was stupid and said, 'But if you have a CD player in it you won't be able to hear the sound of the engine.'

I thought he was taking the mickey. Who pays thousands of pounds for a car if you can't listen to music when you're in it? I said to him, 'Listen, if you can't put a CD player in it just give me my money back.' The colour drained from his face as he imagined thousands of pounds in commission disappearing down the drain. He returned it double-quick, with the CD player installed. I'd rather ride a bicycle than drive a car without music.

I've always loved music and the club scene. It comes from my dad. I've said how I would pose around in his blazer and brogues, look in the mirror at myself and prance around the house to his Freddie Jackson and Marvin Gaye records. The first record I ever owned was a New Kids on the Block album (a present by the way!) and then I got Michael Jackson's *Bad*

album, which I played all the time. I knew every word. The sleeve got all ripped up because I pulled the record out so often.

When Dad drove me to football he'd put old reggae on, proper roots reggae, which was his big thing. I loved that too. I also liked jungle, which was a mix between garage and hardcore, with old raga dubs. I used to listen to DJ Brockie, DJ Ron and Grooverider on the radio. I loved R&B too.

The club scene when I was in my late teens was fantastic. There was Koo and Buzz Bar in Leicester Square, 5th Avenue in Ilford and, my personal favourite, the Coliseum, which was the best place around for garage music. It was also at the time high up the league table of the roughest clubs in England. There were a lot of heavy-duty guys who got in there.

I went once with Incey, Wrighty, Jamie Redknapp, Robbie Fowler and Steve McManaman and for me it was a perfect night out because there was quality music, birds everywhere and a wicked vibe. The lads were into their music, but Jamie was in a panic and kept asking if it was safe to go in. Me and Wrighty were like, 'Yeah, man, it's all right. You get nothing but love in there. The people will be sweet with you.' So in we went and everyone was black except Jamie, Robbie and Steve. They looked even whiter than usual in that place. Within an hour they were gone.

If I'd told them about some of my experiences we wouldn't even have got them through the front door.

I used to park behind the club and one night, when I was about 19, I was driving with my mate Justin towards the main gate when this fella went hurtling past.

We looked down the road and could see he was heading for a dead end. Seconds later, four men ran past after him, followed by another guy with a towel covering his arm, and we knew the bloke was in trouble.

They caught the guy up, start bottling him, then all moved

out of the way. The guy was on the floor going, 'No, no, no' and suddenly – bang! I don't know if he was shot or not. Might just have been a frightener. But we couldn't hang around in case they turned on us.

I hit the accelerator and drove like mad. We were shaking and didn't know what to do. We could call the police but first up we knew we had to help the bloke if he'd been shot, so a few minutes later we drove back round to have another look. It was like it had never happened.

Everybody was gone, all five of the men chasing, and the bloke on the ground. What could we tell anyone now? To this day I don't know whether that guy is dead or alive.

It wasn't unusual for a gun to go off in or outside the clubs I went to. I remember hearing a gunshot as we stood in a queue for a rave once. We ran off for about five seconds then raced back because we were worried we would lose our place!

Sometimes a gun would go off in the Coliseum just because someone wanted to salute the record being played. Everyone would scatter for a few seconds then the dancing would start up again. How they got the guns in I don't know, because there were these big metal detectors on the front door. It was like going through security at Heathrow airport.

I've seen people get stabbed in there and saw one girl hit another with a baseball bat outside the club, on the same road where the bloke was attacked.

Yet none of those incidents stopped me going back. It had the best house, garage and R&B music. You couldn't ask for better. It was like anywhere. If you wanted trouble you could go and find it. It wasn't anything to do with the club itself or the management. But if all you were looking for was a good night out with your mates, then that's what you got.

When I first started going clubbing my mum warned me it could be trouble. She's a big worrier, but very streetwise. She was going to blues and reggae dances when she was 15. She always told me not to leave a drink lying around in case it got spiked, never to take drugs and never to smoke anything. It was good advice which I've always followed. She never mentioned the guns though.

I'm lucky that I get invited backstage to gigs and it's great being able to talk to the artists. I've met quite a few of them, like Mariah Carey, 50 Cent, Kanye West and Usher. I spoke to Craig David, who's a big football fan, at Party in the Park a few years ago and must have bored him and his manager to death with all my questions.

I love rap music. The Notorious B.I.G. was and still is the man for me, even though he's dead now. They are still re-mixing his music.

Me and Wazza went on stage at a 50 Cent concert at Manchester Arena and introduced him and his group G-Unit. I was quite nervous about doing it, but 50's manager really wanted us to. It was a hell of an experience. I'm going to be able to say to my kids that I've been on the stage with 50 Cent and I'm proud I had that opportunity.

We got some stick in the media because it was just after Wazza had been sent off for clapping the ref in United's Champions League draw against Villarreal and England had been beaten by Northern Ireland. What are we supposed to do, hide indoors every time we don't get results? The night of the game, and into the next morning, I got very little sleep, running and re-running every aspect of the game over in my head. But you've got to move on at some point. Meeting 50 was amazing. The chance to spend a bit of time with a guy who tops the charts every time he puts a new record out doesn't come along every day. I talked to him before he went on stage and he was so focused, a real professional.

My mate Courtney Richardson suggested that we should

start up a record company and go out and get our own new acts to promote. I thought it was a great idea. It would help Courtney's career and be a good hobby for me.

We set up White Chalk Music and decided to find some acts by staging a talent contest in Manchester – our own mini *X Factor*. We handed out leaflets in the street, left them in shops and went on the local radio to promote it.

When it came to the auditions at the Dance House Theatre, there was a huge queue snaking out on to the street, even though it was a freezing cold Sunday morning. I had been nervous, wondering if anyone would turn up, but the response was brilliant and the BBC and Granada came down to talk to the kids.

The judges were me, Courtney and my aunt Audrey, a vocal coach who does her own showcases and was once signed up to a label. She knows the industry. The auditions went on from 9 in the morning till 7.30 at night. We had to shut the doors in the end because the theatre couldn't stay open any longer.

Those who were successful went through to three heats, with 20 acts in each, which were held in the Contact Theatre in Manchester. In the week leading up to their heats we gave the performers vocal coaching and choreography lessons. The top three from each heat went through to the final and there was a lot of local interest.

People like Wylie, Estelle and Lethal B came to watch and perform. A girl group made up of Shola Ama, Kele Le Roc and Chanelle performed a Breast Cancer fundraising song as well.

It was inspirational for the children taking part, to see people they had watched on *Top of the Pops* and other music shows performing and then mingling backstage with them.

We had rock bands, rappers, soul singers and even a classical singer. If you were good enough you got in, whatever type of music you were performing.

The final at the Opera House Theatre attracted 2,000 people. There were cash prizes and loads of freebies from my sponsors Nike and Ben Sherman and every contestant in the final got a watch made by Klaus Kobec.

The winners were Melody, Harriet Wood and Nia Jai and they all got a chance to work with White Chalk. I rented a building in Manchester and put a proper studio in, then me and Courtney brought in local boys Mark Menzies and J'mez – who had produced and written their own songs – to run it. We also got another guy on board – Kevin Simpson, who used to be Jamiroquai's manager.

J'mez runs NVQ music courses for teenagers and we are hoping to get more involved in community projects to help disadvantaged kids. I would love the acts we find to become big stars, but the most important thing is to give the kids a focus in life. If they become successful then that's a bonus.

I'm fairly hands-on, but not to the extent that it detracts from my football. I leave the day-to-day business to the others.

I've started writing songs as well, but just for my own satis-faction, to know I can do it. I've no intention of trying to make a commercial success of it. I'll be sitting in my car and will start writing lyrics on my phone or I'll get a pen and paper out on a plane or in my room when we're on trips.

But I'm never going to be another Notorious B.I.G.

Beating the Racists

I heard him making monkey noises and asked Emile and Kieron, 'Can you hear that geezer?' They could, you couldn't miss him. He was doing it throughout the game and his mates were laughing and occasionally joining in. I'd have loved to have given him a right-hander, but we're not allowed to do that, are we?

If I named the player who came out with the most racist abuse I've ever heard on a football field, no one would believe it. I guarantee you'd be astonished.

Legally I couldn't ever reveal the bloke's identity because I couldn't prove anything in a court of law, but I've heard it loud and clear with my own ears.

It happened when I was at West Ham and involved a black player in our side who was up against a very well-known opponent. Every time our player got the ball and was attacking him, the guy's going, 'Come on, you black bastard. Try to get past me, you coon,' all sorts of racist stuff, and I'm thinking, 'Am I hearing this right? I can't be hearing this right.'

But it went on throughout the game and our player told me that defender did the same to him every time they played in order to intimidate him. He even admitted that sometimes it worked, which made it all the more depressing.

Those two players are still very much involved in the game and the player concerned comes over as quite a nice bloke. You wouldn't imagine he could come out with such crap but he does. He probably reckons it's all part of the game.

Well, not to me it isn't. It's bang out of order and I think our player should have reported him. Maybe I should have done something about it, but I was young at the time and didn't want to get involved. I'm disappointed now with how I turned a blind eye to it.

I'd like to think if it happened today I would make an example of him. But at the time the player was a seasoned professional, with a good reputation and I thought calling it on with him could ruin my career. And, of course, proving it is very difficult – it's your word against his.

Some people tolerate racism. My heroes are the ones who wouldn't tolerate it at all.

The first time I learned about Martin Luther King, the black civil rights leader, was at Camelot school, through a teacher called Mr Bakhir, who I've seen since over the years. When I moved on to Blackheath Bluecoat school it used to frustrate the hell out of me that they didn't teach us more about Martin Luther and those like him. Mum and Dad filled the gap by buying me loads of books about the American civil rights movement. I couldn't put those books down.

What Martin Luther King stood for fascinated me. He wanted black people to have equal opportunities and at the time it was a big thing for him to go out on a limb like that.

The first professional football match I ever saw was at Millwall's old ground The Den when I was ten years old. The ground had a bit of a reputation for trouble and some racism but I went because they were playing Liverpool and I loved watching John Barnes, a famous black player.

One of my dad's mates on the estate, Bill, knew I liked Barnes and got tickets for me, my mate Ahmet and Dad to go with him. It was Dad's first game as well. I liked Bill, but he was a real Millwall hardman. You would see him on the estate after games, bleeding with a cut head or a busted nose.

Liverpool won the game 2–0, John Barnes scored, and I started cheering. Bill told Dad to keep me quiet or we could get in trouble. At the end Bill goes, 'Julian, take the boys home. I've got to go and have a fight' and off he went.

He was a normal, decent bloke most of the time, but a proper hooligan at the football. He loved the game but he enjoyed the aggro as well. You never know what makes people want to be hooligans. I watched a TV show about Chelsea hooligans and loads of them worked on the Stock Exchange, so there are no class boundaries. If it's in you, it's in you. Bill would say, 'It's the buzz, it's the fucking buzz, mate.'

It would never have given me a buzz, I know that, yet I've

got mates who have banning orders against them which stop them travelling abroad to watch me playing for England.

There were quite a few of the Millwall mob on our estate. They would come back with tales of how they'd tried to storm the away supporters' buses. I'd ask them why they did it and they'd say the same as Bill, 'Mate, it's just the best buzz ever.'

When I went on loan to Bournemouth from West Ham we played Millwall and, as I went up for a corner, I could hear someone going, 'Rio, you fucking wanker yeeehh.' I looked in the crowd and there's one of the guys I know from home with all my mates still going, 'Ay you fucking wanker Rio, fuck off.' It wasn't aggressive, they were just having a laugh.

When I'm on the pitch, I usually manage to shut out any racism coming from the crowd and not let it get to me. It doesn't mean I'm happy about it though. Barnes was the same. We've since talked about how it made us both more determined to get one over on the idiots. Barnes was a legend on our estate for the time he backheeled a banana on the pitch.

I've never suffered racism the way he or the other black players coming through in the seventies did. I'm almost embarrassed to talk about racism in football because players such as Viv Anderson, Cyrille Regis, Brendan Batson, Clyde Best and Barnes all got it far worse than me.

It's still around though. It's worse abroad, admittedly, but there are pockets of it in England. I used to get people going 'ooh ooh ooh' at me and pretending to be apes, which is what they are.

Some black people will tolerate being nicknamed 'blackie', but I wouldn't have that. If somebody called me that within earshot of my mates at home they wouldn't get out of Peckham without a slap. I'm not having being called 'banana boy' either, which I've heard in the past.

I used to be amazed by this white woman on my estate who was going out with a black geezer. She used to call him a nigger and a useless black whatever all the time. I would be in our flat, listening to her screaming abuse at him, then the next night he'd be walking into their place like nothing's happened. I'm wondering what this fool is doing with this woman when she's got no respect for him. I don't understand why anyone would put up with that.

But, equally, I get annoyed when you can't say the word blackboard or recite the nursery rhyme 'Baa, Baa Black Sheep' in case someone gets offended. What's that about? Let's concentrate on what's really racist.

The Spanish manager, Luis Aragones, seems to fit the bill. He called Thierry Henry a 'black shit' and virtually got away with it. Pathetic.

It seemed to me the Spanish FA didn't give a toss and neither did FIFA. Yet Aragones was insulting one of the most decent men in the game. And, from what I can see, Sepp Blatter, the head of FIFA, also did nothing about it, yet he happily told the world I should be banned for missing a drugs test when I hadn't even taken drugs. In my book he had his priorities all wrong.

I've worked with Thierry on racism campaigns and I know how hurt he was by what Aragones said. I got involved in the 'Stand Up, Speak Up' campaign with Thierry off the back of Aragones' comments. Nike came up with the black-and-white wristband idea and it really caught on.

Then, last season, an MEP called Chris Heaton-Harris approached me about a European Parliament campaign to force UEFA into taking stronger action against the racists. Over 400 MEPs signed a motion calling for tougher sanctions, like docking points and closing grounds. UEFA got all shirty about it and claimed they were doing everything possible.

Their head of communications, William Gaillard, had a go at me for highlighting a couple of matches in Spain which he said were not under their jurisdiction. But the fact is that Spain is a member of UEFA and UEFA could flex their muscles and get involved if they wanted to.

Three days later, Blatter announced a whole series of measures, including points penalties, which he planned to impose against the racists. I don't know if he was always planning to do that, but it was some coincidence.

Even a lot of the sports columnists, who have given me a going-over in the past backed my stance, which was almost as astonishing as what Blatter did.

Our country should be applauded for the way it clamps down on racism. I've given the FA some criticism in this book, but they don't get enough credit for what they've done to drive out racism. The 'Kick It Out' campaign, which has been going on for more than a decade, has sent out a strong, forceful, message that racism will not be tolerated.

I worked on a campaign – 'Give Racism the Red Card' – and in a promotional video I highlighted an incident which occurred at Millwall when I was a kid.

A bloke who was in the stands in front of me was attacking a player, saying you black this, you black that, and wouldn't stop. I asked a nearby copper what he was going to do about it and he shrugged his shoulders. This bloke went on and on and at one point turned round and saw me and said, 'Not you, mate. It's those black wankers on the pitch.' In the end I had to walk out or I'd have punched him.

Racists at our grounds nowadays are looked on as sad, pathetic creatures. They are idiots. Other countries still need educating though, like former Yugoslavia, where there are very few black people and there has been such horrific ethnic violence. There is still a lot of work to do there, as well as across eastern Europe and, of course, Spain.

I played in Barcelona in an Under-21 match against Yugoslavia in March 2000. Emile Heskey and Kieron Dyer were also in the team and Emile, in particular, got loads of racist abuse.

The smaller the crowd, the easier it is to hear racist chanting. It isn't always obvious in a ground packed full with 80,000 unless everyone's at it. But in this game, there were only about 1,000 fans and one guy was egging on others in the main stand.

During the warm-up, I heard him making monkey noises and asked Emile and Kieron, 'Can you hear that geezer?' They could, you couldn't miss him. He was doing it throughout the game and his mates were laughing and occasionally joining in. I'd have loved to have given him a right-hander, but we're not allowed to do that, are we? We just have to put up with it.

When we played against Spain in the Bernabeu in a friendly in November 2004, there was a lot of racism. The game was held a month after Aragones had made that stupid comment about Thierry. I only properly noticed the abuse being hurled at our players once I came off injured in the second half.

We probably had more black players on the field during the course of the game than ever before but the monkey chants were directed at Ashley Cole and Shaun Wright-Phillips.

David James was sitting on the bench and said to me, 'Listen. Just listen to that.' It was unbelievable.

But again, FIFA had little to say about it afterwards. Why? Politics, isn't it? That was the perfect opportunity to make a stand and tell the Spanish FA that they would have to play games behind closed doors or away from Spain entirely. But instead all there was was what many regarded as a paltry fine of something like £40,000.

You can still hear it going on when you watch Spanish league games on TV on a Sunday night. Barcelona striker Samuel Eto'o seemed to be getting abuse at every match last season.

I've been lucky, I suppose, in that, because I'm mixed race, I haven't suffered as much abuse as other black players. People aren't sure from my looks what my origins are. I could be South American or something so, when I'm playing abroad, the morons don't know whether to pick on me or not. Instead, they go for someone darker.

Racism is not just an issue in football, and it's not just about black or white. It's about religion and culture as well. Football can play its part in educating people against racism, but in order to eradicate it from society altogether, schools must do more to teach kids that it is abhorrent.

The world, and Britain in particular, is a much more multi-cultural place than it was 30 years ago. I never think about anybody's colour unless someone mentions it. My dad's black and his fiancée Lisa is white, while my mum's white and her husband Peter is black. I've never had any prejudices about anything at all, race, religion or creed.

Sadly, not everyone has been educated. Towards the end of my time at Leeds I was being honoured as Player of the Year at a special dinner. They hired the Liverpool comedian Stan Boardman, who is well known for joking about the Germans, and he made a few racist jokes.

One of them was about how Woody and Bow had been to a nightclub and when they came out they said, 'I could murder an Indian.' It was only five months after their trial and Leeds, the club and the city, was still very raw.

An Asian guest got up and called him a 'disgrace' and Boardman went, 'Fucking hell, I'm being heckled by Pakis now. Why don't you go back to your curry house or shop in Bradford? Your elephant's waiting outside.'

I only fully realised what had been said when I saw it in the paper a couple of days later. I hadn't been listening properly, as I'd been chatting to people on my table. Needless to say, Boardman's brand of comedy went down like a lead balloon. It would have been completely inappropriate in any situation, not just at Leeds United.

I don't know why some players are always in the papers and others manage to stay out of them. I'm in them far more than I'd like for non-football matters, but I honestly don't go looking for publicity. I love nothing better than a quiet night out.

I know I've had my moments and have been a bit cocky maybe or just daft or forgetful. I admit that and take the flak when it comes.

But there are people who seem determined to make life difficult for me even when I haven't done anything wrong.

Take, for instance, one incident when I went to a club called Odyssey with Wazza and Wes Brown. I was meant to have slapped this geezer, which I definitely didn't do. Then the paper said that I went downstairs and hand-picked some beauties to take upstairs, which I didn't do either. What can I do about a story like that?

You get stupid dizzy birds coming up to you all the time talking rubbish. When you try to get rid of them they'll say, 'What do you have to be like that for? I'm only saying hello.' That same bird then goes to the papers to make an easy buck after trying it on with you.

I've had birds crying in clubs, claiming I've insulted them because I've asked them nicely to leave me alone. They won't take no for an answer so you've got to be hard about it and then they get stroppy and upset.

And some of them will tell the papers they've slept with you when they haven't. I went to a club in London with Dad,

Lisa and Rebecca on Valentine's Day. We were having a drink together and it was a nice evening. Then a bird who was sitting at the table behind ours came up to me and goes, 'Who are you with tonight?'

I said I was with my girlfriend, my dad and his woman and she went, 'Do you want my number?' Rebecca was a yard away, if that, and could hear everything she was saying. Ten minutes later, the girl was standing on the seat with her mate, and they were rubbing their arses on my back. Then they start rubbing my shoulders. Rebecca wanted to knock them out. Lisa had never been to a club with me before and couldn't believe what went on.

I want to be in amongst the crowd. I don't like being shut off in a VIP area. But these days, there's always some dickhead who gives it large. I can't do anything about it because I'll be the one in trouble. I tend not to go to certain clubs now for my friends' sake as much as my own. I don't want my mates to have to get involved to help me and risk getting themselves hurt.

I'm not shy but I don't like it when cameras follow me round. I can't stand the intrusiveness. There's a geezer who regularly stands outside the gate of my house with a camera and I've had a reporter walk up to the house, past the gardener, and demand to talk to me. I wasn't in at the time but how can people do that?

On one occasion, I was in the car with Rebecca and could tell there was someone following me. You get a nose for it. I stopped the car, jumped out in the middle of the road and ran to the geezer's car. He was shitting himself. I said, 'You're following me, you fucking wanker. How would you like it if I came to your house and followed you and your missus around? I'm going to sit outside your house and follow your missus and kids everywhere they go for a day and see how you like it.' I went berserk.

Don't get me wrong, I like it when fans come up for autographs and a chat and appreciate me as a good footballer. That's one of the rewards. And I like the fact that I can make people happy just by signing a shirt or having a photograph taken with them. I understand that because I was made up just getting a glimpse of the great players when I was a kid. It was a proper thrill.

I play football because I love it and I appreciate the respect of my peers and the fans. When someone comes up to me and says, 'Well done,' it's a good feeling. Even if someone says, 'Oi you're shit' I don't mind it too much because at least they have an interest in the game. It's their opinion.

Football has given me so much. I've been able to support my family and I don't have to worry about money. I wake up in the morning and I want to go to work. There are some days when I briefly consider giving it up and going to live on a remote island. I felt a bit like that last season after we got thumped by Middlesbrough and then lost to Lille in the Champions League in the space of five days. But I'd never actually give it all up.

To be truly happy, your job has to be going well. If it's not it can be depressing no matter how much you earn. One of the stupidest things you hear from fans or pundits is, 'How can he make a mistake like that when he's earning £100,000 a week? He obviously doesn't care.' What's the money got to do with it? Everyone makes mistakes.

And we do care. We care a lot. You don't get to play for Manchester United if you don't care whether you win or lose. Comments like that make me laugh.

That week when we lost at Middlesbrough and Lille, it was hard to go out of the house. I felt ashamed to walk up the street. I had to drive to the quietest shop I could find where the old woman behind the counter didn't know who I was so that I could buy some milk and bread.

At times like that it's not easy to go out in town. You just think all eyes are on you, there's nowhere to hide except in your own house.

Playing for United makes things a thousand times worse. If ever we lost a game at West Ham we'd still go out, but it's not so easy to do that at United. The bad times are much worse than at any other club, but the good times are so much better as well. It's a well-worn phrase but you have to take the rough with the smooth.

Nowadays you can't just be a footballer. There are other aspects which go with the job, like the obligatory sponsorship appearances. A lot of players would be perfectly happy if they never had to make any public appearances or speak to the media. I'm not really like that. I like to be able to put my own point of view across. But the media, by which I mean radio and TV as well as the papers, has gone so far over the top about every aspect of the game they have forgotten where the middle ground is.

The pressure put on young kids from an early age, for instance, is enormous. Theo Walcott has suffered from the media attention ever since he broke through at Southampton. When he signed for Arsenal and got picked for the World Cup squad it got even more intense. Yet he is only just starting out in the game. It was similar for Wazza when he was a kid.

But I'm a realist and I know the media can't really ignore players like Wazza and Walcott. I haven't got the answer. I just think it would be good if the attention eased up a bit and youngsters were allowed to develop at their own pace.

I believe clubs should let the media into training grounds every day, like they do abroad. It would help both sides understand each other better in my opinion. We would become more familiar with one another.

I had no problem with the open-house arrangement at West Ham. But incidents like the one when John Hartson kicked Eyal Berkovic made closing the doors necessary. In my view the people filming it should have had more respect and gone to the manager with the recording first.

There are always stories about bust-ups in the back pages of the papers but if journalists were regulars at training they would see it happens every day and it wouldn't be such a big deal. The relationship between the players and the media is at an all-time low now because the players don't trust them. And, of course, the media guys don't know players the way they did years ago.

We have become remote figures to the fans as well. Punters find it difficult to relate to our lifestyles, whereas 30-odd years ago their lifestyles were much more similar. It's why we get so much more stick now when things go wrong.

The media attention on a footballer's life away from the field aggravates me. I would happily sacrifice half my wages to avoid that. Real football fans don't want to know about that kind of thing.

I enjoy some of the attention and I suppose you cannot pick and choose, so I wrestle with that dilemma all the time.

And if a player's girlfriend or wife wants to be in the limelight and he wants it as well that's a totally different scenario. If they are embracing it, they're asking for whatever comes to them. We should have the choice, but we don't get it.

I'm so glad I've got a girlfriend who is not a celebrity because life is a nightmare when your partner is as well known as you are. I couldn't do the Posh and Becks thing. I'd hate it. All eyes are constantly on them. When Becks is by himself it's bad enough, but when you add Victoria to the mix it's manic. He can't even go down to the local pub for a beer. I'm glad I can. I'm recognised all the time, but it's not going to be on Sky

News if I've been out for a drink. With Becks, they'll report that he ordered two pints and bought some chicken crisps. He did occasionally go out while at United, but it had to be places where he knew everyone. His missus once took the kids to Pizza Hut and I read about it in the papers. Crazy. I don't know how they deal with it.

You can't choose who you fall in love with, but I was lucky I found Rebecca. She has no aspirations to be famous at all. If we book a table in a restaurant we don't want to be in the middle of the room, we would rather sit in the corner. We love holidaying in places where we can be anonymous. But if I go out in Manchester city centre, especially during the day, I'm followed by photographers like the Pied Piper.

I'm not moaning. There are many positives which outweigh the negatives. And I have courted my own publicity by writing my column in the *Sun*. I did it because I like people knowing exactly what I thought rather than making assumptions about me.

Players are easy targets and one incident summed up just how vulnerable we are. The day before the vital England v Turkey Euro 2004 qualifier at Sunderland I had to leave the team hotel to give evidence at the Crown Court. I had been in a nightclub with Dubes and two days later the police turned up at Thorp Arch saying they wanted to question me about a rape case. I said, 'What are you talking about? What have I got to do with a rape?'

It turned out a girl who was in the club while we were there had gone outside and been abducted by a guy claiming to be a taxi driver. He drove off with her, beat her up and tried to rape her. Apparently he was saying, 'Don't blame me, blame Michael and Rio. Michael and Rio have told me to do this.' Then he told her his name was Martin Luther King. Seriously!

He rang the papers, telling them he had a story about how Dubes and I made him rape this girl.

He defended himself in court and when he got me in the witness box he goes, 'Rio Ferdinand, do you know me?' If it hadn't been so serious and awful for the girl I'd have thought Jeremy Beadle was going to pop out.

I said, 'No, I don't know you. I don't know nothing about you.' Then he says, 'Do you know this girl?' I told him I'd never met her before. I was in there for about 20 minutes and that was it.

The guy went down and it came out after the verdict that he already had previous for raping a woman at gunpoint. But mud sticks. Key 'Rio Ferdinand' and 'rape' into Google and you'll find about 50,000 entries!

If the public wonder why people in the public eye become aloof, it's because of situations like that. I explained how a guy tried to sell a story saying I'd tried to buy drugs off him. No wonder we become paranoid.

These days, when a bloke I don't know comes up to me in a club my first thought is, 'What is he trying to get out of me? He could be off talking to some fit birds.' That's unfair on those who genuinely want to talk, but I've become wary.

I've always been one of the most easily accessible guys because I try to live as normal a life as I can.

I try not to judge people before I get to know them, but there are plenty of players who won't bother talking to people they don't know. I don't want to ever get like that, but I can understand why it happens.

Maybe I'm too easy-going. Mum has always said I'm too naïve and trusting. She might be right.

Front Page News

There must have been more than 20 geezers with baseball caps and hoods on. I'd thought there were only two blokes there. My heart started pumping furiously, it was scary, but I was high on adrenaline and there was no backing down now.

England went on an end-of-season tour to America soon after we'd lost to Arsenal in the 2005 FA Cup final, but I pulled out because of injury.

There were rumours that the manager had told me I couldn't go as a punishment both for my missed drugs test and having not signed a new contract. It was all rubbish. I'd been playing the back end of that season with a bad foot and had to have an exploratory operation. Luckily, there was no serious damage. I just needed to rest it.

I hate missing any England games and the gaffer knows it. He would never pull me out of an England squad if he knew I was fit, although he has told me at times that he would prefer me not to play the full 90 minutes. I'm sure he would like all his players to take as little part as possible in friendly internationals for the sake of Manchester United, but try telling that to the players who want to get as many caps as possible for a country they've dreamed about playing for their whole lives.

Not that being away from the England scene kept me out of the papers. I've never been on the front pages so much and that's saying something.

My run of publicity actually started before the Cup final when I had an altercation with a photographer who seems to follow me round London. Jody Morris and I and a couple of mates had gone out for the day and we came out of a bar in Hampstead, where you'd never normally see a cameraman, at about midnight.

The bloke was clicking, clicking, clicking away while we were walking and getting on everyone's nerves. I was carrying a bag full of CDs and I swung it round to shoo him away. I then remember his camera dropping to the ground and the photographer getting into a scuffle with one of my mates.

There were headlines which claimed I'd said to Jody, 'Kill him . . . Stamp on his head.' That wasn't true. But having caused all the trouble, the photographer goes to the papers and it's another black mark against me for nothing.

Next up I got done for overtaking a police car at 106mph on the M6 in Stafford. It wasn't as stupid as it sounds. Well, the speed was, but I wouldn't normally overtake a cop car. It was actually an unmarked car – mind you, I did flash at him to get him to move out of the way.

It didn't have a big blue light on the roof and an orange stripe down the side, but you would never have known that from the way it got reported. I got banned for 28 days and was fined £1500.

I wasn't in court for the hearing. I'd gone to Malawi, with David James, Gary Neville and our respective partners on behalf of the FA to work with kids suffering from Aids. A driving ban doesn't worry you too much when you see the hardships these children are suffering.

If I explain that the most thriving business was coffin building you get the picture. We went to a school for a question and answer session and the kids really believed that because we came from a wealthy country there was no Aids in Britain. They thought money just stopped it but we had to put them right on that and explain about safe sex and not to use dirty drug needles and the like. It was heartbreaking to see some of the kids who were ill.

When I returned from what was an eye-opening experience I went off to Sweden with a mate. We were in this bar and the owner invited us into his VIP area. It was crowded with Swedes asking for autographs which wasn't a problem for me, but some pushing and shoving started – I honestly don't know why, although apparently there were a few local characters in that night – and, to get out the way, I had to jump up on the sofa. When I stepped back down it all started again and punches were being thrown. I dodged one with a swerve Amir Khan would have been proud of and security came to help get me away.

But the story came out that I'd jumped on the settee with a glass, saying 'Who wants some?' which was a load of bollocks. I didn't throw a punch, I didn't have a glass in my hand and I didn't give anyone any aggro. I was just trying to stay out of the way. I was also meant to have been headbutted and have a black eye and blood on my face. Rubbish, my good looks were intact.

Enough? Not quite. Next up we had 'Rio Hotel Rampage' after I flew back from Sweden to Jody Morris's wedding at the Grove Hotel in Hertfordshire. We were in the bar the night before the wedding. Admittedly we were there for a good few hours and we were a bit pissed. About 3 o'clock in the morning, there were five us left having a laugh and messing about – me, Jody, Dubes and a couple of Jody's mates.

One of those lads picked up a fire extinguisher and ran off down the corridor, followed by the other one with another fire extinguisher. Security start flying about asking who it was running around. One of Jody's mates knocked on a random door and sprayed the guest with the extinguisher when he opened it. Being sensible, I took a fire extinguisher off the second lad, put it on the floor and went on to my room.

The next morning I was asked by the manager to go down to reception and explain what had happened. He said that the guy who was sprayed had at first identified the attacker as a short white guy with dark hair, then he came back again and said it was me, a 6ft 3ins black bloke with braids. He later admitted in the papers he couldn't identify who had sprayed him.

I found out who really did it and the lads told the manager, but it didn't make any difference. A witness went to the papers and I was blamed for being part of the whole thing.

Hands up, I've not always been Mr Innocent. I've caused a few problems with a bit of drunken revelry but whenever I have, it hasn't reached the papers. Maybe someone up there is evening up the score.

Dubes and Jody always seem to be there whenever I'm involved in any strife, but they are good mates of mine. I've known them for years. People might say they are a bad influence, but who knows? It might be me who is the bad influence on them.

I've known Jody since going to the England youth trials and got to know Dubes through Jody because they were at Chelsea together. None of us are malicious or go out with bad intentions. We just seem to do the wrong thing at the wrong time once in a while and get ourselves into mischief.

Mostly we just have a laugh, like when I met Jody and one of his mates in a pub in Fulham. They'd been there a couple of hours and I was late because the train had been delayed. They had a drink on the table waiting for me and said I had to down it in one as a forfeit. They wouldn't speak to me till I did. I gulped it down and found out what it was – chilli vodka! My throat was burning, it was like when they drink a bottle of Tabasco in the cartoons.

My eyes were watering and I must have drunk four pints of water in the next five minutes. They were rolling about on the floor cracking up, crying with laughter, and I'm sitting there going mental. I wanted to kill them.

Another time, Jody came up to my house in Manchester and we had a right stupid night. We went out for a few beers then came back for some more. We were mucking around outside on the forecourt, beside my Navigator Jeep and the Aston Martin. He got on top of the Navigator then tried to jump down to the roof of the Aston Martin. He was so pissed he fell back off the Aston Martin on to the floor. He did himself a bit of damage and could hardly walk. It was a mad night and the stupidity wasn't over yet.

At about 1a.m. we went back into the house and went through Jody's phone, ringing people and leaving messages.

We rang Terry Byrne, who used to be a masseur for England and works for David Beckham, then we called Peter Reid, Ray Wilkins, Dennis Wise, Dubes and Dominic Matteo and they're only the ones I can remember.

I like Wilkins, I thought he was an unbelievable player even though he was nicknamed the Crab because he had a reputation for always passing the ball sideways. So we left a message saying, 'Ray, pass it forward. Just for once, please pass it forward, give the strikers a chance. Make us happy.' Half an hour later we rang again and left another message which said, 'Ray, have you passed it forward yet?' Ray never realised it was us until I told him at Jody's wedding. He saw the funny side.

The message we left for Terry Byrne had further consequences than we'd imagined. We told him we were going to come round his house and get him.

Jody rang Terry a couple of days later and said, 'Did you get a phone message the other night?' He explained how we'd been pissed and had left messages for people. Terry was mortified. It turned out that he had sent someone round to lean on a geezer who he thought was threatening him!

I love a bit of banter, as do all the lads in the changing room, including Wazza, who's always good at coming back with an answer whether it's to his team-mates or criticism in the media. One morning there was something not very complimentary in the paper about him and he went out and had an unbelievable game, scoring one and setting up another. Some people can do that whereas others crumble under pressure.

He'll never be one of those big 'I am' types however much

he achieves in the game. His approach to life is similar to Ole Gunnar Solskjaer's, who scored United's winner in the 1999 Champions League final. Ole will go down in Old Trafford history, yet it hasn't gone to his head. If he walked into the dressing room and you didn't know who he was you would assume he was a YTS player who'd got lost. Wazza's the same.

It's the lads who aren't as good as they think they are who are the big-heads. If someone's appeared on the front cover of a magazine he knows for a fact that it will go on the wall in the changing room accompanied by some jokey message. You even get hammered for writing articles in the Man United magazine. And if someone's done a cheesy photo, like Ronaldo did for Pepe Jeans with his naked body out on show, he'll get slaughtered. We told Ronny he was gay. There was one hilarious picture in the newspaper of Wazza standing up and Ronny on his knees in front of him. One of the lads made out that Wazza was getting a blow-job and it went straight on Ronny's locker.

Ronny gets the most stick because he's the easiest to wind up. We call him the pretty-boy or Chico because he looks like that bloke from *The X-Factor*. When Ronny wants to he can speak good English but he doesn't always understand it if we talk too fast, especially Wayne and Wes with their accents.

We'll sit in the corner looking at him and laughing and he'll get all defensive, going, 'Why are you talking about me, you lot? You idiots.' Quinny Fortune would wind him up, telling him his jeans were too tight and that he could see everything.

I was sorry to see Quinny go. He was another lad who, when he was barely a teenager, was being talked about as the best young player in the world. I remember watching him play for the Spurs youth team after I'd finished on another pitch with my district side. I'd heard so much about him. He was a number 10 then, playing behind the front man, and was unbelievable.

But injuries hampered his career, even though he still did very well and was appreciated by his fellow pros at United. We will miss his humour. He was no respecter of reputations. He dug everybody out.

Our striker Louis Saha gets stick for everything – his gear, his barnet, you name it. Fletch, on the other hand, gets a coating for being too scruffy. Even the captain gets it. One of the funniest things I've ever heard is the recording of a phone call made by a college kid to Gaz, which ended up on the internet. Gaz went nuts, demanding to know where he got the number from. Some of us downloaded it on to our own mobiles.

I've been a victim too. The lads put up a picture of me and Plug, the ugly kid from the Bash Street Kids cartoon strip in *The Beano*. It was intended to show the comparison between the two of us. I couldn't see it myself!

One man who gets left alone is Giggsy. He's too much of an institution but he's a funny bloke with a dry sense of humour.

There's a lot of banter involving games on the PlayStation especially on long away trips. Fletch and I are partners and we absolutely tear the life out of everyone else. They can't handle us. Pro Evolution Soccer is our favourite and I reckon I could have a career as a commentator because my commentary when we're playing is unbelievable.

We usually play two against two, with me and Fletch on one team and Wazza and Wes on the other, while Sheasy and Alan 'Smudger' Smith are also a regular pairing. The rule is that the winner stays on and me and Fletch can be on for ages. Once we were on for two or three weeks and only lost one game.

We even held a mock press conference in which Wazza and

Wes had to explain their poor performance. It was just like the real thing and I filmed it on my mobile. Wazza and Wes were being questioned about the problems between them and what was going on. Wazza said he wanted to transfer-list Wes and bring in Smudger. It might sound silly but it's the sort of stuff which keeps us kids amused.

On England duty, Wazza and I are partners. John Terry's not a bad player, although I battered him in a one-on-one game. Anton's stuffed him as well, so clearly JT can't deal with the Ferdinands. Funny thing is he officially endorses the game on the front cover of the case!

Before the video games came along we used to have quizzes on the bus and the gaffer was brilliant at them. He is one of the best at general knowledge I've ever come across. He knows about animals, trees, countries, kings, queens, cookery. You name it, he knows it.

Mind you, Nicky Butt could give him a run for his money. He's not too shabby. I can hold my own and I pride myself on having been told I got one of the hardest ever questions right on *A Question of Sport*. They showed a picture of a stadium and I was asked whose ground it was. It was Boca Juniors and everyone in the audience was staggered when I came up with the answer, as was the presenter Sue Barker. How could I not have got that one? It was the home of Maradona!

Having a laugh with the boys whether at United or England became very important to me when I was getting a hard time from the supporters over signing my new contract.

We played away at Clyde in a pre-season game in July 2005 and the booing I'd experienced towards the end of the previous season had got worse. They were singing 'Chelsea rent boy', 'One greedy bastard', '100 grand you're having a laugh', 'Rio for Chelsea' and 'Sign the deal you fucking twat'.

Those were the ones I could make out. I'm sure there were others.

Three days later we played at Peterborough and it was louder still. One lot had a banner which they hung at the back of the stand telling me where to fuck off to. Every time I got the ball they were booing. I was gutted.

I phoned Pini straight after the Peterborough game and told him it was becoming too much. I didn't want to leave, didn't even think about it, I just said to Pini, 'Please, you need to get the contract sorted.'

But the United officials couldn't meet us for a while and I had to hang on. We went on tour to the Far East and everything calmed down a bit. But it cranked back up again when we travelled to Antwerp for their Centenary game.

When you run on to the pitch there, the fans are on either side of you, as if you're in a cage. You're close enough to see into each other's eyes. I could hear our fans on one side shouting, 'Rio, you fucking tosser' as I walked out, while their fans were smiling at me and cheering.

When my name was mentioned on the tannoy the 'boos' from the United fans were deafening.

At the end of the first half, I jogged off to the sounds of, 'Fuck off Rio, you greedy bastard,' and a geezer chucked a plastic glass full of beer all over me. I called him a fat twat and we had a brief argument before I continued on into the changing room. It was all doing my head in.

I carried on playing and we won 6–1 but, as I walked out of the ground, there was a small group of about ten United fans beside our coach.

I recognised the geezer who'd chucked the beer over me straight away and he went, 'Rio, can I have a word?' I carried on and got on the bus and sat looking out at him, while he's going through the window, 'I just want to talk to you.' I went down to the front of the coach, stood on the step at the door and asked what he wanted. He said he hadn't thrown any beer over me, but I knew he had and I told him he was out of order. He asked why I hadn't signed and I said, 'I've told people I want to sign. Now fuck off. I'm not talking about it until I've actually signed.'

He wouldn't give up, 'Yeah we love you. We want you to stay but when you going to sign?' Gaz Neville was getting on the coach and goes to the bloke, 'He's a fucking Man United player and while he wears the red shirt you fucking support him. He's said he's going to sign so just wait.' Gary Neville always sticks up for the players, as he had done over my missed drug test, and you just think to yourself 'Respect!'

The hold-up over the contract was about all sorts of things – personal image rights, wages, the Glazer takeover and setting a date to sit round the table. The United officials were away in America and when they came back Pini was away. It got to the point when I just wanted to give in, grab a pen and sign so all the nonsense would go away.

The main problem was that the Glazer takeover delayed all our negotiations. Sorting out all the details about how the new regime was going to work out was the most important thing for chief executive David Gill. The club's future was a bigger issue than me. Obviously.

The fans seemed to believe for some reason that, not only would the Glazers be upping ticket prices, but that I would be pocketing the increase. They were worried about what was happening to their club and I could understand that. Yet there were other players at United who took far longer over their contracts than I did. It wasn't like there was any hurry either. I still had two years to go on my current deal. My contract had become big news because of situations that arose such as the meeting with Kenyon. At one point during that pre-season, things got really out of control. I was in the house on my own watching TV one night when the door-buzzer rang.

I have security cameras which show who's at the front gate but I couldn't see anyone. I thought the camera was either broken or there was a hand over it. When the buzzer went again I got up and went to the entry-phone in the kitchen. The bloke at the gate said, 'Is Rio Ferdinand there?' so I said, 'Who's speaking if you want to speak to him?'

He goes, 'Oh, just a couple of people who want to talk about signing the contract.' I told him to get his hand off the camera and he's going, 'Can you not just come out here and speak to us?' and I'm going, 'Take your hands off the camera.' I put the phone down and he rang the buzzer again. I was looking at the screen but he wouldn't take his hand off.

I was angry by now that he was taking liberties at my home and grabbed a stick about a metre long to defend myself with if it came to it. I went out the side door near the kitchen and, like Spiderman, jumped on to a wall so I could look over the gate and screamed, 'What the fuck do you want?'

There must have been more than 20 geezers with base-ball caps and hoods on. I'd thought there were only two blokes there. My heart started pumping furiously, it was scary, but I was high on adrenaline and there was no backing down now.

They'd been drinking in a nearby pub and I could smell booze on them. I went, 'Take your hoods off. I want to see your faces.' They did, after I promised I wouldn't go to the police, and then they said, 'We're Man United supporters and we think the Glazers are taking over the club, taking our money. They're going to raise prices and you won't sign your new contract because they won't give you £170,000 a week.' That figure was going up all the time!

I replied, 'For one, I've not asked for that kind of money and for two, how many times have I said that I'm going to sign for United? I've told the manager, the manager's said it in the paper and I've said it to the other players. What more do you need?'

They were all in their mid-twenties to mid-thirties. They were proper United fans, they wouldn't have been at my house otherwise. I understood that they were concerned but I still wasn't happy and said, 'What if my missus had been here by herself? She'd be shitting herself. You might have been coming to rob the gaff.'

Then we heard police car sirens going because one of the neighbours had phoned the cops and they ran off, although they did thank me first for having the balls to come out and talk to them! The police asked what had happened and I told them it was just a few fans who wanted a word and it was nothing to worry about.

I'd had people come to my door for autographs before, but never to confront me like that.

Pini stirred things up some more when he said in the *Sun* that the club had to give a little and that if I didn't sign I'd just let the contract run to its end in two years and then, of course, I'd be entitled to a free transfer. Agents have to do things like that, but it didn't make my life any easier. It was embarrassing, but Pini's got his job to do. The gaffer also increased the pressure by saying it was time I signed, which he was entitled to say.

Again I said to Pini, 'Can we not get this sorted?' and he was saying, 'There's no agreement. We are at different ends of the ball park.' I told Pini I was coming to the next meeting with him to see for myself what was going on. That was quite unusual because normally it's left to the agent and the club to sort it out.

So one Friday morning we all sat round the table at the Carrington training ground and the manager said, 'Let's get this sorted and get it banged out before we leave today.' Figures were bandied about and we made a lot of progress. David Gill said he'd get back to us.

The manager and Pini got along fine throughout the whole saga. They are old friends, and there was no animosity between them.

When I first met Pini he spoke about Alex Ferguson like he was one of his brothers. There's a picture of him and the gaffer on the mantelpiece in his London flat. They eat out a lot together when the boss is in town.

Pini's always lived the high life ever since I've known him. When I first signed up with him at West Ham he took me and my family to the Ritz in London. I had lobster and then a platter of fruit was put on the table like I'd never seen before. Everything imaginable was on there, fruits from all over the world. It was an amazing sight. It would have kept me going for a month. Pini sat in his chair with this big fat cigar, like someone out of *The Godfather*. A waiter came up and spread a napkin on my knee and called me sir. It was like another world to us.

At the beginning of our relationship he said to me, 'As long as you play well then my job will be easy.' It's kind of gone like that really. You hear stories about agents saying you've got to go here or there but Pini has never pressurised me into anything. He will tell me if a club has asked about me and will tell me what he thinks. He'll never suggest that I move unless he feels it's right for my football career.

A lot of Italian and Spanish clubs came to him in my last two years at West Ham asking if he could get me to join them. Financially it would have benefited me and Pini to go to one of those clubs. But, on each occasion, he felt it was not the right time.

He reckoned I still needed to learn my trade at an English club before even considering moving abroad. When I was weighing up leaving Leeds for Manchester United he told me that although United were one of the biggest clubs in the world, at the end of the day the decision lay with me and I had to feel right about it.

I signed my new contract at Old Trafford a week after the meeting at Carrington. On the way into the stadium there were loads of fans outside the superstore asking if I was going to sign. When I finally scribbled my name on the bottom of that document I looked at David Gill and said, 'Thank goodness for that. It's over. It's taken too long.' He replied, 'You're telling me.'

When I went back out people were asking if I'd signed and when I said I had they were cheering. It felt good. I rang Rebecca then my mum, dad and brother to give them the news. Rebecca had felt the strain of it all, especially after I'd told her about the fans coming round to the house.

There was plenty of criticism about how much I was getting, and there's no pretending it was not a lot of money because it was. But money has never motivated me. I'm too in love with football. Whether we win, lose or draw, I hardly sleep after games because of a combination of adrenaline and the fact that I run through moves in my head wondering if I could have done better.

Two days before any game I focus my mind solely on the match, role-playing it through my head. I try to push my body to the limit so I can achieve my aims. Then, afterwards, I analyse it all – good passes, bad passes, headers, interceptions, their goals, our goals, everything.

If we go out after we've lost I can be talking to people but it's obvious I'm not really there, because I'm still thinking about the game. I go into a trance. The thought of not playing terrifies me.

Do I think I earn a fair wage? Well, there are many people who deserve to earn more than me like doctors, nurses, fire-fighters and policemen. Playing football doesn't warrant the money we earn. But that's what we get and I'm lucky I'm in this business. We are in a game where there is a lot of money sloshing around. You have a value to the industry in which you work and why should you undervalue yourself?

I have days when I feel unhappy and lonely just like anyone else. Money doesn't shut out those feelings although of course it takes away a lot of the stress that those without money have in their lives.

I didn't choose football for the money. I chose it because I loved it and am good at it. I don't feel I should be embarrassed by the rewards it gives me, and I'm not.

But just because I signed a new contract – it didn't mean everything was sweet.

SEVENTEEN

Dropped and Humiliated

David Beckham texted me, telling me not
to worry, to work hard
and I'd be back in the team.
I remember replying,
'My World Cup's finished, man.'

A **week after my new contract** was agreed I went to Denmark with England and we got stuffed 4–1. We were an utter shambles.

We didn't prepare properly for the game, that's for sure. I mean mentally rather than physically.

It was the first week of the season and there was a bit of 'It's just a friendly, it doesn't matter. When the serious games come along then we'll play.' There was too much of a jokey atmosphere in the changing room as well.

At that time of year you are still easing into the mode of playing week in, week out and you don't want to get injured. It's not a good time for a friendly. But if you are playing for your country, whatever the circumstances, you've got to be able to go out there and prepare properly.

David James got criticised for his performance after he came on for Paul Robinson in the second half and conceded all four goals. Afterwards, he admitted he hadn't done his own usual preparation. By saying that, he opened himself up to more criticism. He was being honest but I thought it was a mistake on his part because he wasn't solely to blame. We all were.

Managers and players can't win with international friendlies. The number of substitutions which go on in the second half always disrupts things, especially when Sven used to change up to ten players until the rules limited the number of substitutions he could make.

As a young player you don't mind because it means you will get a cap at some stage in the game. But if you're going to grow as a team, so many changes aren't a good idea. You need continuity in the team and while once in a blue moon all the changes will work, you can sometimes get battered as we did against the Danes.

From a club manager's point of view it's much better that we play 45 minutes, but as a player you want to be out there

Me and Frank. Under-21s. Still in the squad!

First cap!

Goal bound...

...looking good...

...keeper's got no chance...

...goal! Nice moves.

Getting the
better of Rivaldo

RIO BUTTED

Rio hit in bar brawl

VIDEO SEX SHAME OF ENGLAND SOCCER STAR

3 LIONS ON THE TOO

Keegan rejects prefer to go on a bender than watch our boys

HERE WE RIO AGAIN

FRIDAY: He's butted in bar

MONDAY: Cop quiz on 2nd row

EXCLUSIVE: NEW SOCCER

RIO IN RUINS

- Eight-month ban leaves him broken
- His Euro 2004 dream in tatters
- United to fight 'savage' decision

RIO HOTE RAMPAG

New shame as police quiz star

SunSport EXCLUSIV

RIO: I'M GUTTE

- 8-month ban stays as FA reject appeal
- Man U star says: It's taken my hope away

RIO'S DRUG TEST SHOCK

RIO'S BINGE

- He's on the tiles until 5am on eve of crunch hearing
- He snogs married blonde during a bender in club

£50M RIO

United break the bank to net defender

RIO TO THE RESCUE

By Harry Harris and Matthew Dunn

MANCHESTER UNITED have invested an astonishing £50million to make Leeds defender Rio Ferdinand the most expensive British player for the second time in his career. Ferdinand will sign a five-year deal worth £9m basic — £90,000 a week and with...

By Richard Tanner

RIO FERDINAND finally broke his Manchester United goal duck and was then told by Sir Alex Ferguson: "Now score some more." The defender began the 4-0 rout of Wigan that

TURN TO PAGE 78, COLUMN 1

Rio roars back

Ferdinand returns style but Gerrard England doubt

By IAN LADYMAN

MAN UNITED 1 LIVERPOOL 0

HEAD MAN . . . it's all over as Ferdinand nods the winner
Picture: RICHARD PELHAM

HIS NAME IS TRIO

Ferdinand nets number three

NEIL CUSTIS
AT OLD TRAFFORD

WHEN Rio Ferdinand finishes his autobiography, you can bet this moment will fill a chapter.

He is working on it right now but the final part will have to be swiftly rewritten.

Indeed, this last-minute winner completed his rehabilitation in the eyes of all Manchester United fans.

Some turned on him during the eight-month ban for missing a drugs test.

Others questioned whether a player once dubbed the new Bobby Moore was anywhere near that.

Now after a trio of goals in nine and increasingly impressive

Thirdinand

RIO BAGS WINNER BUT NEVILLE FACES TAUNT RAP

ARM THE MAN . . . Ferdinand

Back after eight
months out...

The boss

The heat

The tournament.
World Cup 2006

Looking ahead
after the
World Cup.

the whole 90 minutes. Before we go on international duty the gaffer will jokingly say, 'Play ten minutes this time and then get off.' It's fair enough because the club is his priority.

The England manager is in a difficult position because he has to please everyone and it can't be done. Right from the start of his time as England manager, Sven had a policy of protecting players by making a lot of substitutions. That meant that the club managers expected it from him every game. He made a rod for his own back.

It was a bad feeling coming off that pitch in Copenhagen. They were playing keep-ball at the end, taking the mickey.

The following month we played against Wales at the Millennium Stadium in a World Cup qualifier with the Denmark result still being talked about in the media. Becks was given a new deep-lying central-midfield role and I thought it was an interesting idea to play him there. It meant that Shaun Wright-Phillips, who at the time was in brilliant form, got a place he deserved in the team.

Sven brought him off when he was just getting into it, which was a strange move. Becks had just started finding him with his long-range passes and their defence looked worried. Still, we won the game with a goal from Joey Cole, although it took a worldy of a save by Paul Robinson from John Hartson's header to make sure.

It was good to be up against Johnny again, but he didn't see much of the ball and although Giggsy caused us a couple of problems here and there it wasn't the hardest of outings.

We were criticised for our performance which was fair dos, really, because we weren't great, but we were never under huge pressure either and we'd got the points. But the critics had their day when we went on to Belfast and lost to Northern Ireland the following Wednesday.

We knew it was going to be a tough game. The Windsor

Park pitch was really sticky but that was no excuse because, on paper, we were easily the stronger team. Their fans were right on top of us, it was raining hard and everything started going wrong.

Wazza got frustrated with the situation because things weren't happening for the team. He shouted at the ref when he gave a free kick to them which should have been for us. It was a poor decision and Wazza said so. Becks moved in to calm it down and Wazza told him to fuck off.

As we were going off at half-time, Becks said something else to Wazza and I joined in saying, 'Wazza, just relax, man,' and he told me to fuck off as well! If you knew how many times team-mates say 'fuck off' to each other during a game you'd be amazed. It happens all the time. The fact that the cameras are always on Wazza makes him look worse than he really is.

In the dressing room Wazza apologised to Becks and when he came out for the second half he patted Becks on the back. There was no grudge or anything like that and I didn't feel it had an unsettling effect on the team at all, even though we lost.

You had to hand it to David Healy for the way he took his goal. He'll be a hero over there for a hundred years. To be fair they could have had another one near the end when they thrashed a shot right across goal. I was praying for Michael Owen to come up with the goods and save us but it didn't happen.

When that final whistle went I knew we were going to get mullered and rightly so. I wanted the ground to open up.

It was deathly quiet on the coach. Everyone was deep in thought, examining what they could have done better and what the team could have done better. I spoke to the coach, Steve McClaren, and said that people needed to be told more forcefully what their jobs were. I felt it was too quiet in the dressing room and everyone needed a kick up the backside. He did not disagree.

I suppose up to then we'd taken it for granted that we'd be going to the World Cup and this was a big wake-up call.

There was a huge inquest into the defeat and Wazza's temperament. Ten months earlier, in the friendly in Spain when Ashley Cole and Shaun Wright-Phillips got racially abused, Wazza had been slaughtered for losing his cool. But I honestly wasn't worried about Wazza's behaviour.

After the Northern Ireland defeat we were up against Austria the following month. There was some speculation that I could be dropped because it was the first time in ages that me, Sol Campbell and John Terry had all been available for the two centre-back places. And I wasn't exactly having a blinding time at United.

But I had one of my best training weeks of the season, felt really sharp, and thought there was no way I could be left out. Sol had only played three games since coming back from injury, so I didn't expect Sven to take a chance on him, whatever he thought of my form.

In training me and Sol got swapped around on both teams, which was unusual. Normally, you get an idea of who's going to play and who's not, but it was still quite vague at that point. Sven told us during the session that one of the three of us would be on the bench, but didn't say who. I still felt confident I would get the nod though.

Then, the next day just before training, I got the dreaded finger. He pulled me aside and said, 'Rio, it's hard to tell you this, but you're not going to be playing in the game. I'm picking Sol and John Terry.'

I stood there, stunned. What with my poor United form, this put the tin hat on it. It was ironic that I'd told McClaren people needed kicking up the bum and it was me who had been kicked hardest.

Sven said: 'When you're playing at your peak, you're the best, but you have to work hard and start playing consistently. Get your form back and then you'll get back in the team. But right now I'm going to give someone else a chance. You know what you've got to do to get back.'

Sven had to make a decision and I understood that, even if I didn't agree with it, but I was absolutely gutted and training that day was very difficult.

Afterwards, I just stayed in my room and went to sleep. I was meant to go home to see Rebecca, but I couldn't even do that. I didn't want to speak to anyone.

David Beckham texted me, telling me not to worry, to work hard and I'd be back in the team. I remember replying, 'My World Cup's finished, man.'

I was embarrassed, my pride was hurt, and it made me take a long, hard look at myself. I realised that I'd become too relaxed with the relief of signing the new contract at United.

It's not that I thought I was better than JT or Sol, I would never say that. I knew I had no divine right to be in the side. But for the sake of your pride you want to be playing. You don't want to be sitting on the bench or in the stand. I'd done all that at the beginning of my England career and had been a regular on the team for a long time.

Sometime later, I was on television and said that I'd wanted to come back to shove it down Sven's throat and prove to him that dropping me was wrong. I didn't mean it to come out quite the way it did, but that was the attitude Sven would have expected, I'm sure.

I spoke to Rebecca that night and was quite emotional. I said, 'I'm not going to play in the World Cup. That's it. Sol and JT are in for good now. '

Rebecca doesn't know much about football. She knows I don't usually like talking about it with her, so it would have been a shock that I was. That's how bad things were!

In the changing room before the match I tried my best to be bubbly, but I was lower than a snake's belly. Unbelievably,

Sol had to come off injured after an hour and I had to get out there, stop feeling sorry for myself and be solid.

I didn't want to do anything wrong. I made a couple of interceptions, won a header from a corner and did basic defending. It went well. We took the three points through a penalty by Frank and learned later that night that we'd qualified for the World Cup – at least as one of the best runners-up by virtue of Holland beating the Czech Republic. It meant the day finished a hell of a lot better than it started.

We had a few drinks to celebrate, but I wasn't in a big party mood. I was sure that if Sol was fit for our final qualifier against Poland he'd play.

Unfortunately for Sol, he had to go home and that gave me the chance to properly re-establish myself. Honestly, I was gutted for Sol because he's a mate and you don't want to get in a team through somebody being injured. But if the opportunity comes, you have to take it.

Sven pulled me to one side before the Poland game and said, 'Show me what I know you can do.' I was fine. We won to top the group and I had put myself in a position where if anybody wanted the shirt off my back they would have to fight me for it.

Signing my new deal at United wasn't like a light switch that made everything right again with the fans. They still had to be convinced of my commitment. I hadn't expected the transformation from supposed sinner to saint to come overnight. I knew it was going to take time and that some supporters may never change their opinion.

When we lost 4–1 at Middlesbrough and then away at Lille in the Champions League it was probably the worst week of my whole career. It came not long after England had lost to Northern Ireland and I'd been dropped for the Austria match.

The Middlesbrough defeat was my worst display in a United shirt, but I'd had a couple of dodgy games a few weeks earlier when we lost at home to Blackburn and won 3–2 at Fulham. Those games obviously contributed to my England demotion. I can see that now.

After signing the new contract I felt I didn't have anything to prove. Subconsciously I'd let things go and become too relaxed. Jimmy Floyd Hasselbaink made me look an idiot against Boro. I tried to be too cute and poke the ball out of play instead of blasting it and he scored. The manager subbed me, which was the most embarrassing thing I've ever had to go through as a footballer.

I'm not immune to getting substituted, but if a defender gets brought off then you know he's having a stinker. The boss didn't even look at me as I trudged off, not a flicker.

I watched the game later and his expression said it all. If he'd looked at me he'd have wanted to punch me. I was filled with emotion and embarrassment at the way I'd played.

My bad performances were coinciding with us losing games and we weren't playing well as a team. On Man United TV there was a spot where a player analyses a game. I'd done it many times before, every player has to do it, and it was Roy Keane's turn on the rota for the Boro game.

The club gets to see the show before it is broadcast and on this occasion it was blocked from going on air. I wasn't even aware it hadn't gone out until I saw the papers the next morning.

The reports said that Roy had been slamming a few of the young lads – Fletch, Kieran Richardson, Sheasy and me. Apparently, he had questioned my right to my wages for that performance.

Roy wasn't around much at the time because he was injured, so I hadn't seen him for a few days. But the next morning when we came in he was there and he told the manager he wanted to speak to us and play the tape.

We were all in the changing room and he said, 'Listen, I still wouldn't mind the tape going on air. I would have been happy for it to be played. I think it should have been played. The papers have made a meal out of what was said on the video. I never mentioned anyone's wages and I didn't insult anybody. I judged the performances honestly and if you are not criticising yourselves in the same way then you shouldn't be at United.'

He was 100 per cent right. He couldn't have criticised me any more than I did myself. After the match I couldn't get to sleep until about five in the morning.

We watched the tape together. Roy highlighted the goals and said, 'Rio should have done better there. I've seen him make that mistake before. He should have just dealt with it and got it away. As for the other goal, he should have defended better because he went to the ball with the wrong foot.' It was just football analysis. I didn't have a problem with it.

He told Fletch that his missus could have tackled better than he did, but he said it tongue-in-cheek. He and Fletch understand each other. Keaney kind of looked out for Fletch.

He wanted Fletch to do well and that was the way he tried to get him to do better. I don't believe the media would have made as big a deal out of the tape if it had been played. There would not have been much of a story.

Keaney had just come back from injury and had been due to play in a reserve game, but the manager pulled him out of it. The next day, the gaffer came out after training and said that Keaney had left the club.

We were in shock. I remember Ruud going 'shit'. I never expected Keaney to go, no way. The gaffer didn't explain anything to us. He just said they had come to an agreement for Keaney to move on. Despite what the press had said, I don't think there would have been any dressing-room unrest if Keaney had stayed. We all got on well with him. There's nothing on that tape that he wouldn't have said to our faces.

What is said on the pitch or in training is not personal. If you do take it personally you shouldn't be in football. We will have a go at one another for only one reason, for the benefit of the team. It's not meant to be negative, it's to help us become a winning team.

It was sad the way Keaney went. There's always going to be that feeling that he left under a cloud. I hope the fans will remember him for all he did for the club and what a magnificent player he was.

The players trust the gaffer and if he believes it was the right time for Keaney to go, then it's not for us to pass judgement or question his decision. I never imagined Keaney would ever leave United. He and the gaffer got on well and would have a joke with each other.

I thought he would be the next manager, would stay at United for another couple of years as a player, then get into the coaching side to learn his trade. He'd said that he'd like to be a manager one day, but it wasn't up to him. Now he's in the hot seat at Sunderland I'm sure he'll be a big success.

The day after Keaney left I saw him as we came off the motorway at the same turn-off. He bibbed me and drew up alongside me at the lights. I wound down my window and said, 'What's going on, man? Have you gone for definite?' He said that he had and that he was just going to chill for a while and see what happened. I wished him good luck and said that I hoped things worked out for him and he drove off. A few weeks later he announced he was joining Celtic, a club which had always been close to his heart.

People have the impression that Keaney was a bit of a loner, but he wasn't, he was one of the lads. He spoke to Giggsy and Gary Neville a lot and was good mates with Nicky Butt. Keaney's a family man and always wanted to get home to them but that didn't make him a loner. Whenever the team went out Keaney was there. He wouldn't miss any dos we had as a group. In the changing room he was always one of the loudest, having a laugh but when it came down to the business of football he was very serious.

I've got used to Keaney not being there now, but at first it was strange. He had his spot in the changing room where he always sat, spraying his feet with stuff which hardened the soles. He would also chuck used socks at you when you weren't looking. But he's not there anymore and you've got to move on. No player, no matter how great, plays for ever.

Keaney came back to the training ground once to say goodbye to the lads and the backroom staff. And he had a testimonial between United and Celtic at Old Trafford at the end of the season. He played one half for United and the other for Celtic and gave all the lads a watch as a thank you for taking part. I played central midfield against him in the first half and got him to sign the shirt I wore, which I've had framed.

The match was a fitting occasion for a player who gave such great service to the club and the game. I reckon he was the most influential player there has ever been in the Premier League.

The manager had said in the past that I could be the next captain of United after Keaney. I had had a go at it the previous season when Keaney was injured. But I wasn't considered as captain when Keaney left, even though I was one of the most senior players in the team.

The lads were asking what had happened between me and the gaffer, but the truth was nothing had happened. I was disappointed and figured it must have been because of what had gone on with the contract. Or maybe the manager just didn't see me as captaincy material, simple as that. I'd always said I'd like to be captain at the club, but it wasn't to be.

When the gaffer mentioned a couple of possible captains

to the papers and I wasn't one of them that told me the writing was on the wall.

You can't have what you want all the time can you? That's the way it goes. Shit happens.

Gary Neville got the job and is a great man for it. He's fantastic, he is Mr United. When we were going through our dodgy spell, Peter Schmeichel came out and said that all the United players were interested in was diamonds and cars and that I only ever thought of myself. I thought he was wrong. Football always came first. Schmeichel is a legend at Old Trafford, but I thought that if he'd had something to say, he should have spoken directly to me about it.

I'm always disappointed when an ex-player makes comments like that when he doesn't know the people he is talking about. I was disappointed in him. He was a player I had looked up to because of his magnificent career. Maybe I was an easy target because we didn't know each other. I'd met him in a restaurant when I first went to United but that was all.

It's unusual for ex-United players to come out on the attack so forcefully. But at the time he had a job to do on the BBC. It was wrong of him to get so personal though.

When we beat Chelsea at Old Trafford in November, thanks to Fletch's header, I stayed out on the pitch longer than usual, applauding all sides of the ground. I wanted the fans to know that I appreciated them. It was a small turning point for me in my relations with the fans.

My actions weren't premeditated, it was just something I felt I had to do at the time. Hopefully, the supporters can see by the way I play that I'm happy to be at United and I wear my shirt with as much pride as anybody else. I can see myself staying at United for the rest of my career.

EIGHTEEN

Savage Amusement

No punches were thrown, but he was whingeing on, going, 'What you doing? What you doing?' After the game, which we won to put us through to the final, we shook hands and I thought that was the end of it. Wrong, very wrong.

With United beating Chelsea and peace having been established with most of the United fans, I had a renewed confidence when England played Argentina in Geneva. It was a fantastic match and I witnessed a genius called Riquelme at work in their midfield.

He pulled all the strings. I'd seen him play before and thought I knew all about him. But Diego Forlan, who used to be at United and was Riquelme's team-mate at Villarreal, told me he was better than I realised.

Diego was right. Riquelme was rolling the ball this way and that with his studs and at half-time Ledley King said he couldn't get near him. Ledley wasn't the only one. Playing Argentina is always a blinding game and although this was just a friendly, there was something special about it.

They took Riquelme off when they were leading and ended up losing. It was a smash and grab by us, with Michael Owen heading a couple in the last three minutes. That game summed up what Michael is all about. You might not see him for 85 minutes then – bang, bang – we've won. It's amazing how many headers he scores for a little bloke. We missed that poacher's instinct when he got injured at the World Cup.

Peter Crouch coming on helped make a difference as well. He took two players with him, giving Michael the freedom to get the equaliser.

Crouchy had been getting some flak in the press, but he is a good footballer. He has a proper all-round game and great feet. Not just for a big man – he's got great feet, full stop. He's a nuisance.

I thought we deserved a draw, but to win was remarkable. The country believed in us again and the media was saying we were going to win the World Cup. One game doesn't make you into World Cup winners, but everyone was getting over-excited. I wasn't about to get carried away. It was too early to judge.

It's always nice to beat the Argies, though, especially as we later heard how they'd been jumping around on the bus before the match singing songs and supposedly calling us all sorts of names. Well, they got their answer.

After the traumas of the Denmark and Northern Ireland defeats to then go and qualify for the World Cup and beat Argentina was a major turnaround.

I scored my first goal in 140 games for United against Wigan on 14 December 2005. The ball came in from a Giggsy corner on the right and he drifted it in towards the near post. I met it and guided it towards the goal over my left shoulder. The keeper got a hand to it, but it wrong-footed the defender and went in.

It was an unbelievable feeling, I can tell you. I went bananas when I scored that. The manager said afterwards that it was about time I scored and I couldn't disagree with him. I'd spent enough time in the box at set-pieces. It had been coming, though. I had been getting on the end of a few and Ruud and Wazza had both scored goals after I'd headed on.

My next goal against West Brom came 12 days later and was a proper header. The ball came over and a defender, Curtis Davies, came with me. I jumped just before him and thumped it into the net over the keeper. We'd been working on my runs in training, a lot more than we had before, and it had paid off.

My problem had been that I would run past the front post well before the kicker even stepped up to the ball. I was never going to score from there, even if I did connect with the header. Usually it would just sail over the top of me and then I'd have to sprint back 60 yards. It was pointless me being up there, really.

You'd think I ought to have known where to run, but I'd never put much emphasis on getting goals. That wasn't why I was in the team. I'm pretty sure the boss would have liked me to stick a few more in though. And eventually he got his wish. I became a goal machine. Sort of . . .

The goals were coming thick and fast by my standards and the one against Liverpool in January was one of the highlights of my career.

The build-up to Liverpool games is at least on a par with the derby against City and slightly ahead of a match against Arsenal.

When you're walking down the road the week before a game, every Man United fan you meet goes, 'Make sure you beat those scousers.' There is an unbelievable atmosphere during those games. The noise is deafening.

This one wasn't a great match – in fact, it was quite boring, but the tension in the air was crackling. Neither team really opened the other one up. Then I went up for the corner as full-time approached and Gary Neville said to me, 'Go and bang one in.' And, of course, I always listen to Gaz.

The ball was brilliantly delivered by Giggsy. It just hit my head and I guided it in. If you look at a replay my head nearly sinks into my shoulders I get so crunched up. The keeper had no chance, couldn't hope to keep it out, and I exploded.

It doesn't get much better than to score a last-minute winner against Liverpool in front of the Stretford End. I thrust my arms in the air and the lads jumped all over me. I managed to stay standing acting kinda cool, going, 'Yeah, this is what it's about.' Then I got a burst of energy and ran down the touchline with Wes Brown on my back. After about ten strides my thighs were killing me and for the next couple of minutes I couldn't move. *Roy of the Rovers* stuff, no doubt about it.

I had made a bet with Anton that whoever scored the most goals in the season would win £1000. When he went 1–0 up he rang and asked if I wanted to make it £5000. But his youthful confidence was misplaced. I won 3–2 but I still haven't got any money. The Sky TV show *Soccer AM* presented me with the worst trophy I've ever seen to mark the achievement.

It was a massive football which must have been about a size 8, sprayed gold and mounted on a bit of wood. It's on the bar in my house because I like to remind Anton who won, but it's a shocker, it really is.

When we played Burton Albion in the FA Cup third-round replay – after we'd only managed a 0–0 draw at their place, one of the surprises of the round – the manager put me on as sub in midfield.

I came up against my old mate Andy Ducros who had been called up with me to train with the Euro 96 squad and had played with me in the England youth team. We hadn't seen each other for years. He's only about 5ft 4in yet as a teenager I remember him playing up front for Coventry against West Ham in the Premier League.

It was good to see him again. He was a great little player when he was a kid. He had a good touch and skills and I called him the new Peter Beardsley. But it didn't quite work out for him. He played well in that game, although at one point he did ask if I could stop running around because he was not used to the pace at the top level any more.

Good lad Andy though, unlike Robbie Savage.

At half-time in the second leg of our Carling Cup semi-final against Blackburn at Old Trafford in January 2006 I jogged past Savage and told him to stop acting like a tart, stay on his feet and pack the diving in because, as far as I could see, he'd been rolling around on the pitch giving it some drama.

As I was going down the tunnel I sensed him running up behind me. I turned round, he made some smart-arse comment and we ended up pushing and shoving each other and at one stage he fell down. And that was about it until loads of security piled in and stopped us. No punches were thrown, but he was whingeing on, going, 'What you doing? What you doing?'

After the game, which we won to put us through to the final, we shook hands and I thought that was the end of it. Wrong, very wrong.

Soon after, we played a Premiership game at Blackburn and I was in midfield against him. Other than a mistake with a back-header which cost us a goal, I didn't play that badly. But, somehow, they won 4–3 and I got sent off.

I first got booked for a challenge on Morten Gamst Pedersen who, in my view, made a meal out of it and went down holding his knee. Then when the ball was bouncing around near the end I ran through to take it. Savage was coming in from one side and Pedersen from the other. All three of us had our feet at the same height and me and Savage came together, sideways on.

How I could have kicked him hard enough to send him down, grimacing in pain, I don't know. But down he went, landing on my calf, and I heard him scream.

Straight away I knew something was going to happen because of Savage's behaviour. I saw the referee pulling out his card and the only person he booked was me. Unbelievable.

Savage was on the floor, rolling around, and I'm sent off to the changing room for a second yellow.

I barged through the door and was so pissed off. I'd never been sent off before in my life, not at school, not for my youth team, not for anybody. Now that record was gone and in my mind it was through Savage's acting which, unfortunately, has become part of the game.

I was totally gutted and I felt cheated as well because of the way he'd gone down. I was crying and started chucking drinks round the changing room. I kept saying to Alby, our kit man, 'How can I be sent off for that? That's never a sending off.'

Alby was going, 'I know son,' while running round cleaning up after me, making sure it was tidy before the manager came in. Good bloke, Alby. No reason to piss the boss off even more. Losing was enough.

To make it worse, my calf was buggered. I could hardly walk.

When I was on the coach, one of my mates texted me asking how come Savage had been carried off on a stretcher. I didn't know. The lads said he'd gone off with his arms crossed like he was in a coffin. We'd barely connected with each other and he's gone off on a stretcher, how the hell does that happen?

I would be embarrassed with myself if I acted like that. If I saw Anton do that in a game I would hammer him. I get embarrassed enough when Anton does his silly dance after a goal, so if he did that and went down too easily, like he'd been poleaxed, I'd muller him.

I quite enjoyed my little spell in midfield and thought I did quite well. But I'm better as a centre-half and you should play where you play best. Given time, I could be a midfielder, but I got into the West Ham team playing centre-half and I got moves to Leeds and Manchester United by being a centre-half, so what's the point in changing a formula that works?

If I was living in a fantasy world and could pick where I wanted to play I'd be a number 10, just off the front man doing outrageous skills, better than Ronaldinho and Zidane.

I sometimes wonder what would have happened to my career if I'd played a different position. I doubt I'd have done as well. Maybe in the midfield holding role I'd have done okay, but as an attacking midfielder I wouldn't have got to the top. I'm too old for a drastic change but if the manager wants me to do it and feels it's right for the team then I will.

We went out in the FA Cup fifth round at Liverpool thanks to a Peter Crouch header. I didn't play in the game but I had an eventful day all the same.

Me and Sheasy were both injured and decided we wanted to experience the game as proper fans. We turned down tickets in the directors' box and decided to go in the away end at Anfield. We went with one of Wes Brown's mates, Leon, and a guy called Abu who was our driver.

The car had tinted windows but they weren't that dark and we had to crouch down in the back seat so the Liverpool fans wouldn't see us as we came towards the ground. We had to leave the car in Stanley Park and walk the last few hundred yards. I had a cap on, a scarf round my face and a coat with a big hood. All you could see were my eyes. I looked like a proper wrong'un! The adrenaline was pumping as we walked towards the gates when suddenly these coppers sprang out and demanded we all take our hoods off so they could see our faces.

Sheasy protested that we couldn't, but one of the coppers just snatched my hood and cap off my head. The Liverpool fans went absolutely mad when they saw who I was. I felt like I was completely starkers!

The match commander appeared and gave us an escort to the away end, for our own safety. The fans followed us all the way, pointing out who we were.

When we got inside we put our hoods, cap and scarves back on, so we'd be anonymous, and took our places among our own fans.

When Crouchy scored, our supporters were showered with urine and coins by the Liverpool fans in the upper tier. We were lucky we were far enough back to escape from it but it wasn't pleasant for those in front of us.

I'd forgotten what it was like to be a proper fan and what different characters you get. Some supporters, on both sides, had obviously not come for the football, they were just there to shout abuse at each other.

Mind you, I was shouting at the ref as well and I felt helpless when Alan Smith got badly injured and I was not around to see how he was. Nobody clocked us until near the end when, because it was so hot and we were sweating like mad, we removed our hats and scarves.

The fans were amazed to see us and demanded we give them a song. I did mine and then Sheasy came out with some lame little chant and the fans started singing, 'What the fucking hell was that?' I was gutted we lost, but it was an amazing experience to be a fan for a day. We even got kept in for half an hour at the end!

Our only chance of silverware for the season was the Carling Cup. We were expected to beat Wigan in the final, but we had completely dominated the previous season's FA Cup final against Arsenal and had lost on penalties, so we weren't taking anything for granted.

In the Wigan midfield was Graham Kavanagh. I'd had a word with him earlier in the season when we played them at their place and asked whether he remembered me from the Middlesbrough days. He did. He even remembered the mad hair with a high top I had at the time.

Wigan had beaten Arsenal in the previous round and were going well, but in the end we won comfortably. We played well on the day – the big players performed and we scored the goals.

I'd been in two cup finals previously and lost both so it was definitely a moment to savour. It's always good to get some silverware on the table, whatever people think about the merits of the competition.

I refused to swap shirts at the end, even though a couple of their players asked me. I wasn't being ignorant but it was my first cup final success and I wanted my shirt to go with the medal, which takes pride of place alongside my Premiership one.

That wasn't the only thing I won last season, though. I picked up over £100,000 cash from a bookies' runner who delivered it to me in a paper bag. I cannot describe how much of a buzz I got seeing all that money lying on the passenger seat of the car.

I don't have a clue what the geezer who runs the betting operation – which is a special one for footballers – looks like. He could walk past me in the street and I wouldn't know him. But it was a safe and very easy way to have a flutter.

You just texted him on your mobile saying '£5,000 on the three-legged nag in the 2.30' and it was done. I would keep the sums totted up in my head, but every now and again they would text you your balance. Then there would come a point where they either texted you saying, 'Any chance of some of the money?' or you texted them saying, 'Can I collect?'

It was weird not dealing in actual money. We just texted a figure and they texted us a figure back. It was five or six months before I collected on a load of bets that I'd placed on foreign football, horses, greyhounds and rugby league.

I've always liked watching greyhound racing. I used to go when I played at West Ham. And I'm quite into rugby league. I watch it on Sky on a Friday night.

Getting the money was like something out of a film. This geezer just turned up in a car park and handed the money over to me in a Gap bag. There were all these £50 and £20 notes.

No matter what I've earned, I've never seen that sort of money in real cash. It was amazing. I couldn't stop looking in the bag. I was laughing. I still can't get my head round it now. I earn a great deal of course but you don't actually see it there in front of you. It's numbers on your payslip.

I drove home very slowly. God knows what the police would have thought if they'd stopped me for speeding and found all that cash on the front seat.

When I got home I told Rebecca to look in the bag and she went white. She thought I'd robbed a bank and went, 'What are you doing with that, how did you get it?' I explained where it came from, paid some bills and put the rest in the building society.

It was great, but that's it. I've had my fun. I'd be very lucky to pull off a coup like that again and I don't want to take the risk of having to hand it back.

The gaffer pulled me aside and asked if I was involved in any of the betting stuff being reported in the papers. I said I'd had a few bets and he wanted to know if they were big amounts. I told him the truth, that it was a few thousand here and there and the gaffer said, 'My advice to you is to quit while you're ahead.'

He didn't have to tell me that, I was going to do that anyway. I'd never really gambled before. I used to bet, and lose, on the Grand National every year. My uncle used to go down the bookies on a Saturday and did the pools as well, but that was the extent of it in our family.

I don't know how much other players bet but everyone's threshold is different. We all have different perceptions of what we think is a big or small punt. If I was betting some of the figures you see in the papers I wouldn't be able to sleep at night.

I'll gamble up to a few thousand a time. I do realise that

is a hell of a lot of money and I'm not being flash about it, but it's all about what you can afford to lose. You would never catch me betting six figures. I'd be too nervous and my mum and dad would kill me if they found out.

I play in the England card schools occasionally, but I'm not religiously involved. It's only every now and again. I don't have an addictive personality. If I was told tomorrow that I couldn't have a bet for the rest of my life, it wouldn't bother me. I can go into a casino and not play the tables. I'll have a meal or a drink instead.

I've only been betting on foreign football for the last year or so because there's a lot of live games on the TV from all over the world and a little flutter adds a bit of interest. I don't do any of those complicated bets. It's win or lose. I might bet on six teams to win throughout all the leagues in Europe and do an accumulator, but that's as technical as it gets. I can't be bothered with all that first corner, first throw nonsense.

I do feel some of the restrictions put on players gambling by the football authorities are ridiculous. If you want to have a little bet on a game, what's the problem? That said, I don't think we should be able to bet on our own games, that's probably too much to ask.

But I honestly don't believe footballers would throw matches.

There are 22 players out there and millions of fans and you're going to throw a game for a few thousand pounds? You've got to be some stupid idiot to do that. It's also very difficult to fix a team sport. The best chance is to bribe the ref otherwise I don't see how you can be in control of the bet. As has been proved in Italy, getting to the refs is the only way to ensure success. That's why Juventus were relegated.

In one West Ham game the ball went straight out for a throw-in from the kick-off. People said it was a scam, but to pull something like that off you'd have to win the toss first, that's only a 50-50 chance. Then you'd have to make sure the ball went out. Somebody could easily have stopped it.

I've never known players to fall out over betting. I've been involved with England, Man United, Leeds and West Ham and I've never witnessed an argument about money.

And, despite certain stories I've read, I haven't seen any players betting £30,000 on the turn of a card. If it did happen no one told me. I have known players lose £30,000 at cards, but that's over a period of time.

We don't have any cash on the table. What a shame that was not the case all those years ago in La Manga when I was £800 up and Hoddle made me go to bed before I could get back into the room. We use poker chips these days which have a value not necessarily related to the figure on the chip but usually the games are for a few hundred pounds not thousands.

Footballers get criticised if they lose a big bet because it is argued they could have done something better with it, but a lot of players I know give thousands and thousands to charity, and don't brag about it.

Sportsmen should be allowed to gamble if they want. It's their money and they can do what they like with it.

Sheikhen but Not Stirred

The story had no effect on what I thought of Sven as a boss and didn't make me have any less belief in him as a manager. He still wanted to win the World Cup and was going to do his job to the best of his ability.

It was announced Sven was to give up the England manager's job even before we got to the World Cup.

He got done in the *News of the World* by the so-called Fake Sheikh who was an undercover reporter. Sven told him that Becks wanted to come back from Real Madrid, Michael Owen had only gone to Newcastle for the money and I was lazy.

My first feeling was that he'd been stitched up. I couldn't see the point of a paper doing that when we were on our way to the World Cup and the nation should be getting behind Sven and the team. But I also wondered why Sven would say those things to someone he didn't even know.

He shouldn't have been discussing personal details about players with a stranger. I got a message to ring Sven at home and Nancy answered. She put Sven on and he said, 'Rio, I guess you've seen the paper. All I can say is I'm sorry about what's been written and they didn't print all of what I said. I also talked about your capabilities and how good you are and I said that because you're so good, you don't need to work as hard as others, so you can become lazy sometimes. I'm sorry.'

I told him that he didn't need to explain himself to me and that I wasn't hurt by what he'd said, which I wasn't. It was done. He couldn't go back on it and it wasn't a big problem as far as I was concerned.

This lazy tag comes up all the time but I don't think I am. I have a style that makes me look that way, but I cannot help that. I'm as dedicated as any player. Rebecca might say I'm lazy for leaving dirty plates and glasses around the house, but that's about it.

As for what was said about Michael and Becks, that was their business.

The story had no effect on what I thought of Sven as a

boss and didn't make me have any less belief in him as a manager. He still wanted to win the World Cup and was going to do his job to the best of his ability.

The next week there was another story in the *News of the World* about Sven and his agent, Athole Still, saying managers and clubs were allegedly involved in dodgy transfers. I knew the mere fact there was another story was going to be trouble. Sven had ridden the first one out but now things were obviously going to be a lot more difficult for him. It was one story too many.

I thought he might have to go there and then, but instead it was agreed he would leave after the World Cup.

I'd always had a feeling that he would go then anyway, whatever happened. I felt that if we won the World Cup he would leave as a hero and if he didn't he would want a fresh challenge and the FA would probably want a change too.

The media are very hard on England managers. Both Terry Venables and Glenn Hoddle were forced out over issues not related to results. For me the England manager should be judged on what he does with the team and the rest of it is secondary.

I used to think that went for the players too, but I have realised that we do have a responsibility off the field because children look up to us and want to be like us. It took me a long time to understand that.

I didn't think announcing that Sven was going would affect our World Cup chances. It had happened in previous tournaments with Bobby Robson and Venables and both times England had got to semi-finals – Robson at Italia 90 and Venables at Euro 96.

It didn't diminish my desire to play for England and try to win the World Cup and I'm sure that went for the other players as well. You do it because you have the Three Lions on your shirt. You do it for your country. I don't think the announcement did affect us in the end even though we only reached the quarter-finals. It was nothing to do with the fact that the manager was going to leave.

I liked Sven and I thought he brought a good ambience to the England squad. The Hoddle regime was more regimented and less enjoyable even though he was a great coach.

Sven never said much at training but his views and opinions came through his coach, Steve McClaren. Sven told Steve what he wanted and Steve relayed it to the players in training.

There were accusations in the media that the players picked the team but it was more the case that Sven would consult us. He'd ask senior squad members our opinions and what we thought of a certain formation he was going to play. He wanted us to feel comfortable with it. If we didn't, he might have a re-think but in the end the final decision was always the manager's.

Most of the time the players had no problem with changes. Players can adapt to different formations as they prove week in week out with their clubs. As I've said, Sir Alex has asked me to play in midfield a few times and that is fine by me.

It was said that Paul Scholes retired after Euro 2004 because he didn't like where Sven wanted him to play. But I think Scholesy had just had enough of travelling and wanted more time with his kids.

The FA put themselves under huge pressure by saying they were going to name the next manager before the World Cup. They didn't need to do that. It was unfair on the new man and unfair on Sven as well. For three months the story was never out of the headlines. I thought we should have been concentrating on the World Cup.

I wasn't bothered who got the job, whether they were English or foreign.

Big Phil Scolari clearly had it in his grasp at one point and his record spoke for itself which was why the FA went for him. And if they'd got him it would have been very interesting, given what happened in Germany.

Scolari had won the World Cup with Brazil, got the host nation, Portugal, to the European Championship final and was up there with the best managers in international football. It was obvious why they were trying to bring him in. Scolari had loads of photographers following him round when it became clear he was the favourite and he dropped out of the race saying he didn't want his privacy invaded. I can understand that. The media scrutiny the England manager has to deal with is like nothing else. When it was finally decided to give the job to Steve McClaren I was quite happy. All the players agree that he is a fantastic coach.

We beat Uruguay in a friendly in March by 2–1 thanks to a late winner from Joe Cole. I didn't have the best of nights. I tried to go round my old United team-mate Diego Forlan early on, he robbed me and I only just got back to tackle him. It didn't get much better. It was like I was playing with two left feet. It was one of those nights.

It crossed my mind that my place could be in jeopardy again but I was in good form for United by then so I reasoned that would count in my favour.

And we'd chalked up another win, our fourth in a row. A good habit to get into. I felt we had the potential to win the World Cup, but I didn't want to talk about it publicly because I thought it would bring bad luck.

I knew having been to two World Cups would stand me in good stead and I felt it was a great opportunity for us. I figured that if we approached the tournament right, avoided injuries and got a bit of luck on the day, as every team needs, then we'd be all right.

Former chief executive Adam Crozier had said when Sven

took charge that the plan was to win the 2006 World Cup. Now the day of reckoning was approaching. The quality of the team spoke for itself. Our fans and the foreigners weren't saying we could win it just because Crozier had said it all those years ago. They were saying it because they could see the team's potential with their own eyes.

But bad luck gave us a kicking earlier than usual, on 29 April to be precise, when Wayne Rooney famously broke a metatarsal against Chelsea at Stamford Bridge. We were getting stuffed but Wazza was still chasing and as he burst into the box he went down.

At first I thought it was a penalty but no one was appealing and I expected Wazza to get straight back up as he usually does. After a couple of minutes, I realised there was a problem and me and Gary Neville ran over. Wazza was still on the floor and I kicked him on his arm. That might sound daft but sometimes if you kick someone and they don't move it means the pain is serious. Wazza twitched a bit and went, 'What?' and I said, 'You all right?' He said, 'Yeah, I'll be okay,' and, although he got carried off, I thought it probably looked worse than it was. We were 3–0 down and that was bothering us more than anything else.

When we got to the changing room Wazza was on the bed with ice on his foot and his mood had changed. He said, 'I think I've broken it. It feels the same as the last time.' He'd suffered a similar injury at Euro 2004.

The day was going from bad to worse. We'd been hammered by the team who had confirmed themselves as champions by beating us and I just wanted to get out of there. Also my old mate Joe Cole had beaten me rather easily for one of their goals with a nice bit of skill, which didn't help my mood.

I was worried about Wazza. I was praying that he would be fit for the World Cup. On the way home I kept saying to him, 'Is it all right?' and he kept saying, 'It doesn't feel right. I feel like I've done something bad to it. I feared if it was broken he might miss the World Cup.

I spoke to Wazza the next morning on the phone and he confirmed the worst. But he said that Dr Stone, and the physios, thought there was a chance he could make it to Germany. That was something to hold on to, which was good. But in all honesty, I'm one of those 'what will be, will be' types. I wanted Wazza with us but if he wasn't then we'd have to make do.

Wazza isn't the sort of bloke who gets depressed, or if he does he doesn't show it. He wasn't crying about it. He was determined to get on with his rehabilitation. He knew that even if the bone healed in time there would still be a battle on to regain his fitness. He was prepared to work as hard as he could. But was he going to be as sharp as he was before? Was he going to have that same explosive power? Time would tell.

We met up in Portugal at the magnificent Vale de Lobo complex to begin our World Cup preparations and the lads couldn't resist taking the mickey about a picture of me having my hair done which appeared in the papers.

I had been sitting in the hairdressers, waiting to get my braids put back in and because it was quite a nice day the door was open. A photographer must have been tipped off and a car pulled up at the door. Before I knew it, a geezer in the back started snapping away. I couldn't run out and have a go because my hair was all over the place. Imagine what a picture of me running down the road would have looked like? Kids would have been crying with fright for years if they'd seen that. And who could blame them!

I was lucky in one sense because the season had finished at United so my team-mates weren't around to stick the picture on my locker. But the England lads let me have it, calling me Diana Ross.

I got them back though with my World Cup wind-ups show which we produced for ITV.

The plan was to play tricks on seven different players: David James, Ashley Cole, Wayne Rooney, Gary Neville, Peter Crouch, Shaun Wright-Phillips who unfortunately missed out on selection for the World Cup, and David Beckham.

We did Gaz Nev first, getting him for traffic offences. We set up in such a big underground car park that it took a whole day to wire up all the cameras. I was sat in a van nearby where I could watch the monitors.

After chasing Gaz into the car park with sirens blazing, an actor posing as a Scouse policeman showed him a picture of his car. He goes, 'Do you know why we stopped you?' and Gaz goes, 'No,' and he says, 'Well today you were doing 70 in a 60 zone.' Gaz's facial expressions were a picture. I was crying with laughter.

The fake copper says, 'I'll tell you what, instead of me giving you six points just take a photo with me and I'll forget about the six points.' Gaz goes, 'No, fuck you. I'll take the six points. I ain't having a photo with you. I'll have the six points and I'll do you for bribery.' He just wouldn't have it. It was so funny.

And then when the copper told him the exhaust emissions from his Range Rover were over the legal limit I thought Gaz was going to blow his own exhaust pipe!

I did Gary first, knowing that he is a responsible lad and that if he didn't react well to it we'd have to rethink the programme. Fortunately, he cracked up. If I had felt that anybody was going to be made to look an idiot I wouldn't have done it.

The actual hits took about 20 minutes but they were a long time in the planning. They were a combination of my ideas and those of the production company.

With Ashley Cole's hit the hardest bit was getting him there. He'd been set up to help record a charity record, but at the last

Becks was going for a meeting with adidas one afternoon after training in Manchester and we took our chance.

My driver Jason was the chauffeur and he brought along his mate who's an actor. We made him out to be another driver. On the way to the adidas shoot the guy says, 'I've got to drop something at the police station because I had a crash earlier, I hope you don't mind.' Becks gets a bit irate, starts swearing, tells the driver it's out of order and rings his agent.

The agent rings me and says I should stop because Becks was getting really upset. But it was a wind-up, that was the point, so I decided to let the camera run and see where it took us.

I hadn't anticipated what would happen next. Suddenly, as Becks' car rolled up to the lights, he jumped out while the vehicle was still moving!

He was in Moss Side, which is a notorious area, but he just ran across the road and down the opposite lane. I was in the car behind and jumped out after him shouting, 'Becks! Becks!' He turned round but a lorry went past at the same time and blocked me from view so he carried on running. I kept shouting and eventually he turned round, realised it was me and stopped.

He was standing there with a confused look on his face and said, 'What's going on here?' I said, 'Flipping hell, you've just got merked, man,' which is a London term for when someone's used a bit of skill and tricked you.

Becks saw the funny side and was laughing, but later that afternoon I heard that the papers were going to run a story about how Becks thought he'd been kidnapped. That sounded serious, but he told me he'd just been worried that he was late for his meeting and was getting annoyed. He never realised it was a wind-up at any point. As he'd been playing in Spain he hadn't seen any publicity about the show so he was caught cold.

minute he said he couldn't do it because he was doi
and had to attend a sit-down session with his writer
ring Ash and plead with him not to let us down.

The idea was that he had to help produce a cha
in an area for deprived kids with behavioural problem
he arrived there was a producer in the studio who sho
the buttons he needed to press to start and stop the so

Ash is in there for a couple of minutes on his ow
the producer comes back and goes, 'The song's gone. V
the song gone?' Ash says, 'I ain't done nothing. I press
button you told me to press.' Then the guy goes, 'You
understand, this is my livelihood. I've got a top Am
producer coming over today. He's spent loads of money o
package and you've gone and deleted it.'

The American producer comes in and goes, 'Are you g
to play the track?' and the other guy says, 'The track's g
Ash is beside himself and the producers are going nuts. T
I jump out and I think Ash was more relieved than anyth
else.

I loved the one that we did on Wazza, where he went
open a kennel at the dog shelter and a vet asked him for son
help with an operation. When the vet goes out, the dog (whic
was stuffed, don't worry) 'snuffs' it on the operating table. Th
kid whose dog it is then blames Wazza for killing his pet. Wazz
was panicking there, I can tell you.

The one with Becks caused the most hysteria. It led to headlines that Becks feared he'd been kidnapped!

I'd spoken to the guy who looks after him, Terry Byrne,
and he'd cleared it. We needed to get it 100 per cent right
because it cost about £60,000 to set up the equipment. There
were four cameras in the car and they had to be all rigged up
so you couldn't see them. We almost had to take the car apart
and rebuild it.

We had been followed by a paparazzi guy that day and I reckon he was the one who put the kidnap theory about. The geezer had said he'd consider not putting out any of the pictures he'd taken, but in the end he did.

He's got a job to do, I suppose, but I was annoyed he'd gone ahead and published them.

The programme got mostly positive reviews, although a few slagged it off. All I can say is that they must have no sense of humour. It went down great with the players, they were buzzing about it. And the viewers must have liked it because ITV repeated it a couple of months later.

I love a prank and I'm sure the lads will be working on ways to get me back but that's okay. If you dish it out you've got to take it.

I remember one time when me and Frank turned a fire extinguisher on Steve Lomas and John Moncur during a pre-season tour with West Ham. Steve really suffered because it went all over his bed and he had to sleep on wet sheets.

They got us back though. After training the next day there was a horrible smell lingering around my gear and I discovered somebody had done something very unpleasant in a book which was lying in my kit-bag. I never did find out what happened in the end of that story – needless to say I threw the book away. As for the culprit I'm guessing it was Moncs, although no one owned up.

The wind-ups show was the first programme I'd ever made and I loved it. It gave me a taste for doing more in the future. I wouldn't mind trying my hand at presenting or hosting shows more regularly one day. I wouldn't do just anything though. The vibes would have to be right.

The Beckhams held a party before we went to the World Cup which was a cracking do – sit-down dinner, followed by music and dancing and a star auction. I bought a Harley Davidson for £50,000 in the charity auction and I don't even ride a bike! I'm not allowed to ride for insurance reasons. And it's got nothing to do with being banned from driving so many times. It's a football thing. So that we don't get injured. The bike was an investment. It's got an England emblem on it and is signed by the whole World Cup squad.

The singer P. Diddy was one of the star guests and he offered the audience three choices to either record a song with him in America, party with him in New York for the weekend or stay at his house in the Hamptons with all his staff and be treated like a king.

The bidding got to about £100,000 and Wazza was battling it out with Sharon Osbourne, then he went, 'No, that's me finished. I'm not doing it.' So I told him, 'I'll go halves as long as he knows that we're both going.' Wazza kept on putting his hand up and when it got to £140,000, P. Diddy went, 'If you go to £150,000 you get all three offers.' I shouted to Wazza, 'Put your bloody hand up now!' He did, and we got it. I don't know when we'll get the chance to take up the offer, though. One thing's for sure, we're going to have to wait till Wazza's 21. To enjoy the partying on offer we're going to want to go to a few bars and clubs, and it's a 21 age-limit in the States!

It was the first Beckham party I'd been to. People think I've been to every single one of them, but I haven't because I don't usually like going to such glitzy events. But the team had been together for a week at the warm-up camp in Portugal and were really getting on well. Becks is a good lad and I'd got to know his missus a bit better out there. So I went along, although Rebecca couldn't go because she wasn't feeling great due to the fact she was now seven months pregnant.

There were so many different faces at the party and it was a great night. Me and Frank Lampard were sitting with our mouths open just like that time all those years ago when we went out with Jamie Redknapp and his team-mates.

James Brown walked past and Ozzy Osbourne, then Robbie Williams. It was unbelievable that the Beckhams were mates with all these people.

P. Diddy didn't know who the hell I was when I went up to chat to him but it was special for me to meet him. When James Brown started singing I was on the dance floor straight away and I reckon I'm a better dancer than he is! Robbie Williams sang for about 40 minutes and the whole floor was packed. Usually at these types of events people are so pretentious but this was different. No one had to be on their guard because it wasn't a public event.

I'm a huge *EastEnders* fan and at the party I was delighted to meet Ross Kemp who plays Grant Mitchell. I said to him, 'I can't believe I've met Grant,' and he told me how he'd seen me in Monaco a few years before but didn't have the balls to come and speak to me. I told him I knew how he felt – I almost bottled going up to him at the party.

Ray Winstone was there too, an absolute legend. I think he's brilliant, the most undervalued actor we've got.

The only disappointment that night was that they shut the bar at 4 a.m. We could have kept going till breakfast!

During the weeks leading up to the World Cup I got to know some of the newcomers in the squad, like Aaron Lennon, Scott Carson and Theo Walcott, none of whom I'd met before. When the squad had first been announced on 8 May, I was dazed for a good couple of hours.

Everyone picks their own squad in their head and I hadn't even thought about Lennon or Walcott, or Stewart Downing for that matter.

To me, Theo came from absolutely nowhere. I asked Harry

Redknapp about him. He had been his manager at Southampton before he was transferred to Arsenal and Harry said that he was so quick he could run through a puddle without making a splash.

When we later did one-on-ones with the youngsters in training, it was the quickest session I've ever had in my life.

It was almost laughable watching Theo and Aaron. None of us could match them for pace. They had rocket heels. It was funny the next day when Sky television showed a clip of the session. The only one they used was of JT being done twice by Aaron. I got away with it and JT was not happy.

I'd played against Lennon once and seen him in the Under-21s and he always looked very good. I was texting my mates saying, 'Lennon is waiting to be unleashed.' He was nicknamed Azza, which was a bit confusing given that Wayne's nickname is Wazza, but somehow we got by.

I could understand why Lennon had made the squad, but I wasn't sure about Walcott.

In my mind it was hard to justify his presence when there were other options like Darren Bent, the top English goalscorer in the league, and Jermain Defoe, who had often been in the team and the squad before.

With there being question marks over the fitness of two of our strikers, Rooney and Michael Owen, it was strange that we only took four front men. You would have expected another one, especially if a kid like Theo was being included. Like everyone else in the country, the players were stunned that we were bringing a lad who was untried for England.

No disrespect to Theo, but I felt it was like asking a Sunday League player to turn out in the Premier League. This was a pressure-cooker situation. There would be massive crowds of up to 70,000, let alone the millions watching on TV, and you just don't know how a 17-year-old kid is going to react, particularly one who the manager had never seen play. Surely it would have been better to take someone who knew how to get a goal at the top level.

In any other country, Bent would have been on the plane. You would have thought that his goal record during the season would have booked his ticket. But Darren didn't even make the standby list.

Jermain was nominated as the twenty-fourth man in the event of any injuries or Wazza not getting the okay to take part. Jermain was first class during the run-up to the tournament. He was there in Portugal and in Watford and Manchester for our two friendlies and was fantastic. You wouldn't have known that he wasn't in the squad. He was probably our best striker in training and, as I watched him, I was thinking, 'How can he not be going?'

Theo did all right, but you can't expect a young kid to come in and dazzle at training every day – it doesn't happen. He showed glimpses of what he was capable of, but he'd no experience in top-class football.

I could sort of see what the manager was thinking, that he could bring Theo on in the hundredth minute and he would frighten the life out of people. But we had Aaron to do that, a player who had proved himself in a Premier League season with Spurs. In the event, Theo didn't kick a ball in anger at the World Cup. I doubt that would have been the case if Bent or Defoe had gone.

I felt sorry for Theo because no blame should have been directed at him. It wasn't his fault he'd been picked. When I went to a World Cup at 19 I had more experience than Theo and it did me the world of good being there, finding out what the preparation before matches was like, how the squad operated etc. Theo could have travelled as an unofficial twenty-fourth man, knowing he wouldn't be playing from the outset.

He would be getting the experience of being around the World Cup scene but without the pressure.

There was an England B game against Belarus at Reading for the fringe players and those coming back from injury like Michael. We lost 2–1, but Crouchy played well and showed that he was going to be a worthy addition to the squad.

Those games are difficult because everyone is trying to do well for themselves and it's not as much of a team effort but Aaron Lennon was a shining light. He was unbelievable. His pace scared defences. I wouldn't have liked to face him in the World Cup heat, with your legs tiring so badly.

We beat Hungary 3–1 at Old Trafford in our first World Cup warm-up game. They scored a blinding goal from 30 yards but we played some decent football, with goals from JT, Stevie G and Crouchy and I was quite happy with the shape we were in. We then hammered Jamaica 6–0 on the Saturday and there was a carnival atmosphere at Old Trafford.

The game was a non-event once the first goal went in but it was still nice to get a good win under our belts before we left home. Crouchy scored a hat-trick in that game and became a cult figure.

His celebration robot dance will go down in history. I told him he should have done the Bogle, which is a Jamaican dance, but I don't think he has the rhythm for it. We'd seen him do the robot at Becks' party, and egged him on to do it in the match. Let's say it was a dance that suited Crouchy, and no one else. People warm to Crouchy because he's someone who can laugh at himself. He's a good lad.

He'd already scored two when we got a penalty and he took it. But he got too cocky and chipped it over the bar. I thought, 'What are you doing, man? Just put it in.' Their striker, Deon Burton, who I knew from years back, said, 'He's not going to make many friends taking liberties like that.' Professional footballers can't stand it when opponents get too cocky.

Luckily, Crouchy got another chance and produced a great finish to get his hat-trick. I was really happy that he'd scored that one because it took the heat off him. I also played a ball through for Michael Owen to score, which was a big moment for him. It was his first goal of the year after all his injuries.

In the sunshine, the crowd cheered each goal and then applauded Sven at the end. The mood was good.

We were under no illusions though. We knew a result like that didn't make us world-beaters.

CHAPTER
TWENTY

Great
Expectations

We'd played two games, got a maximum
of six points, had not conceded a goal,
qualified for the knockout stage with a
game to spare and made our best start to
a World Cup for 24 years. And we'd
avoided a possible upset. What more did
they want?

As we prepared to fly out to Germany the whole nation seemed to be obsessed with Wazza's injury and whether he would play or not.

You would have thought we were going with a squad of one and if Wazza didn't make it England would not be able to take part in the World Cup. The intense scrutiny on him was out of control. He had steadily been improving and everyone got very excited when he scored with a bicycle kick in training. But he had not had any physical contact with any other players. That was going to be his big test.

I admit he was doing a lot better than I had expected and was probably ahead of schedule, but at the same time there was a chance that he could break down. It's difficult to hold yourself back when you've been injured and are dying to play again.

There was a lot being made of a supposed rift between Manchester United and England over when Wazza might be able to play, but you could have put your house on a story like that being wheeled out. It goes back years. There's always been this supposed United v England warfare going on. But at the end of the day it was always going to be the doctors' decision whether he went or not, whatever either side said.

Wazza was desperate to play and I could understand where he was coming from. But when you're so young and exuberant you don't think about the consequences there could be if you come back too early. Wazza wasn't bothered about all the politics of who said what to whom, he just wanted to get out there.

I was nervous for him when he flew back to Manchester for a scan which would determine whether he would be able to play in the World Cup. It was going to break his heart if he was told he was out.

I saw him when he got in the car to go to the airport and wished him all the best. Then I was texting him during the day asking what was going on, but his phone was off. Can't say I blame him. We all had our fingers crossed for him.

We eventually found out he'd got the all-clear and when he walked through the front door of our hotel in Baden-Baden he apparently said, 'The Big Man's back.' That's what he calls himself, the Big Man. When he's describing himself after games or training he'll go, 'And the Big Man got up at the far post,' or, 'The Big Man shot at goal.' Funny thing is he's not really that big a bloke!

It was good news and the lads were happy for him.

Wazza would have been in contact with Sir Alex all the way through the process, I'm sure of that – and why not? The boss had to play a big part in it because Wazza's a Man United player first and foremost – they pay his wages. If your player is at the World Cup and there's a possibility of him putting himself at risk for the following season then the club has a right to have a say in what happens. United would not have tried to harm England's chances just for their own benefit. They were thinking of Wazza.

I was looking forward to the World Cup. I just wanted to get on and get the tournament started. The build-up wasn't without one embarrassing moment though.

The night after Wazza was passed fit Channel 4 ran a spoof documentary entitled *Sven: the Cash, the Coach and His Lovers* which, believe it or not, was being shown in the treatment room at our hotel while me and Wazza and a few others were getting a massage. We were shouting at the TV saying what a load of old crap it was and that it should never have been shown. We were hammering the birds in it and giving former FA secretary Faria Alam some stick.

There was this bit where 'Sven' was having it away with her over the kitchen table and I was having a right go at her. Wazza was tapping me on the shoulder, but I just carried on

until I looked round and realised why he'd been trying to attract my attention. Sven had just walked in the door.

Everyone started laughing, including the boss, and I said to him, 'Listen, boss I swear to you I was just saying that it's out of order making a programme like that, it's a liberty.' I was as red as a beetroot. Sven replied, 'If, and I mean if, it was true, maybe that is not the position I would have done it in.' Brilliant! Everyone in the room was cracking up and Sven walked out laughing. We didn't know he had that sense of humour. We'd seen a different side to him.

By the way, my lookalike in the programme was poor – I'm much better looking! I reckon they should have used Alistair McGowan, who does a great take-off of me. People wonder if I'm offended by it, but I'm not at all. If anything I'm flattered.

I met him at an awards ceremony one time and I think he was a bit worried about what I was going to say but I congratulated him on his work. I love his programmes. He's a funny bloke.

The facilities where we stayed at the Buhlerhohe Schlosshotel near the beautiful town of Baden-Baden were fantastic. It was a wonderful mountain retreat. The setting was perfect and the training pitch just up the road was excellent. We could not have asked for any more. Preparation-wise everything was sound.

We had a geezer out there called Bill Blood who's a masseur from Chelsea and he made my trip. I reckon he'd be worth £10 million on the transfer market. No one knew him apart from the Chelsea lads, obviously, but right from the first day he was cracking jokes. You'd get on the massage table and go, 'Come on, Bill, give us a joke,' and he would be off. The massage room was always the centre of activity, the hub of the banter. We'd go in there to watch games even if we didn't want the massage.

We also had an arcade area. I tried the golf simulator but I was bang average. I preferred the table tennis where I let a few of the lads know who's boss.

Theo beat me a couple of times on the Pro Evolution soccer game, but I was just easing him into the squad, as you do. I couldn't terrorise the lad on his first trip, could I? It got worse one night, after a match. Me and JT stayed up till five in the morning playing it. He must have beaten me three or four times and I have to say I didn't have the best of sleeps after that. I went to bed feeling really deflated. Honestly!

Joe Cole and Wazza are the worst losers at the game I've ever seen though. Joe will try and bite the control pad out of frustration and Wazza will punch the life out of anything in his sight or break the pad. It's the highlight of beating him.

While I enjoy the games I can survive without them. But I cannot do without my iPod. As long as I've got my music I'm happy. I couldn't function if I lost it.

I always go to training with my headphones on and get into a zone with certain songs. I just get a vibe that helps me concentrate.

When I was banned from driving and had a guy to take me to the ground on match day I used to have certain songs always playing in the car. They were from an album called *The Firm*, which had on it Nas, Foxxy Brown and Jay-Z.

They got me into a mindset I liked, a little bit aggressive, on the edge, even though you don't really see that side of my game when I play.

We had our own World Cup CD in Germany. Everyone in the squad picked their favourite track. I had 'Renegade' by Jay-Z and Eminem, a wicked song which gets you pumping. But there was some dodgy stuff on there as well, songs you could not believe were anybody's favourite. How about Michael Owen's choice, 'The Winner Takes it All' by Abba, or Paul Robinson's, 'Sweet Caroline' by Neil Diamond. Even Stevie G had an iffy one – Survivor's 'Eye of the Tiger'.

I watched a recording of the opposition the night before

every game. You could get DVDs of the teams you were playing, showing the goals they'd scored in their qualifying campaign, all their free kicks, corners and penalties.

The next morning it would be breakfast, then pre-match stretches, then lunch. On a match day I'd have a breakfast of porridge or Coco Pops with chopped banana on top. Anything you wanted was on hand. For lunch I might have Coco Pops and bananas again, then simple pasta. If I was feeling especially hungry it would be a bowl of pasta and broccoli with cheese on it, olive oil and lemon, as well as some bread and probably a little bit of chicken or fish, followed by a strawberry yoghurt with loads of honey. It was my own special diet.

Everyone is different. Some players have egg on toast and beans, some have pasta with mashed potato and beans and chicken and others have loads of toast.

With it being so hot at the World Cup we also drank loads of water and power drinks like Gatorade or Lucozades. From the time we woke up on match days to the game itself, I reckon we'd drink at least a couple of litres. There was always a great long queue for the toilet on the bus on the way to the stadium.

Most of our matches were in the late afternoon or evening, so after lunch we would go for a sleep, after which I'd have a shower and do some stretching in my room by myself with music blaring.

Wazza would come in about 20 minutes before we were due downstairs for the team meeting and we'd sit there and chat, not necessarily about the game.

Steve McClaren would go through the patterns of play and Sven would do his main team talk before we got on the bus.

He would tell us how he wanted us to play, but the main point was always more or less the same. He'd say, 'Make sure you go out there and get three points and win.'

On arrival at the stadium some players would go out on

the pitch to have a look around. It's only at big tournaments or cup finals that players tend to do that. I don't do it normally. In Germany I think I did it once. I preferred to be in the changing room and would either have my headphones on or be listening to the team music.

Ashley Cole has his headphones on constantly throughout the whole warm-up even when he's having a massage. Some players retreat within themselves, while others are buzzing around talking, having a laugh and doing mad things with the ball.

Steve McClaren and Sven were always walking around talking to individuals about certain things they wanted from them, like who would do what with set-pieces and so on.

We would then go out for the warm-up, come back in and, just before going out for the game, the manager would sit down with us and give us another talk – he'd be a bit more animated than he was in the hotel.

We had a little huddle in the changing room before every match. We'd all link arms and Becks would say a few things and different people would have a word afterwards like myself or JT.

Our first match was on 10 June, against Paraguay in Frankfurt and it was hot. Boiling hot.

We had talked in the months before about how the climate in Germany was going to be better for us compared to the stifling heat we'd faced against Brazil in Japan. So what happens? We come to the Paraguay game and it's the hottest day of the year, 38 degrees centigrade pitchside, over 100 degrees Fahrenheit.

It scares you a little bit and you start thinking about the heat rather than the game itself. My dad texted me beforehand and said, 'If you think about the heat, you'll let the heat beat you.' It helped me focus and I kept telling myself, 'Forget the heat, man, just play your game and you'll deal with it.'

Conditions were tough though, right up there with the

Brazil game four years earlier. There was not the same humidity, but it was absolutely roasting. It might be an old line but you really could have fried an egg next to the dugout.

I was breathing hot air and that was hard work in itself. I thought, 'If I do any more of this breathing I'll be knackered!' Thank God we scored early, after three minutes, when Becks' free kick was headed in by their captain, Carlos Gamarra, because in the second half I couldn't move. I was out on my feet, everyone was the same. When we looked at the video afterwards it showed the defence and the midfield weren't going forward at all.

Their striker Nelson Valdez was useful and had good movement and I was worried he might have enough in the tank to catch us out, but we survived.

I sat down in the dressing room afterwards thinking, 'This is going to be a long tournament. A really long tournament.' The good thing was that no more of our matches were going to be kicking off so early in the afternoon.

After the game, we'd drink buckets of water and have snacks to get our energy levels back up. I usually had a chicken and mushroom Pot Noodle. There's also chocolate bars, Jaffa Cakes, sweets, bananas, muffins, sandwiches, oranges, apples, milkshakes, energy drinks and water. All sorts. We had ice baths which are brilliant because you get in them for ten minutes and you come out feeling like a new man. A few people, like Jamie Carragher, even got in them at half-time.

Just as an aside, one very strange thing happened in that game. We had been joking in training the day before about whether we could hit this giant TV screen which was suspended high above the middle of the pitch. Somehow our goalkeeper Paul Robinson managed it with one of his clearances during the match. I reckon he did it deliberately just to prove it could be done. He's got a hell of a kick on him but there was no way any of his normal clearances would have gone that high. Annoyingly, Robbo's bit of fun meant the referee bounced the ball and insisted we kick it back to them, so proving he could do it wasn't too helpful!

It was good to come off with a win because Paraguay play in that heat on a regular basis. The atmosphere at the match was rather flat though, it was nothing like Japan or France. We had plenty of fans there, but maybe they had just expected us to win and after all we hadn't played particularly well. The most excited they got was when Wazza went out to do some training at the end. But it was the first game in the World Cup and it's fantastic to win, no matter how you do it.

There was a lot of discussion about whether Wazza would play in the second game, against Trinidad and Tobago in Nuremberg five days later. Sven had apparently told him he would get on at some point but then the FA and the doctors said that it wouldn't be good for him to play.

I wasn't too concerned. Whoever went out there had to perform. If Wazza played, then brilliant, but we had other players who were more than capable of doing the job. I knew how much he wanted to play, though. After the Paraguay game Wazza wasn't happy at all even though there had been no prospect of him getting a kick.

He was standing in the changing room going, 'Oh I can't believe this, this is a joke,' and I was laughing saying, 'Wazza you're nuts.' He's going, 'It's the World Cup. I need to be playing. Just two minutes, that's all I wanted, two minutes.' My mind flashed back to the 98 World Cup when I'd been desperate to get one minute, let alone two, but I never got on. So I knew what he meant.

We didn't play well against Trinidad, not at all.

They had ten men behind the ball and hardly came out although they took some good free kicks and corners and JT had to clear off the line. We got booed off at half-time which was a bit strong. But I suppose the fans had come over expecting us to perform and we hadn't.

Wazza got on which cheered them up and Crouchy scored with a header before Stevie G smacked one in right at the end. Again, we had won the game, which was the most important thing.

But afterwards the TV pundits and the press were saying it was a really bad performance and the mood was really negative. At the press conference I asked whether they would rather us play pretty football without qualifying for the knockout stages or get through. We'd played two games, got a maximum of six points, had not conceded a goal, qualified for the knockout stage with a game to spare and made our best start to a World Cup for 24 years. And we'd avoided a possible upset. What more did they want?

Much was being made of the fact that Michael Owen wasn't scoring but I wasn't bothered by that. He will often grab a goal from nowhere even though he hasn't been involved much in the game.

Injuries permitting, I reckon he will become England's top goalscorer of all time. He is up there with the best out and out goalscorers, but I don't think he was fully fit going into the World Cup. How could he be, given that he had not played a whole competitive match since the previous Boxing Day? I still believe we needed him in the team, though.

Apparently Michael said it didn't work very well for him if there were too many long balls played up to Crouchy and he had to go running around for the scraps. He wanted it played through midfield and so did the rest of us, but it didn't pan out like that. Maybe when we saw Crouchy up there we saw the easy route, the easy target to hit.

We got back to the hotel and sat around discussing why

we weren't playing well. We were like supporters in any pub, chatting about it. There were some questions about whether we were right playing one up front because Wazza preferred to play as a pair, but then again it meant Stevie Gerrard and Lamps could get forward better with a holding player behind them. It was swings and roundabouts. Some of the players felt that the manager's tactics were right, but that we weren't putting them into practice correctly. For the most part, I was in that camp.

You can talk about systems all you want but if you're not playing well then the system means nothing.

After each game, when we walked through the mixed-zone interview area the first question would always be the same, 'You've got the result but you didn't really play well, did you?' It was a recurring theme – and an annoying one. I have to admit that at no point in the tournament did I feel we'd let people know that we were a team to be considered. Not for one minute did I think that. But in my heart I still felt we could win the World Cup – we would just have to improve a lot.

Teams like Argentina and Holland showed what they were about early on although they still went home before the semi-finals. But we never consistently showed what we were capable of, which was a huge disappointment, given the build-up and the belief that we really could do it this time which had swept the country.

Some members of the squad got narked by criticisms from the TV pundits but that didn't worry me. They were just doing their jobs. I'm good friends with Ian Wright, who was a BBC pundit. If they haven't got an opinion there's no point in them being there. Wrighty had his own gripes about Sven and had made some comments about not wanting England to win with him as manager. But I'm sure he said that tongue-in-cheek.

My main criticism of Wrighty was his dodgy gear!

But I took issue with Gary Lineker and Alan Hansen for the way they absolutely butchered one of my all-time heroes, the Brazilian striker Ronaldo, in a personal attack on him. They crossed the line there. He was a bit overweight maybe, but they didn't have to keep harping on about it, making snide little jokes. Ronaldo is one of the best players ever and they showed him no respect. The guy is the top scorer in the history of the World Cup.

The lads were well aware of comments by ex-players like Terry Butcher on the radio and in the paper. He dug Becks out quite a bit but he says what he wants to say. He's an ex-England captain, he's been there before, seen it and done it. He knows what it's all about, although I'm sure when he was a player he didn't like getting criticised by ex-players. But you can't go to a World Cup and not expect criticism. It's part and parcel of the whole thing and it's always going to happen.

I felt we were being too cautious in our play. I think we are a cautious nation by nature. Our wingers are always too honest at club and international level, playing almost like right- and left-backs. We've got to be bold enough to say, 'You guys occupy their defenders and let them worry about you.' But for club and country they will always chase back. The result of that is that our full-backs play even deeper, behind the halfway line for most of the game. You're not going to be able to score two or three goals playing with wingers too far back to have an effect in the other half.

I would tell Joe Cole not to defend and suggest to Becks that he stay as high as he could. A guy like Miguel of Portugal, whose main asset is attacking, is always up there putting pressure on the opponent and sometimes relies on his central defenders to bail him out if he gets caught up-field. I'd be okay with that. You have to take a few risks. The manager, though, had his own ideas and wanted to make sure we were narrow and tight when we didn't have the ball.

Sven paid me a compliment before the Sweden game in Cologne when he compared me to the great Franz Beckenbauer. That spawned the headline 'Franz Ferdinand'. It was flattering and I don't mind admitting it gave me a boost. But you can't get carried away.

I never thought that anyone was going to score against us in open play. I felt confident. I've felt so good about my game for two successive World Cups. I don't get fazed by big occasions at all. It feels like I'm going out to play with my mates on the back grass on my old estate. The pressure doesn't worry me. I realise that everyone in the country is watching in the pubs and clubs but that doesn't make me nervous, it gees me up.

The World Cup has been good to me in terms of personal performances, but of course that is no consolation for coming back without the trophy.

After our stumbles in the first two games we played our best football of the World Cup in the first half against Sweden.

It didn't start too well though. Michael Owen was out of the game after one minute when he collapsed unchallenged. I thought he might have just tweaked something. Then, out of the corner of my eye, I saw him roll off the pitch and he was grimacing. I knew then that he'd done something bad.

When we went into the changing room at half-time we saw he couldn't bend his leg. He'd been told it was knee-ligament damage and he was going for a scan the next day, but he knew he was in trouble and out of the World Cup. The lads were gutted, not only for Michael, but also because he's the one person who can be relied on to score goals.

Michael's injury apart, it felt like it was all coming together at last in that first half. Joe Cole's 30-yard volley put us ahead but then my groin started hurting towards the end of the half and I wasn't sure I'd get through the game. It got worse during the break, despite the treatment and, as soon as I played a ball down the right at the start of the second half it began seizing up.

I feared it was going to tear if I carried on and not long after they equalised through a header from Marcus Allback I went off.

I was panicking that I might be out of the World Cup but I had a scan the next day and the doctors said that although they could see there was some bleeding there was no tear. You never know how long groin injuries are going to take to heal. I had to get constant treatment for the next two days and, luckily, I recovered.

I was sat on the bench when Stevie Gerrard came on as sub for Wazza and had an eventful cameo. He first cleared off the line, then got our second goal with a header which looked like it had won the game. But they equalised in the ninetieth minute when a throw-in bounced right across the box and Henrik Larsson touched it in.

I couldn't believe it. It shouldn't have gone in but it did and the lads were pig-sick. We were still top of the group and it made no difference really but our confidence took a jolt. We'd conceded two sloppy goals. We were deflated, not happy. We should have won. Conceding those goals the way we did might have affected us mentally.

Looking back now, I reckon we were too polite to each other when things went wrong, as they did against Sweden. As I've mentioned, at our clubs, training-ground spats happen all the time, but they don't on international duty. Everyone is too nice because we respect each other as players so much and that respect probably got in the way.

There comes a point when you've just got to hammer each other. A bit of straight-talking might have done us the world of good. There were times when things needed to be said and they weren't.

After the Sweden game the manager said, 'You finished top of the group, well done. But they were two very bad goals and we'll have to work on that.' McClaren said, 'Two shocking goals,' and we had to practise defending corners and free kicks all the time in the lead-up to our last-16 knockout game against Ecuador. It obviously worked because we didn't concede another goal.

The town of Baden-Baden was 20 minutes down the hill from where we were staying and we thought it would be a refuge for us, a chance to get out of the hotel, stroll around and see some civilisation.

But it was not as relaxing as we had hoped.

For a start there were a lot of England fans, which surprised me because we weren't playing any games there. Me, David James and Sol Campbell went into town for a coffee once and suddenly there were 50-odd people standing outside the restaurant taking photos and asking for autographs. We had to leave after an hour because by then the paparazzi were all over us as well.

With hindsight I think it was a bad idea to have our families in the town so close to where we were staying.

My mates were ringing me asking what was going on with all the birds going out partying, and I was telling them it wasn't a problem. They became known as the WAGs which stood for Wives and Girlfriends, and the paparazzi attention on them was phenomenal. It's always a bit of a pain when you're on the receiving end of such treatment. There is no escape, nowhere to run, nowhere to hide and, of course, it put the players on edge at times, which wasn't helpful.

A lot of the players, like me, thought it was good to have the families there. But towards the end the mood changed and some of us were saying that having them so near wasn't such a great idea.

If it was up to me in 2010, which it won't be, then I would put it down to a players' vote. I would be voting against having the families so close. They could maybe come for a visit after the first three games, stay for one night, and then go to their base in another part of the country. The World Cup only comes round every four years and the players need to be 100 per cent focused on the football. No distractions at all.

It's hard for a player not to worry about his missus or his kids. Especially when they are in a foreign country. You're always wondering what's going on, hoping they are all right. If Rebecca goes out to a restaurant or a club and I'm not at home, I like her to text me to let me know she's in, she's locked the door and put the alarm on. I want to know she's safe. I don't sleep properly until then.

Although I had different friends and family members coming over for every game, I didn't feel under pressure to socialise with them. Being pregnant, Rebecca wasn't really taking part in the social scene out there anyway. It would have been too much like hard work for her.

She wanted to be careful. We had a hospital on standby out in Germany, in case there were any complications with the baby or it came early. Rebecca doesn't like all the stuff that goes with being involved with a footballer anyway, like the paparazzi and so on, so she tries to stay as far away from all that as possible. She gets on with all the girls though.

The Brenner's Park Hotel, where the wives and girlfriends stayed, along with a lot of the press, was a beautiful place but it was too open.

You'd get people staring in from the opposite river bank and the paparazzi could sit there all day, snapping away to their hearts' content. There was too much access to the families and I thought they should have been put in a smaller hotel. The press were right there, so they knew exactly what was going on. Nothing went unnoticed. I don't think the press and the families should have been in the same place. It wasn't a good idea.

There's always going to be animosity because the press are seen as the bad guys by our families. Some of them have it in for certain players, rightly or wrongly, and it's normal for family members to be protective of their loved ones.

Unfortunately the World Cup will be remembered in England more for the WAGs than for what the players did on the pitch.

The manager decided on a 4-5-1 formation for the Ecuador game and, although it wasn't going to get the very best out of Wazza, there was no one more capable of playing the role than him. Wayne can play in any formation, but he's better off as one of the two up front, or playing behind the front-man.

I was quite confident about the formation, hoping that the wingers would stay high and that one of the midfielders would join in, because that's what we had worked on in training.

Ecuador could have gone ahead early on when Agustin Delgado, who used to play for Southampton, flicked it on and I couldn't go up with him because I wasn't close enough. JT went to head it and miscued and Carlos Tenorio got away. He should have scored, but Ashley Cole came from nowhere, made a great sliding block and the ball bounced up and hit the bar. I breathed a sigh of relief. It was the only time I thought we might concede a goal in open play.

Becks was physically sick on the field but he never complained about how he felt during the game and it didn't stop him coming up with the free-kick winner. He struck it low into the bottom left-hand corner, although the keeper should have saved it. He was a mile over the other side of the goal and still managed to get a full hand on it with his dive, but it sneaked in.

Again it had not been a very good performance but I kept believing that the next time it was going to kick in. We couldn't go through a whole tournament playing so crap.

I felt we should have played better and won by a couple of goals against Ecuador. Even playing one up front as we did we had the players to make that formation work. But it would not come together. We had to get it right in our quarter-final against Scolari's Portugal. It just had to happen, otherwise we'd be out, no two ways about it.

TWENTY-ONE

End of the Dream - Again!

I sank to my knees and the tears started flowing. I couldn't stop them. I couldn't understand how we were out of the World Cup. They weren't better than us. All the emotions came flooding out and I thought about what I could have done better, how I'd let everyone down and how my pride was crushed.

The lads all believed we would beat Portugal. Everything was in our favour. We had the better players, it wasn't too hot, the stadium roof in Gelsenkirchen was closed, which helped, and everyone was fit, bar Michael Owen who had flown home.

A lot was being made of the fact that we were up against Scolari again and that his teams had beaten us twice before – Brazil at the 2002 World Cup and Portugal in Euro 2004. Added to that, there was the fact that he had turned down the chance to become England manager.

None of that mattered to me. This was a new game and Scolari was irrelevant. I thought that with their midfielder play-maker Deco out through suspension and Cristiano Ronaldo being a slight injury worry, Portugal would struggle to score.

I also felt that Lamps was ready to fire for us. He'd been getting frustrated because he wasn't scoring and he's the type for whom goals help his confidence. It was getting him down. Frank prides himself on his performance and on his goals. He's like me in that if he's not doing what he should be doing, he gets annoyed with himself. Since he was a kid at West Ham he'd scored goals every season and his goal ratio had gone up every year.

In training he was doing it and I was convinced he would get one. If I'd been having a bet, which of course I wasn't, I'd have put money on Frank to score the first goal. And I thought if we scored once there was no way we would lose the game.

Not a lot happened in the first half. Early in the second Becks went off injured and Aaron came on. Almost immediately he beat the full-back and crossed low into the box. Uncharacteristically, Wazza miscued, but it fell to Joe Cole who put it over the top. It was a good chance, but I thought we'd get more and the winner would come.

Then disaster struck. With just over an hour gone an

incident occurred which will be talked about for as long as the game is played.

Wazza was tussling for the ball and expected to get a free kick, but the referee didn't give one and, as I later discovered, his foot came down, catching the Chelsea defender Ricardo Carvalho in the privates. I couldn't really see what was happening at the time and my first impression was that Wazza was just trying to free himself. Cristiano came running up to the ref and I pulled Wazza away after he shoved Ronny.

Then I turned round and a red card's been shown. I thought, 'What the fuck's that for? I don't understand, what's he done?' I reckoned that the only thing it could be for was the shove Wazza gave Ronny. It wasn't until later, on TV, that I saw Wazza had connected with Carvalho. I don't think it warranted a red card.

Our World Cup hopes were starting to unravel. But you cannot dwell on whether there's been an injustice or not, you have to roll your sleeves up, get on with it, and work out how to play with ten men.

I tried to ask the ref what had gone on but like all the refs at the World Cup he wasn't having it. You tried to speak to any of them and they raised their finger at you and either started screaming and shouting or ran away and blanked you.

I thought we'd have to hang on and take it to penalties and I was confident we could do that.

We had to change things round and I heard Joe Cole saying, 'I can't believe I'm being brought off.' Then he made a 60-yard run, like you do when you want to prove you shouldn't be getting hooked.

Crouchy came on and did really well, battling up there against Carvalho and the other centre-half and winning a lot of balls. He put himself about and tried to bring others into the game, like Owen Hargreaves who was like two players out there the way he was running about. I knew Owen was a good player. After all you don't play for Bayern Munich for all those years, and win trophy after trophy, if you don't have something special about you. But he'd never had a sustained run in the England team to prove himself.

Any England player will admit that it takes you 10 to15 matches to really get the hang of the international game. Owen had been in the squad for five years but had not played in the team consistently. Against Portugal, he turned into a bionic man. He was incredible. It was the best individual performance by an England player for a number of World Cups, never mind just the last one. The media hammered him before the World Cup while praising others who didn't have an ounce of his experience or his record of success.

When you're a man down it almost galvanises you into thinking, 'Fuck this, we've got to win now.' You dig in and no matter what happens you just don't concede a goal. You feel if you can nick one then great, but the priority is to batten down the hatches.

We had a couple of chances. Frank had a volley from a corner and Ricardo saved one of Frank's free kicks, then dived the other way to save Azza's follow-up. I thought that if it went to penalties we'd win, even though our record in shoot-outs was so bad. It wasn't thinking about the law of averages, I just believed we'd do it.

When I came off at the end of extra-time I was asking the ref how long we had before penalties. Not an unreasonable question. But he just ignored me. 'That's just fucking ignorant,' I thought, and told him so. I don't know if he heard me or not, but I reckon his English was good enough to understand.

The manager designated the five penalty takers and I was nominated as number eight in case it went to sudden-death. I couldn't believe it, as I'm one of the top penalty takers in the world! Seriously, I would have liked to have taken one and I'm sure the manager knew it, but maybe he trusted others more. My record in shoot-outs is 100 per cent! I've scored one out of one, the kick I converted in the Community Shield for United against Arsenal.

But Sven didn't come round and ask, 'Who's up for it?' He just picked them. You could probably have said no if you didn't want to do it, but nobody did.

We'd been practising penalties almost every day. Some players were varying their penalties and some were taking them the same way. I was very confident if it came to me to take one. I was going to place mine and was already psyching myself up for it. I had to keep my legs moving because they were seizing up by then. I was at the rigor mortis stage.

They put their first penalty away and Lamps went up first for us. We had our arms round each other in a line and we're all going, 'Come on, Lampsy, you're gonna score.' But his kick was saved by Ricardo, who had also starred in the shoot-out in Euro 2004.

I wasn't worried at that stage, though. I thought Robbo would save a few because he had been doing really well in training. As it happens, Hugo Viana then hit the post for them and when Owen Hargreaves scored we were all square. Everything was going to be fine.

When their midfielder Petit missed altogether, we were in the box seat. If Stevie Gerrard scored, the pressure would be right on them, but his was saved as well. He said after the game that he didn't hit it right, but the keeper made a good save.

We were still level at 1–1, with three penalties each having been taken. There was no reason for panic. Helder Postiga, the former Spurs striker, netted for Portugal and it dawned on me that if Jamie Carragher didn't score we would be in trouble.

Carra had been brought on a couple of minutes before the end, specifically to take a pen. I thought that was the right thing to do. In training he was probably one of the top two or three penalty takers in our team. But when Jamie took his kick he didn't wait for the ref's whistle. I realised straight away. He had to put it back on the spot again and the pressure increased by a hundred times. His kick was saved as well, Ricardo turning it on to the bar.

Now it meant that if Ronny scored we were out of the World Cup.

Usually he goes to the keeper's right and Robbo knew that. He had a dossier on him, as he did on every player. I had a gut feeling as soon as Ronny put the ball down that he wasn't going to miss. This time he put it to Robbo's left. It was a good penalty, to be honest, but it was crushing seeing that ball hit the net.

I sank to my knees and the tears started flowing. I couldn't stop them. I couldn't understand how we were out of the World Cup. They weren't better than us. All the emotions came flooding out and I thought about what I could have done better, how I'd let everyone down and how my pride was crushed. I'm not a crier by nature. The only times I've cried in recent years were at the 2002 World Cup, the FA Cup final defeat by Arsenal in 2005 and this World Cup.

People were trying to pick me up, but I didn't want them to. I wanted them to go away, to leave me to my private grief. I wanted to get up when I was ready and not before, although I knew the other players and staff were trying to do their best for me. I remember burying my head into the pitch and wanting to punch the life out of the grass.

I genuinely believed we were going to win the World Cup and I couldn't get my head around any other outcome.

We walked around clapping the fans but all I wanted to do was hide in the changing room. I was embarrassed. We had so much quality, which was admired all over the world, and our fans had been expecting a lot more from us. I felt for everybody in the stadium and everyone back at home. We'd failed.

We'd gone out at the quarter-final stage, as we had done the last time. There was nothing to soften the blow. We hadn't given the supporters a good time. There was nothing that had excited them other than a couple of goals from Joe Cole and Stevie Gerrard. The fans applauded us, yeah, it's the way the English fans are. They support their team whatever.

But perhaps the hysteria, excitement and mad security which always follows the England team around creates a hype and a belief among fans and players that gets everyone thinking we're better than we really are.

When we were back in the changing room I gathered myself together. The lads were all slumped in their seats. Gary Neville was walking around shaking everyone's hand and tapping people on the shoulder saying, 'Come on, keep your head up. Have a shower and get out of here.'

I thought Sven was going to cry at one point, but he didn't, he held himself together and said, 'Listen, it's been fantastic working with you guys. You've gone out on a penalty shootout which was unlucky. We couldn't have prepared any more for penalties. I thought you were the better team today. You had the better chances and . . .' From there I just went into another world, thinking like I did when I was sat on the pitch about what me and the team could have done better. But it didn't matter what Sven said or what I thought. The World Cup was gone, it was out of our hands.

It was the most sombre changing room I'd ever been in. Four years earlier I'd been taken straight to a drugs test so I hadn't seen what the atmosphere was like, and eight years before I hadn't kicked a ball, so didn't feel it the same way. This time I got the whole rawness.

I got showered and changed and I saw Ronny and said

to him, 'Make sure you speak to Wazza. The people are saying you meant to get him sent off, so make sure you speak to him and iron things out.' He said, 'Yeah, yeah no problem. I didn't ask for him to get sent off. I'll speak to him on the phone.'

I went to speak to the reporters. I felt I had a duty to talk about our exit. I didn't want to be a bitter loser. They were asking, 'How do you feel?' and I was thinking, 'What kind of obvious question is that? Should I answer with, "I'm delighted. I couldn't be any higher. I'm on top of the world"?'

I said I was gutted and this reporter goes, 'Yes, but how do you really feel inside?' I stood there and stared at the guy, thinking, 'What more do you want me to say? Do you want me to get on my knees and start crying, so you can take a picture and put it in the paper? We've lost the game, I'm gutted, it's as simple as that.'

When I got on the coach I put my phone on and I must have had about 50 texts from my mates saying, 'Ronaldo's got Rooney sent off. Ronaldo's out of order, blah, blah, blah.' All the lads on the coach were going, 'Everyone's saying that Ronaldo caused it.'

Rebecca had sent me a text saying, 'Ring me when you want to ring me. I won't call. You just call me when you're ready.' I rang her and asked if she was all right, but she knows I'm not much good in these situations. Then I spoke to my dad, my mum, Pini, Gavin Rose and a couple of other mates.

I was asking, 'What was it like, man? Should we have won?' and the general opinion was that we had the better chances, they never looked like scoring, Ronny got Wazza sent off, and we had the better team on the day.

I asked Wazza if he'd stamped on Carvalho and Wazza said he hadn't done it deliberately. I believed him.

I had a bad blister on the sole of my foot which I had to go and get popped, and my groin was killing me again. So when we got back to the hotel, I went to the physio room for treatment and then I watched the match on TV. Wazza definitely caught him but it was nothing crazy. It wasn't violent.

There was frustration on Wazza's part that he wasn't getting a free kick despite the fact that he was having his shirt pulled. But for some reason the ref didn't give it. After the clash with Carvalho, Ronaldo came over and Wazza shoved him. That's where I think the referee made his decision. I don't think he was going to send him off before then, but I think the shove on Ronaldo did it.

I still wasn't annoyed with Ronny though. If it had been the other way round our players would have run to the ref. We wouldn't have asked for a red card, but we would have run over and said, 'What's going on, ref?'

I said that to the lads and explained that I couldn't really have any animosity towards Ronny. The argument was that he shouldn't have done what he did to a Man United team-mate and I can understand that point of view. But in the heat of the moment, isn't the other player just the opposition, not a club mate?

Wazza was annoyed with the whole situation. Whether he was annoyed with Ronny or not, I couldn't say. He wasn't happy in the changing room afterwards, in fact he was in tears, but he didn't try to storm their dressing room as was reported at the time.

When Becks got sent off in '98 he got hammered by the papers but it didn't happen with Wazza. I'm happy about that. Maybe the fans and the media realised that what they did to Becks was out of order.

Mind you, they did find another scapegoat in Cristiano –

and his biggest crime became the wink to the camera which he was seen making after Wazza got the red card. I still didn't feel any anger towards him for that. Who knows why he was winking? He told me Scolari had said to him, 'Make sure you start attacking them now, this is your chance to win the World Cup.' And he winked and went, 'All right, boss.'

I texted him to see how he was doing and he said he was all right. I didn't ask specifics as I thought he might be under pressure and I didn't want to add to that. Ronny is very much liked in the United changing room. He's always up for the banter.

I will never believe he cheated us.

The manager called a meeting late that night to say thanks for everything, said it had been a fantastic five years and he wished that he could have won. He said Steve McClaren would take us on to be a successful team and that he was sure we'd win something in the next few years.

We also had a presentation for the team administrator, Michelle Farrar, because it was her birthday. Sven made the presentation to Michelle and Becks and Steve thanked Sven for the job he'd done.

We had a few drinks and we didn't really talk much about the game. If we had, we'd have been slitting our wrists.

I wasn't aware that Becks was going to quit as captain the next morning, but I said to him that night, 'You can't walk out on international football. I don't believe in players quitting.'

There had been whispers in the media that he was going to quit after the World Cup. I don't think it's anyone's right to quit the national team. For me, the end comes when you are no longer picked. Becks said to me, 'Never. I'm never going to quit international football.' He reiterated that in his statement when he resigned as captain. We had breakfast together that morning and I still didn't know he was going to give up the captaincy.

I would never have done what he did, but for whatever reason he did, and good luck to him. I'd have waited and seen what the new manager was going to do. As it turned out, when Steve McClaren named his first squad as manager, Becks was left out altogether.

I was surprised by that decision but you have to respect it. It's the new man's regime and he will do what he believes is best for the team. If certain individuals aren't in his plans, then that's the way it goes. No one is immune to being left out. I certainly don't believe it was done to make a statement, or for any professional gain.

I spoke to Becks after the announcement and he was all right. It was obvious he was going to be disappointed. If he hadn't been, that would have been a problem. Being the natural competitor that he is, I'm certain that Becks will want to try and get back in the squad. You can't turn that sort of determination on and off.

JT is a good appointment as captain. He's young enough to stay there for a good number of years. And he's a quality player.

Rebecca came and met me in the morning, we had lunch and then it was time to leave.

Sven made another little speech in the lobby of the hotel saying thanks again to everybody, and he got a round of applause. Then we made our way to the airport. That's when it really hits you that it's all over.

We landed at Luton to drop off the southern-based players then took off again, heading for Manchester. We weren't prepared for what was to come.

That short trip was the worst flight of my life. Halfway through the journey the turbulence started and it was like nothing I'd ever experienced before. We were asking the stewards what was going on and someone asked, 'Are we going to crash?' It was bad. I was scared and worried for Rebecca. We were going up and down like we were on a big dipper and there were people screaming and crying.

In fact, Wazza was screaming the loudest. Every time the plane dropped he came out with the most ear-piercing screech. Stevie Gerrard called one of the flight attendants over and said, 'Can you not just tell us what's going on?' The pilot came on the intercom and said, 'We can't fly into Manchester. We're going to have to land at Birmingham.'

At least it looked like we were going to land, even if it meant a long journey by road afterwards. Then the pilot came on again and said we were diverting to Liverpool. I've never been so relieved to touch the tarmac. We had to wait half an hour before they could sort out all our bags, but that was a minor hiccup. We were alive after all. They offered to fly us on to Manchester when the weather eased but nobody was having that. We got taxis.

The episode just about summed up our World Cup journey. Rocky most of the way with very little to enjoy about it.

I couldn't watch the semi-finals or the final. I was actually sitting outside a bar in Clapham High Street with my mate Gavin during the Italy v Germany semi. When Italy's late goals went in we turned round to see who'd scored but we weren't really watching it. I tried to push it out of my mind. I think Andrea Pirlo played a great ball through for one of the Italian goals but I might be wrong. I wasn't interested. I was still so pissed off that we were out.

The weekend of the final we went to Marbella for Ashley Cole's stag do. Me and Gavin met up with Ashley, Michael Carrick and his brother, one of Ashley's mates, Jermaine Jenas and two of his mates and we just had a good time. We let our hair down and drank. We drank loads. It was good fun chilling on the beach listening to music and having a laugh. It was a good way of getting the World Cup out of our systems.

I got back home before the World Cup final started but I didn't flick it on until extra-time. I was just in time to see Zinedine Zidane's head-butt on Marco Materazzi which was astonishing. It was a sad way to see a great player like that go out. I'd played against Zidane a couple of times and you could see that he had an aggressive side to him. He would kick out every now and again. He was strong and quick and not one of those players who you could physically bully. He didn't take any rubbish, which he proved in Berlin.

It won't tarnish my memories of him as a footballer. Joe Cole absolutely loves him, he thinks he's the greatest there's ever been but I'll always love Maradona and Brazilian striker Ronaldo more.

It was gut-wrenching watching the Italian celebrations and seeing them running around with the trophy. It brought out my frustrations again. I thought we were as good as they were . . . should have been as good anyway. If we had played to our potential.

Any of the teams in the quarter-finals could have won that tournament. In fact when Brazil were knocked out the same day as us it made it even harder to take because I thought we'd never have a better chance of winning a tournament.

It was not a great World Cup. The things I remember were a couple of quality passes by Riquelme for Argentina and Ronaldo's step-over goal for Brazil. I don't know why it didn't have the flair this time round. Maybe everybody's getting defensive because Greece managed to win Euro 2004 with just one up front.

The referees didn't help. They would not listen to the players, handed out cards and awarded free kicks for the most innocuous and feeble challenges and sent players off at the first opportunity.

FIFA had sent a referee round to every national team to explain the rules. He showed us videos of what seemed like perfectly good tackles and he was saying why they would be given as free kicks or even bookings. These weren't tackles from behind, they were from the side, where the player had clearly won the ball, but the opponent might have tumbled over. By the end I felt FIFA were trying to turn the game into a non-contact sport.

I felt sorry for the English referee Graham Poll when he got into trouble for booking a Croatian player three times in the same game. He gave quite an emotional interview on Sky Sports when he got back and said, 'Just leave me and my family alone please.' He got an insight into what it's like being one of us, how you can have TV crews and the press doorstepping you and your family. It wasn't nice for him to have that happen.

He made a mistake, we all do. I've always liked him as a ref because you can actually talk to him. Not like some of those little smiley ones, who say, 'You can't talk to me like that,' and get the yellow card straight out.

You should be able to relate and talk to a ref, as long as you're not swearing or being offensive. Refs can't expect you to not shout on the football pitch. Do they really believe you should come up to them and say, 'Excuse me, sir, can you please have a look at yourself with that decision?' It doesn't happen like that. It's football and emotions run high.

The 2006 World Cup won't be remembered for an outstanding team or an outstanding player. Remember Italia '90, for Gazza, Lothar Matthaus and Toto Schillaci? 1994 was about Bebeto, Romario and Roberto Baggio. Then in '98 you had Michael Owen's goal, and the brilliance of Zidane. In 2002

Rivaldo was the best player in the world, you had Ronaldinho emerging and Ronaldo scoring eight goals in the competition. But nobody in this World Cup made you think, 'Wow!'

The atmosphere was disappointing too. Football is getting too corporate. According to my friends, there was a better atmosphere at the fanfests in the parks, where supporters watched the matches on a giant TV. It was bizarre that people travelled from all over Europe just to watch on a screen. It was a great substitute for those who could not get into the grounds and when we drove past on the way to our matches you could see how brilliant it was.

When I'm finished international football I'm going to make a point of visiting one of those parks, get a beer in and watch the game. It seems like fun.

TWENTY-TWO

What Happens Now?

I wouldn't say I'd failed if I didn't win a major honour with England or the Champions League with United, but I would feel something was missing. These should be the best years of my football career coming up. I can't wait. I also feel I'm starting a new chapter in my life.

Sven took England forward to a certain point, but not a winning point.

The record spoke for itself: three quarter-finals and we were knocked out every time. But we did qualify for every tournament we went in for, so his record stands up there with every other England manager, bar Alf Ramsey who of course won the World Cup.

Fans talked about how he should have been ranting and raving on the sideline, but not all managers are like that. When Arsène Wenger first came to Arsenal and was successful almost immediately he never came out of the dugout.

Personally, I feel that if you haven't played well you need to be told to buck your ideas up. I like a manager who points something out about your game and you go out there and try and correct it. That's how it's been all my club career. If you're not pulling your weight and not playing well the manager needs to let you know. Under Sven that wasn't the case.

I never heard anybody get a bollocking during his time as manager or get so much as a 'Listen, you're not doing this right.' The salary he was paid, supposedly £5 million a year, was brought up all the time, but for me that was irrelevant. The FA had been desperate to get him, so he had to be paid the going rate.

I was sorry to see Sven go because I liked him as a person. He was a really nice bloke you could get along with. He brought a lot of positive things to the squad and encouraged an ambience among all the players which had not existed previously. For young players there can be no better squad to be welcomed into in international football than ours. They feel at home straight away.

There used to be little cliques but not any more.

Before Sven arrived there were separate Man United, Liverpool and London tables and another one for the rest. I used to be on the London table with the likes of Les Ferdinand, Wrighty, Paul Merson and Ray Parlour. Sven got rid of that and decided we should all sit round one table together. He was right. The cliques did not encourage team spirit.

We are in a healthier position now than when Sven got the job but we're still not where we want to be. There are so many reasons for that. I've discussed the fact that our wide men are too honest; they defend too much when they should be looking to get on the attack.

And us defenders could be better in our selection of passes and we should score more goals. That's one of the biggest things we didn't do in Germany, one of the reasons why we didn't win the World Cup. Sven didn't like defenders running with the ball, but maybe there could have been more variation. Steve McClaren is encouraging me to do it now and it's something the manager lets me do at United. Roy Keane used to cover for me in defence whenever I went on a run. But it was not something Sven encouraged.

The bottom line is that we weren't a success under Sven because we didn't win anything. But maybe the reasons for our lack of success go deeper than the manager. We need to teach players from an early age that things like stretching, eating correctly, discipline and preparation for matches are as fundamental as going out and doing skills and learning how to strike the ball properly.

We aren't doing that at the moment which is why we are still playing catch-up in certain aspects with the likes of Italy, France, Germany and Holland. The smallest things add up and can make all the difference.

We have moved on to a new era now with Steve McClaren in charge. It would have been easy for Steve to have changed at the World Cup, knowing he was taking over, getting on his high horse. But he didn't change, he acted as Sven's coach and

never played the big 'I am'. The lads appreciated that and I think Sven did as well.

But now it's Steve's job. We've got players of the highest calibre who have consistently under-achieved with England and hopefully he can sort that conundrum out. We must develop a team framework which accommodates all the positives we have in this country. We also have to learn how to go two goals up and kill games off, instead of getting one up and hanging on for grim death.

We're not the only ones with problems though. Look at Brazil. They've got some of the best players in the world – more than any team. Let's face it, most of their midfielders and forwards would have got in the Italian side that won the World Cup. But the Brazilians didn't play together. Great players don't always make a great team. It's an old saying but it's true.

Steve McClaren is very forceful in his thoughts on the game. There are no grey areas. You know exactly what he wants from you. It would be very hard to find someone who speaks badly of his coaching methods. Time will tell how good a manager he's going to be. He's already introduced some different ideas, but whoever came in was bound to freshen things up. We'd had the same manager for so long.

The appointment of Terry Venables as his assistant was a masterstroke. I saw Terry in a London restaurant not long after it was announced Sven was leaving and told him he should throw his hat into the ring for the manager's job. He didn't really answer, and so when we met up with the England camp for the first time under the new management I asked him if he'd had an idea he was going to be coming back as coach. He said, 'No way.'

Someone of his vast experience is invaluable to us. He's really good on the small details of a game which can have a big impact on the outcome. He demands respect.

And I like the fact a proper sports psychologist, Bill Beswick, has been brought into the backroom team. It will be good to work with him.

We've got to believe we can win the European Championships in 2008. We've certainly got enough quality – players who stand up against the best in the world. Once we've figured out how to do it as a team, then we won't have any problems.

There are still so many things I want to achieve as a footballer.

In the last few years we've come up short at United and I would love to win a Champions League and the Premiership again, as well as the FA Cup, and the Carling Cup. I'm not greedy!

There have been a few changes at Old Trafford as the new season begins, with the likes of Michael Carrick coming in and, of course, Ruud Van Nistelrooy leaving for Real Madrid.

I was disappointed to see Ruud go. He was a good lad and we got on really well. He was a fantastic player for United and had one of the club's best ever goalscoring ratios. He will live long in the memory of our supporters.

I believe we have the squad which can help me get a trophy cabinet full of winners' medals over the rest of my career. And, when I've got them, I'd like to go into coaching and do it all over again with my own team.

I wouldn't say I'd failed if I didn't win a major honour with England or the Champions League with United, but I would feel something was missing.

These should be the best years of my football career coming up. I can't wait.

I also feel I'm starting a new chapter in my life.

That's because on 24 July 2006 Rebecca gave birth to our first child, a 7lbs 13oz boy called Lorenz. We got the name when we were watching the credits to the film *Crash*. One of the actors, who played a car-jacker, is called Lorenz Tate and we just thought it would be a good name.

When Rebecca first told me she was pregnant before Christmas 2005 I was gobsmacked. We'd been trying, but only for a month and I didn't expect success so quickly. We had a little cuddle to celebrate and I jokingly said to her, 'Say thanks, then!'

I couldn't wait for the arrival. I did all the antenatal classes and active birth lessons. I wanted to take part in everything I possibly could during her pregnancy and the birth. It was new to us and we were experiencing something amazing together.

When the time came it rather caught us by surprise, as I suppose it does with most parents unless they've booked a C-section. We had gone into Wythenshawe Hospital the day before to get Rebecca's blood pressure checked and she was advised that the baby should be induced immediately. She had a panic. She didn't have her night bag or baby bag with her which she had carefully prepared. We couldn't believe it was all happening so quickly, one week early.

Rebecca had wanted to give birth as naturally as possible but when the contractions started she went straight for the epidural. I didn't blame her. I felt like having one myself.

We tried to make the experience as relaxing as possible. We brought loads of music on the iPod, with stuff by Marvin Gaye and Barry White. It was a 30-hour vigil, before Lorenz popped his head into the world.

He came out to the sounds of D'Angelo singing 'All right' which I thought was appropriate because he was. At least he was once they'd untangled the cord from round his neck! Within

20 seconds he was testing his lungs with a little scream. It was a fantastic experience to watch Lorenz being born – and I recorded it all on our video camera from start to finish.

I know every parent says it, but seeing your child being born is like nothing else you will ever experience. It's surreal. I was so pleased to have a son. I would have been delighted with a daughter, of course, but on the quiet I was praying for a boy. A mini-me!

I've already been asked many times whether I think he'll be a footballer and my answer is that he will do what he wants to do. There will be no pressure on him. Mind you, he's very aware of his surroundings and from the second day he was looking around the place. Could be he'll make a good passing midfielder.

I don't want to stop at one child. I want four kids at least. Which reminds me, I must remember to tell Rebecca that!

Being a parent alters your focus on life. My love for the game won't ever change, but maybe the coming home and sulking after a bad day at the office will become a thing of the past. I've got big responsibilities now.

It's time to grow up.

Career Statistics

Rio Gavin Ferdinand, born Peckham 7 November 1978

Career
West Ham United trainee. Turned professional 27 November 1995. League debut as substitute 5 May 1996 v Sheffield Wednesday. Loaned to Bournemouth November 1996. Transferred to Leeds United 27 November 2000 (£18 million). Transferred to Manchester United 22 July 2002 (£29.1 million [Manchester United's valuation was £30 million. Leeds United £28.25 million], then record fee for a British player).

Club Honours
West Ham United Intertoto Cup winners 1999
Manchester United Premier League Champions 2002–03, League Cup winners 2005–06.

53 full England caps, 1 goal
1997 v Cameroon (sub)
1998 v Switzerland, Belgium (sub), Luxembourg, Czech Republic
1999 v France (sub), Hungary, Sweden (sub)
2000 v Argentina (sub), Italy
2001 v Spain, Finland, Albania, Mexico, Greece, Germany, Albania, Greece, Sweden
2002 v Holland, South Korea, Cameroon, Sweden, Argentina, Nigeria, Denmark (1 goal), Brazil, Portugal
2003 v Australia, Liechtenstein, Turkey, South Africa, Croatia
2004 v Wales, Azerbaijan, Spain
2005 v Northern Ireland, Azerbaijan, Denmark, Wales, Northern Ireland, Austria (sub), Poland, Argentina
2006 v Uruguay, Hungary, Jamaica, Paraguay, Trinidad & Tobago, Sweden, Ecuador, Portugal, Greece

England Under-21s
1997 v Switzerland, Georgia, Italy, Greece
2000 v Yugoslavia

Season	League Apps	League Goals	League Cup Apps	League Cup Goals	FA Cup Apps	FA Cup Goals	European Apps	European Goals	Others Apps	Others Goals	Internationals Apps	Internationals Goals
WEST HAM UNITED												
1995–96	1	-	-	-	-	-	-	-	-	-	-	-
1996–97	15	2	1	-	1	-	-	-	-	-	-	-
BOURNEMOUTH (Loan)												
1996–97	10	-	-	-	-	-	-	-	1	-	-	-
WEST HAM UNITED												
1997–98	35	-	5	-	6	-	-	-	-	-	3	-
1998–99	31	-	1	-	1	-	-	-	-	-	5	-
1999–2000	33	-	3*	-	1	-	3	-	6	-	1	-
2000–01	12	-	2	-	-	-	-	-	-	-	1	-
LEEDS UNITED												
2000–01	23	2	-	-	2	-	7	1	-	-	5	-
2001–02	31	-	2	-	1	-	7	-	-	-	12	1
MANCHESTER UNITED												
2002–03	28	-	4	-	3	-	11	-	-	-	5	-
2003–04	20	-	-	-	-	-	6	-	1	-	1	-
2004–05	31	-	1	-	5	-	5	-	-	-	5	-
2005–06	37	3	5	-	2	-	8	-	-	-	15	-
Totals	307	7	24	-	22	-	47	1	8	-	53	1

* Does not include 2–2 draw with Aston Villa and subsequent 5–4 win on penalties; match ordered to be replayed as West Ham included an ineligible player.

Other matches
1996–97 Auto Windscreens Shield
1999–2000 Intertoto
2003–04 Community Shield

Picture Credits

Credits are listed according to the order the pictures appear on
each page, left to right, top to bottom.
'RF' denotes photographs belonging to Rio Ferdinand or his family.

Section 1
Page 1: Mark Guthrie; page 2: RF, RF, RF, RF, RF, RF, Action
Images; page 3: Bournemouth v Bristol programme 26 December
1996; page 4: Getty Images, Colorsport, Colorsport; page 5:
RF, RF, RF, RF; page 6: RF, RF, RF, RF; page 7: RF, Rex Features,
RF; page 8: RF.

Section 2
Page 1: Colorsport, Getty Images; page 2: Getty Images, Action
Images; page 3: Action Images, Mark Robinson, Action Images;
page 4: Getty Images, Rex Features, Getty Images; page 5: RF;
page 6: Action Images, RF; page 7: Action Images, Action
Images, Getty Images; page 8: Empics.

Section 3
Page 1: Getty Images, Action Images; page 2: Rex Features,
Colorsport, Rex Features; page 3: Rex Features, Getty Images;
page 4: The Sun, The Sun, News of the World, The Sun, The
Sun, The Sun, The Mirror, The Sun, The Sun; page 5: Daily
Express, Daily Express, Daily Mail, The Sun, The Sun; page 6:
Action Images; page 7: Action Images, Action Images, Getty
Images, Action Images, Getty Images; page 8: Getty Images.

Inside front cover: Action Images, Action Images, Getty Images.

Inside back cover: Rex Features, Action Images, Empics.

Index